OPERATION CATAPULT

OPERATION CATAPULT

WINSTON CHURCHILL AND THE BRITISH ATTACK ON THE FRENCH NAVY AT MERS-EL-KÉBIR

BILL WHITESIDE

NAVAL INSTITUTE PRESS
ANNAPOLIS, MARYLAND

Naval Institute Press
291 Wood Road
Annapolis, MD 21402

ISBN: 978-1-68247-969-8 (hardcover)
ISBN: 978-1-68247-968-1 (eBook)

Library of Congress Cataloging-in-Publication Data is available.

♾ Print editions meet the requirements of ANSI/NISO z39.48-1992 (Permanence of Paper).
Printed in the United States of America.

34 33 32 31 30 29 28 27 26 9 8 7 6 5 4 3 2 1
First printing

All maps created by Chris Robinson.

To Barbara,
to Brittany, Steve, Liam, and Phoebe
to Billy, Daneen, William, and Nelly,
and to the memory of my parents.

"We shall not hesitate to sacrifice our villages." I have heard these words spoken. And it was necessary to speak them. When a war is on a village ceases to be a cluster of traditions. The enemy who holds it have turned it into a nest of rats. Things no longer mean the same. Here are trees three hundred years old that shade the home of your family. But they obstruct the field of fire of a twenty-two-year-old lieutenant. Wherefore he sends up a squad of fifteen men to annihilate the work of time. In ten minutes he destroys three hundred years of patience and sunlight, three hundred years of the religion of the home and of betrothals in the shadows round the grounds. You say to him, "My trees!" but he does not hear you. He is right. He is fighting a war.

—ANTOINE DE SAINT-EXUPÉRY

FLIGHT TO ARRAS

CONTENTS

MAPS

ACKNOWLEDGMENTS

My fascination with Winston Churchill was sparked by a gift from my mother: a copy of *Winston Spencer Churchill, Alone: 1932–1940*, the second volume in William Manchester's Last Lion trilogy. As I read more about Sir Winston in the decades that followed, one small story stuck with me. Every author briefly mentioned the Royal Navy's unlikely attack on French ships in July 1940—every author, that is, except Manchester, whose book ends two weeks before this incident. Given Britain's recently ended alliance with France and Churchill's deep affection for the people he called Britain's "dearest friends of yesterday," that assault seemed terribly out of character.

Later, when I had my own small business and the freedom to manage my schedule, I decided to learn everything I could about that story—first as an intellectual diversion during my business travels, and eventually as an obsession. As I learned more about the clashes of personalities, loyalties, trust, and honor between seamen and statesmen in the months and minutes leading up to the attack, it became a story I wanted to share and then a book I just had to write.

One of the most surprising, delightful, warming, and rewarding aspects of this process was how open and welcoming archivists and historians are to unpedigreed researchers and writers like me. My archive-rat days—at the wonderous Churchill Archives Centre, the Franklin D. Roosevelt Presidential Library, the Arthur J. Marder Archives, the Imperial War Museum, the National Maritime Museum at the Royal Museums Greenwich, and other hallowed sources of history—were, without question, my most enriched days. The Hesburgh Library at the University of Notre Dame was another incredibly helpful resource.

As my writing sideline evolved into a new late-in-life career, I was blessed by the kindness of more guardian and guiding angels than I am able to mention here. I would like to express my particular thanks to:

Lee Pollock, the longtime Executive Director of the International Churchill Society, for his kindness in making me feel welcome in the world of Winston Churchill, and for his thoughtfulness in opening doors to help me spread the word with my writing and speaking.

When William Manchester's declining health prevented him from completing his trilogy, he asked Paul Reid to write the final volume, with Manchester listed as coauthor. Their joint work, *Winston Spencer Churchill, Defender of the Realm: 1940–1965*, ties a brilliant bow on the Last Lion series. As I stuck my toe into the world of Churchill authorities, I had the great fortune to connect with Paul, whose thoughtful encouragement provided an immense boost to my confidence and a sense that I might actually belong "in the club." (Paul, by the way, tells the story of the clash between the navies in *Defender of the Realm*.)

I approached the Naval Institute Press with a windy proposal, a single self-published book to my name, and a manuscript that was not only too long but also divvied into way too many chapters. Despite those flaws, Padraic (Pat) Carlin, NIP senior acquisitions editor, sensed something and nurtured me through NIP's evaluation and development processes with a patient and knowing hand on the tiller. From the first day that Pat responded to my query, every "next step" in the process worked exactly as I would have hoped, due in no small measure to Pat's guidance.

Vincent P. O'Hara, a naval historian with seventeen books (and counting) to his name, subjected my manuscript to an exacting review. His direct and informed criticism and suggestions helped add significant degrees of precision and polish to the quality of my finished work.

Jeff Ikler created a spark and fanned the flames for my first book when he invited me to join him on his podcast, *Getting Unstuck—Cultivating Curiosity*, and then had me back multiple times. The most in-depth discussions I've ever had about history and writing have been with Jeff. Jeff is such a naturally caring individual that he probably has little idea what an incredible boost his encouragement and support have provided.

Chris Robinson, a talented (as well as patient and flexible) cartographer, created the maps that add valuable perspective to this story.

This book draws on the experience, talent, and writing of others. I am grateful to those mentioned below for their kind permission to quote from their works.

Sir Winston Churchill, *The Second World War*—Volume I: *The Gathering Storm*, and Volume II: *Their Finest Hour*. Reproduced with permission of Curtis Brown, London, on behalf of Portland Churchill Ltd © Winston S. Churchill / Portland Churchill Ltd.

Major General Sir Edward Spears, *Assignment to Catastrophe, Volume II, The Fall of France—June 1940*. Reproduced with permission of copyright holder Patrick Aylmer.

Michael Simpson (editor), *The Somerville Papers* and *The Cunningham Papers, Volume 1—The Mediterranean Fleet: 1939–1942*. Reproduced with permission of The Navy Records Society.

John Colville, *The Fringes of Power*. Reproduced with permission of the Licensor through PLS Clear.

The New York Times for permission to quote from "Pittman Approves British Seizures," July 5, 1940.

The papers of Vice Admiral Sir James Somerville reproduced with permission of the Master and Fellows of Churchill College, Cambridge.

The papers of Arthur J. Marder reproduced with permission of University of California, Irvine Special Collections and Archives.

The papers of Vice Admiral Cedric Swinton Holland reproduced with the permission of Royal Museums Greenwich.

When I self-published a previous book, a group of exceptional friends (many of whom I have yet to meet) took a chance on me as an unproven author. Their encouragement helped motivate the writing of this book, and I owe it to them to name them here: Debbie Anderson, Jon Anderson, Marc Bailey, Tom Benning, Todd Bettencourt, David Blakelock, Cathy Bolton, Jeff Carlisle, Vicki Christopher, Pete Conrad, Peter Cotton, Ed Covert, Sharon Crawford, Bob Davis, John Davis, Barbara Denham, Steve Diebold, John Dillingham, Donald DiPalma, Michele Dulin, Larry Dunn, Rick Elder, Walt Fyk, Bruce Gibson, Tom Gielow, Len Gott, Carl

Haag, Prof. Hagesh Havanur, Gerry Hayden, Joy Hemming, John Higgins, Anthony Iannarino, Bruce Jacobsen, Matt Jaskolka, Thom Jones, Sara Komisin, Russ Laskowski, Peter Lotto, David Luettgen, Susan Marchetti, Skip Nees, Mark Nishan, Carolyn Olans, Billy Oppenheimer, Jessica Outlaw, Tom Redder, Barry Rellaford, Mark Rhodes, Jeff Schultz, Ray Scott, Lynn Seal, Daschel Sferra, Noah Sferra, Steve Sheather, Dave Smith, Don Smith, Denny Snyder, Leanne Torrance, Katie Ward, Harold Weinstein, Tom Whelan, Ellen Willertz, and Harry Zeiser.

You should know how thankful and blessed I am that my wife Barbara endured the deficit of time and attention that I imposed as I worked on my book while she managed our home, our travels, our family—generally everything in our life—and enabled me to focus on my often-selfish avocation. The absolute luckiest strike in my life was meeting, loving, and marrying Barbara.

Our son Billy and our daughter Brittany—along with their spouses Daneen and Steve—are my greatest source of joy and pride. I once wrote that a parent could not be any more blessed than I am . . . and then the births of our grandchildren Liam, William, Nelly, and Phoebe multiplied those blessings many times over. This book is for you.

PART 1

UNION

CHAPTER 1

WINSTON IS BACK

CAPTAIN LOUIS MOUNTBATTEN assembled his officers on the destroyer HMS *Kelly* for an instructional session on the morning of September 3, 1939. The British captain spoke to his men about an innovative station-keeping device that enabled ships at sea to maintain fixed positions relative to other steaming vessels, an invention for which he held the patent. As Mountbatten wrapped up his lecture, an aide handed him a piece of paper. He silently read the message, slipped the sheet into a pocket, paused briefly, and announced, "I usually say, 'Now I have given you the basic principles of operating my gear. If war should at this moment break out, you know enough about it to work it.'"

After a pause, he concluded, "Well, war has at this moment broken out."

The slip of paper handed to Mountbatten was a signal that read, "From Admiralty to all concerned at home and abroad. Most Immediate. Commence hostilities at once with Germany."[1]

First lord of the admiralty is a political appointment, roughly equivalent to Secretary of the Navy in the United States. Historian William Manchester described James Stanhope as "a Gilbert and Sullivan first lord, celebrated for his ignorance of ships, of naval strategy, even of the sea. 'Tell me,' he once asked a sea lord, 'what is a "lee" *exactly*?"[2]

Stanhope's appointment ended without fanfare on the day that war was declared. Two days earlier, Prime Minister Neville Chamberlain had bowed to public and parliamentary pressure and invited Winston Churchill to join his cabinet, an offer that mentioned no specific portfolio. On Sunday, September 3, after Chamberlain announced Britain's declaration of war against Germany, he asked Churchill, who had served as first lord of the admiralty before and during the previous war—from 1911 through 1915—to oversee the Royal Navy once again.

Churchill, who believed "the opening hours of war may be vital with navies," plunged right in.[3] A naval officer observed Churchill's return to the admiralty that evening. "As soon as Winston reached his old room he told me to look and see whether there was a chart case fixed to the back of a large sofa at the east end of the room. There was: I pulled out the charts and Winston looked at them and said they were the ones he had used up to the time he left the Admiralty in 1915."[4]

Churchill's return was announced to the fleet that night in a three-word cable. "Winston is back."

British journalist Robert Blatchford, writing for his own small newspaper in 1914, defined an island as "a piece of land entirely surrounded by the British Navy."[5]

One-hundred-and-seventy-four years earlier, Scottish poet James Thomson wrote a tribute to British naval supremacy. His poem was set to music and is sung with vigor to this day. The second stanza of *Rule, Britannia!* declares,

The nations, not so blest as thee,
Must, in their turns, to tyrants fall;
While thou shalt flourish great and free,
The dread and envy of them all.
"Rule, Britannia! Britannia rule the waves:
"Britons never will be slaves."

By the summer of 1939 there were too many waves for Britain to rule on its own. With a vast global empire to protect, and with potential seaborne threats from Germany, Italy, and perhaps even Japan to contend with, the Royal Navy's obligations were stretched beyond reason. After centuries of discord, Britain and France were now allies. At this critical point in history, collaboration with *la Marine nationale* (the French Navy) was a natural and welcome development against the tyrants—Adolf Hitler and Benito Mussolini in particular—who aspired to enslave Great Britain and the rest of Europe.

Reciprocal naval missions were opened and staffed with attachés posted to London and Paris. Naval liaison officers were stationed in key ports, with French-speaking British officers deployed to Bizerte, Brest, Dunkirk, and Toulon, and *capitaines de la marine francaise* installed in Dover, Gibraltar, Malta, and Plymouth. The navies activated a common cipher for secure communications one week before the two nations declared war on Germany.[6] They sailed freely into each other's ports, where they could "expect to be victualled and refueled."[7]

Forty-nine-year-old Captain Cedric Swinton Holland, who had served as Britain's naval attaché in Paris since 1938, helped develop the liaison program between the French and British navies. During that period of relative calm, Captain Holland's liaison responsibilities also included the navies of Spain, Portugal, Belgium, and the Netherlands.

Holland, the son of an admiral, was an affable leader who bore the nickname Hooky, which derived from his uncommonly sharp and prominent nose, with assured grace. (A 1949 personal letter from the former Captain Mountbatten—then Lord Mountbatten of Burma—began with the salutation: "My dear Hook.")[8]

Holland, to his dismay, had been excluded from a British expedition to summit Mount Everest in 1922.[9] A letter from the Royal Geographical Society informed him that due to the "great strength of the climbing party" and the Society's inability to provide transportation for Holland and his gear, the innovative high-altitude wireless telegraphy experiment he had proposed was rejected.[10] Seven men would die in that attempt to summit Everest thirty-one years before Sir Edmund Hillary and Tenzig Norgay finally conquered the mountain. This stroke of misfortune potentially spared Holland for the critical service he was to provide the Royal Navy in the summer of 1940.

An athletic, charismatic officer who led with instinctive informality, Holland routinely joined his men for physical training on the flight deck of the aircraft carrier he commanded later in the war.[11] His buoyant personality led to genial relationships with his opposite numbers in the French General Staff. Holland's counterparts in Paris appreciated that both he and his wife Barbara embraced their culture and spoke their language fluently.

In the month before the outbreak of the war, Holland transferred his work quarters from the British Embassy to the French Ministry of Marine on the Rue Royale. From that point on, his liaison attachment was to the French Navy alone. During the final days of peace, Captain Holland was a welcome participant in the daily meetings of Admiral of the Fleet François Darlan, the head of the French Navy, and his chiefs of staff. Darlan often asked Holland to serve as an intermediary in communications with his direct British counterpart, First Sea Lord Admiral of the Fleet Sir Dudley Pound.

In London, Holland's opposite number, Vice Admiral Jean-Ernest Odend'hal, head of the French Naval Mission, settled into a small suite of offices in the admiralty headquarters at Whitehall, the area between Trafalgar Square and Parliament Square in London. The admiralty, the ministry of defence, and other key ministries and agencies had their headquarters at Whitehall. By the time their governments went to war with Germany, the French and British navies had a solid framework in place for effective collaboration.

On September 4, 1939, the day after war was declared, Captain Holland and the British Naval Mission followed key departments of the French admiralty when they relocated forty miles outside of Paris to the small commune of Maintenon. There was a hopeful sense that Maintenon was safely out of the path of the inevitable German bombing attacks on the French capital.

The move to Maintenon was neither impetuous nor haphazard. Planning for this transfer had begun in 1938. The French admiralty and the British Naval Mission settled into new headquarters on the grounds of the Château de Maintenon. The Maintenon facility was equipped with secure domestic communication capabilities, as well as a direct link to Whitehall. This new naval headquarters was assigned a secret name, "Marceau," a secret that was short-lived. Before the month ended, Marceau was brazenly mentioned on Radio-Stuttgart, a German-based propaganda station that broadcast into France.[12] Marceau was run with naval discipline and shipboard affectation. The several hundred people who worked at the facility were not allowed to live with their families. Nor could they "go ashore" without permission.[13]

This spirit of cooperation between the French and British navies was reinforced by their leaders, both political and military. In early November, Winston Churchill and Admiral of the Fleet Sir Dudley Pound—who, as First Sea Lord, was Britain's senior naval officer—traveled to Maintenon, where they met with members of the French admiralty to sharpen plans for joint operations.

In his history of the war, Churchill acknowledged the primacy of Admiral François Darlan. The French Navy's tonnage, morale, and prestige had receded after World War I. Churchill wrote that Darlan "deemed himself the French Navy, and the French Navy acclaimed him their chief and their reviver."[14]

During the meeting at Maintenon, Churchill expressed concern about the imminent danger presented by the German battleship *Bismarck*. Churchill expected the *Bismarck* to begin marauding the Atlantic in a matter of months, which would threaten the Allies' merchant ships even more so than it would their navies.

For all its naval might, Britain did not yet have a ship that matched *Bismarck*'s size, speed, and firepower. France had a solution in the making, and Churchill implored his ally to sustain steady progress on the construction of the *Richelieu*, a battleship that was scheduled for completion in the fall of 1940.[15]

With the *Richelieu* many months away from her commissioning, the French and British agreed on an intriguing combination of resources. The *Dunkerque*, one of the newest and fastest battleships in the French fleet, was briefly paired with HMS *Hood*, the most revered ship in the Royal Navy. A British signals team was quartered on the *Dunkerque*; a French team sailed on board the *Hood*.[16]

Churchill offered to share a British technical innovation with Darlan. By the late 1930s, the British had the most advanced underwater listening technology in the world. ASDIC, short for Anti-Submarine Detection Investigation Committee, was a seaborne detection system that was the British equivalent of sonar.

Churchill, celebrated for his interest in military innovation, first witnessed a demonstration of ASDIC as a member of Parliament. The technology's ability to spot submerged menaces astounded him, and he wrote, "I never imagined that I should hear one of those creatures asking to be destroyed."[17] Churchill extended an offer—which Admiral Darlan accepted—to install ASDIC devices in the roughly fifty French anti-submarine vessels currently in service.[18]

As the meeting at Marceau drew to a close, Churchill expressed gratitude to his "French colleagues and comrades for the very remarkable assistance which they have given to the common cause since the beginning of the war," and he added his specific appreciation for assistance recently provided by France to a vulnerable British convoy. In doing so, he singled out the services of the *Dunkerque*, which provided "the only means by which the German raiders could be warded off."

On November 8, shortly after his return to London and six weeks before he hosted a dinner at the admiralty in Admiral Darlan's honor, Churchill stood before the House of Commons to address a shocking naval loss and to brief members on the war from the Navy's perspective. Three weeks earlier, a German U-boat snuck into the presumably impregnable British naval base at Scapa Flow in Scotland's Orkney Islands and attacked the battleship HMS *Royal Oak*. After she was struck by a salvo of three torpedoes, the *Royal Oak* sank in just thirteen minutes. Of the 1,234 men and boys on the *Royal Oak*, 835 were killed in that surprise attack in the early morning hours.

After his prepared remarks, in the course of replies to questions from members of Parliament, Churchill saluted a rebuilt French navy, "which has not for many generations been so powerful or so efficient."[19]

Churchill added, "Under the long care of Admiral Darlan . . . a magnificent fighting and seafaring force has been developed. Not only have we been assisted in every way agreed upon before the war, but besides a whole set of burdens have been lifted off our shoulders by the loyal and ever-increasingly vigorous co-operation of the French Fleet."

At the time of this early-November 1939 speech, Britain had 158,000 men on the continent of Europe, a paltry commitment in comparison with the 900,000 *poilus* [soldiers] that France had deployed to fight the land war against Germany.[20] The Allies understood that the Royal Navy and the Royal Air Force would provide Britain's most significant contributions while France bore the brunt of fighting on the ground.

The French Navy's extraordinary cooperation moved Churchill to add, "It seems to me a wonderful thing that when France is making so great an effort upon land she should at that same time offer to the Allied cause so powerful a reinforcement upon the seas."

The *Dunkerque*, which Churchill had singled out with praise and gratitude, had an established kinship with the Royal Navy. When Britain celebrated the coronation of King George VI with an international naval review at Spithead in May 1937, the British welcomed the *Dunkerque*, then the newest ship in the French Navy, as a guest of honor.

Another participant of significant note in the King's naval review was the pocket battleship *Admiral Graf Spee*, which represented Germany in the peaceful waters outside of Portsmouth more than two years before the navies went to war.[21] After the outbreak of hostilities, the *Dunkerque* and her British sailing partners would hunt for the *Graf Spee*. Her demise would help avenge the loss of the *Royal Oak* and would be the centerpiece of the most celebrated Royal Navy operation in the first months of the war.

CHAPTER 2

UNTIL THEY WIN OR GO DOWN WITH THEIR FLAG FLYING

CAPTAIN HANS LANGSDORFF, the commander of the *Graf Spee*, lacked the cutthroat moral compass of a German U-boat commander. Instead of attacking defenseless merchant ships with no warning, Langsdorff operated under traditional prize rules. After a warning shot or two, the German captain provided British crews a brief window of time to abandon their vessels and then sank the forcibly abandoned ships by a combination of shellfire and torpedoes. Some crewmen were cast adrift; many were taken on board as prisoners. None were forced to go down with their ships.

In *Der Seekrieg: The German Navy's Story, 1939–1945*, Admiral Friedrich Ruge wrote, "War at sea envisages the destruction of the enemy's resources, not of its population." He added, "England's weakness—her absolute dependence on supplies from overseas—was to be exploited."[1] Adolf Hitler codified German naval strategy in Directive No. 1 of the Supreme Command: "The Navy will concentrate on commerce destruction directed especially against England."[2]

During three months in the autumn of 1939, the *Graf Spee* sank nine British merchant ships. Her chivalrous marauding affected British morale more than it impacted Allied shipping and supplies. Nonetheless, joint Allied hunting parties, which included shifting combinations of the British aircraft carrier *Ark Royal* and the French battleships *Dunkerque* and *Strasbourg*, pursued her with unchivalrous intent.

After three months of fruitless pursuit in the north and south reaches of the Atlantic Ocean, three British cruisers confronted the German commerce raider off the coast of Uruguay near the mouth of the River Plate on December 13, 1939. The *Graf Spee* was severely damaged in the ensuing battle and sought refuge and repairs in the port of Montevideo.

According to the 1907 Hague Convention's Rights and Duties of Neutral Powers in Naval War, a warship's stay in a neutral port could not exceed twenty-four hours. Local authorities, on their own volition, extended *Graf Spee*'s stay to seventy-two hours, still well short of the time required to return her to battle-ready condition.

Captain Langsdorff was aware that British warships awaited his wounded vessel at the mouth of the river. The British admiralty fueled the apprehension of Langsdorff and the German admiralty with the transmission of unencrypted cables suggesting that reinforcements, including the *Ark Royal*, were nearing Montevideo, when, in fact, they were not within immediate sailing range.

The standoff in the south Atlantic captured the attention of the world. A front-page *New York Times* story about the approaching battlefleet carried the subheading "French *Dunkerque* Also Said to be on Way to Montevideo—Big Holes in Reich Ship."[3] Like the *Ark Royal*, the *Dunkerque* was nowhere near Montevideo. In fact, she was headed in the opposite direction, en route to Canada, on a mission to deliver a portion of France's gold reserves for safekeeping.[4]

Langsdorff considered a suicidal run for open water with his guns blazing in the hope of taking down one or more British or French ships. On the evening of Sunday, December 17, however, Langsdorff and a skeleton crew eased the *Graf Spee* into the shallow waters just outside the mouth of the River Plate. The German crew dropped anchor, set the timers on explosive charges, and abandoned their ship to an inglorious end with her keel nestled into the mud and her turrets and mast poking above the sea.

Two days later, wearing full dress uniform and laying atop *Graf Spee*'s battle ensign in his hotel room in Montevideo, Langsdorff killed himself with a bullet to the head.[5] In a letter found near his body, the German captain wrote, "I can now only prove by my death that the fighting services of the Third Reich are ready to die for the honor of the flag."[6]

Adolf Hitler would have preferred to see that proof in the form of a sea battle. He admired the Royal Navy's traditional willingness to fight to the end, and he later lectured his admirals on the symbolic value of "dying gallantly."[7] Langsdorff had ignored orders from Hitler and *Grossadmiral* Erich Raeder to break for open water and take on the assumed flotilla of Allied ships at the mouth of the river. In the aftermath of *Graf Spee*'s scuttling and Lansdorff's suicide, Raeder issued an order: "The German warship and her crew are to fight with all their strength to the last shell, until they win or go down with their flag flying."[8]

When the *Graf Spee* docked in Montevideo, Captain Langsdorff released the prisoners he had retained on board—sixty-two British merchant seamen whose ages ranged from fifteen to seventy-two. They had been held captive in the weeks (and, in some cases, months) since the *Graf Spee* intercepted and sank their ships. As the British consular staff greeted the newly freed crewmen, several of the liberated men mentioned that hundreds of additional prisoners remained on board the *Graf Spee*'s supply ship the *Altmark,* which was still at sea.

Because Germany lacked overseas colonies and a network of naval bases, supply vessels were used to support extended voyages. The *Altmark* had provisioned the *Graf Spee* with food, fuel, and other necessities during her long voyages through the North and South Atlantic Ocean. While Captain Langsdorff retained some captured seamen on the *Graf Spee*, he routinely transferred a greater number to the *Altmark*, which, in the wake of the sinking of nine British merchant ships, carried 299 British prisoners. The prisoners had endured months at sea in repulsive conditions. They were penned in a single windowless hold, and subsisted on a diet of "black bread and watery goulash." They relied on "brimming forty-gallon oil drums which were almost never emptied" for their bathroom needs.[9]

To this point, the Royal Navy had not been aware of the existence of the *Altmark*, a ship classified as an oil tanker and a supply vessel, not a warship. With *Altmark* revealed as a floating prison, she became the focus of an intense hunt.

The German admiralty ordered *Altmark* to return from South America to home waters in the North Atlantic, and to maintain total radio silence through her journey of 8,000 nautical miles. She cruised at slow speed in the South Atlantic through the rest of December and much of January before heading north. The pilot of a British search plane finally sighted her off the coast of Norway two months after the scuttling of the *Graf Spee*.

Captain Philip Vian, on HMS *Cossack*, led a squadron that attempted to intercept the German support vessel, which had taken refuge in a narrow Norwegian fjord. In response to British demands to search the *Altmark*, Norwegian authorities asserted that they had already inspected the German ship, found her to be unarmed, and had not discovered any prisoners on board. In those circumstances, Norway would permit the *Altmark* to make her way to Germany through Norwegian territorial waters.

A German naval historian later offered the wry perspective, "The status of *Altmark* as a merchant vessel flying the naval ensign and carrying prisoners of war in neutral water was somewhat obscure in international law."[10] Winston Churchill, still first lord of the admiralty, was adamant that the British prisoners be rescued, and sought authorization from Lord Halifax, Britain's foreign secretary, to intercept the *Altmark* in the Norwegian fjord. Halifax concurred within five minutes of Churchill's request. Churchill later wrote, "That was big of Halifax."

Churchill added that although "I did not often act so directly," he bypassed the first sea lord and the admiralty and issued a direct order to Captain Vian that unless the Norwegian navy helped him take the German ship into custody, "you should board *Altmark*, liberate the prisoners, and take possession of the ship."[11]

After the *Altmark* attempted to ram the *Cossack* and then ran aground in the fjord, Captain Vian's ship came alongside, and in an echo of the days of cutlasses and casks of rum, a British boarding party leapt across to the German ship. As British and German crews skirmished on the *Altmark*'s deck, a British hand opened the hatch above the hold in which the prisoners were crammed. Through the sounds of the fracas on deck, the prisoners heard the unmistakable voice of a countryman: "Any Englishmen down there?" When the questioner heard a chorus of assent, he replied, "Come up, then." And then much louder, "Come up . . . THE NAVY'S HERE!"[12]

When the crews of the British ships that had cornered the *Graf Spee* returned to Britain, they marched through London crowds that "were such as there had not been since . . . King George's Jubilee." A Londoner wrote in a letter to a friend, "People kept on running forward and touching the men as they passed. One white-haired old man . . . kept on clapping them on the shoulder or shaking them by the hand and saying, 'Well done, boy!'"[13]

Churchill glowed in the aftermath of the *Altmark* affair: "The rescue and Captain Vian's conduct aroused a wave of enthusiasm in Britain almost equal to that which followed the sinking of the *Graf Spee*. Both these events strengthened my hand and the prestige of the Admiralty. 'The Navy's here!' was passed from lip to lip."[14]

After shuttling French gold reserves to Canada, the *Dunkerque* participated in the most remarkable of all the joint operations between the French and British navies during the war. *Dunkerque* took the lead in a joint convoy that protected seven British troopships carrying Canadian soldiers to England. The voyage was noteworthy for the command structure of the blended fleet.

As the senior officer in this ad hoc squadron, French Admiral Marcel-Bruno Gensoul, sailing on the *Dunkerque*, was its acknowledged leader, marking one of the few occasions in history when British warships sailed under a French admiral. Captain Cedric Holland, on a seagoing hiatus from his role as British Naval Attaché, had been elevated to the acting rank of vice admiral for the duration of the voyage to ensure an effective liaison between the two navies. Holland flew his temporary flag on the World War I vintage battleship HMS *Revenge*.[15]

As they neared the coastlines of their respective nations, the French ships veered south on their way to Brest. The British ships continued to Southampton. Before the two squadrons diverged, their leaders exchanged congenial farewells.

Gensoul signaled, "Hope that we may have an opportunity of meeting again. I congratulate you on the way you handled the convoy."[16]

Holland replied, "I look forward happily to serving under you again."

In a report to Admiral Darlan, Gensoul shared that Holland was "[a]n infinitely courteous, loyal and able collaborator."

No one would have foreseen that in less than seven months Captain Holland would attempt to negotiate the surrender of Admiral Gensoul's squadron to the British, and that Royal Navy battleships—including HMS *Hood*—would fire their 15-inch guns on Gensoul and the *Dunkerque*.[17]

In the interim, the two compatible, and even amiable, allies worked through intermittent bursts of friction. Cedric Holland sparred with a French staff officer over the deployment of French naval assets; Admiral Darlan carped about the "isolationist and unapproachable attitude" of the British commanding officer at Gibraltar until he was sacked.[18] These small disputes were viewed as the natural product of different naval cultures, and the bonds that joined the two navies remained solid.

In contrast, turmoil at the highest levels of the French and British governments in the spring of 1940 threatened the stability of each nation, as well as that of the formal alliance between Britain and France just as the war with Germany was about to ignite.

CHAPTER 3

FACTS ARE BETTER THAN DREAMS

AS NOBLES AND NOTABLES filed into Westminster Abbey for the coronation of King George VI on May 12, 1937, a British military officer caught the eye of the man at his side. The officer gestured toward an unfamiliar figure and asked, "Who is that little man with the Japanese face?"

French author André Maurois glanced up and replied, "That little man is the future Premier of France."[1]

Paul Reynaud, who stood five-feet, three-inches tall, would fulfill André Maurois' prediction less than three years later when the French Chamber of Deputies elected him prime minister by a margin of one vote.[2]

Reynaud's diminutive stature was considered a factor in his demeanor as well as a physical attribute. French diplomat André François-Poncet claimed, "he has all the faults of men under five feet three. He elbows his way ahead for fear that he won't be taken seriously."[3] Reynaud was a dynamo whose energy startled his new subordinates. General Maurice Gamelin remarked that in contrast with Reynaud's predecessor Édouard Daladier, "who couldn't make a decision at all, here we are with Reynaud who makes one every five minutes."[4] Reynaud, a Sorbonne-educated lawyer who was born in the south of France, was, in fact, so distinctly French that the brows above his perpetually quizzical eyes embodied grave and acute accent marks.

On the day after Reynaud's ascent to power, Winston Churchill wrote to congratulate his friend of long standing: "I cannot tell you how glad I am that all has been accomplished so successfully and speedily. . . . We have thought so much alike during the past three or four years."[5]

Churchill and Reynaud had indeed thought much alike . . . to the extent that one diplomat described Reynaud as "something of a French

Winston."[6] During the 1930s, when most leaders were hesitant to poke the German tiger, the two men expressed their disdain in word and deed.

Churchill scorned the September 1938 Munich Agreement, which ceded Czechoslovakia to German annihilation, with a scathing rebuke in the House of Commons, noting that Czechoslovakia had "suffered in every respect from her association with the Western democracies," and that Britain had "sustained a defeat without a war."[7]

Reynaud's outrage at the Munich Agreement was even more pronounced and tangible. He resigned his post as Minister of Justice in protest. Historian Julian Jackson wrote that Reynaud was "a brilliant parliamentary performer, with a gift for the telling phrase or snappy formula."[8] However, in terms of substance, he "tended to dazzle rather than persuade." As Winston Churchill would learn, Reynaud also ricocheted between extremes of optimism and despair.

In the two decades since the Allies defeated Germany in World War I, the tactics by which they won the war—static defensive lines and massive bombardments—were accepted as conventional wisdom in France for how to win the inevitable next war. Reynaud was one of the unheeded voices who argued instead for mobility and speed.

Reynaud's belief in a swift, mobile military aligned with the writings of his protégé, Colonel Charles de Gaulle, whose book *Towards a Professional Army* promoted the deployment of tanks as if they were cavalry, a revolutionary concept at the time.

Reynaud embraced de Gaulle's argument for an alternative to the conventional French approach to fighting a war, best exemplified by what Reynaud condemned as "the soft pillow of the Maginot Line."[9] The Maginot Line was a series of mostly underground fortresses, described by journalist Clare Boothe as "sunken earth-bound battleships" that, in keeping with their belief in the invincibility of static defensive positions, the French assumed would deter a German attack.[10]

According to legend, de Gaulle's book sold just seven hundred copies in his country. A member of the French general staff dismissed the viability of tanks as weapons with the notion that "(t)here are only two bridges in France that can support the weight of an armored division."[11]

To France's future misfortune, *Towards a Professional Army* received a more favorable reception in Germany where it influenced the tactics of Panzer leader General Heinz Guderian, whose armored divisions would race across the fields and bridges of France in the spring of 1940.

On March 28, 1940, just one week after ascending to the premiership, Reynaud traveled to London for a meeting of the Supreme War Council. Prime Minister Neville Chamberlain's British delegation included Winston Churchill in his role as first lord of the admiralty. The most significant outcome of the meeting was a joint statement about the obvious reciprocal commitment of Britain and France: "Both Governments mutually undertake that during the present war they will neither negotiate nor conclude an armistice or treaty of peace except by mutual agreement."

As Winston Churchill noted in his history of the war, "This pact later acquired high importance."[12]

By May 1940, France and Britain had been at war with Germany for eight months. Although all three nations were nominally combatants and actively clashed at sea, this period was known as the phony war, the *Sitzkrieg*, or the *drôle de guerre*, depending on one's nationality. Since the adversaries were still more inclined to drop propaganda leaflets than bombs, it was also called "the confetti war." Regardless of its name, it was a war in which few battles were fought on land. But that was about to change.

Rumors of a massive German invasion of its western neighbors surged throughout the spring. In a March 30 radio address, Churchill warned that the neutral countries of Belgium, Holland, and Luxembourg might, at any moment, "be subjected to an avalanche of steel and fire."[13]

Reynaud hoped to resolve a leadership crisis before serious shots were fired. During his seven weeks as prime minister, Reynaud had lost faith in Generalissimo Maurice Gamelin, the leader of all French military forces. In addition to Gamelin's passive prosecution of the war, the Allies' disorganized and ineffective response to Germany's invasions of Norway and Denmark in early April had been a fiasco.

In a one-hour harangue during a May 9 cabinet meeting, Reynaud argued for General Gamelin's dismissal and stated that if Gamelin remained at the head of French forces against a German invasion, "we are certain to lose the war."[14] When he received scant support for his plan to sack his top general, Reynaud declared, "I shall have to consider the government as having resigned," which meant the dissolution of his cabinet and the fall of his government. Reynaud asked that his resignation remain confidential until the following day, when he intended to seek the approval of the Chamber of Deputies to form a new government.

Gamelin learned of the prime minister's barrage of criticism a short time after the meeting's end and drafted his own letter of resignation. And thus, in the early morning hours of May 10, 1940, the resignations of the French prime minister and the commander-in-chief of its military hung in purgatory and simmered in temporary secrecy while the full military might of Germany massed at the frontiers of Belgium, the Netherlands, and Luxembourg, poised to rain an avalanche of steel and fire on all three nations before dawn, and then roll into France.

Across the English Channel, Neville Chamberlain's fate as Great Britain's prime minister also hung in the balance. Chamberlain had endured two days of acrimonious debate for his meek—it would be quite fair to call it phony—prosecution of the war, most recently after Germany launched its surprise attack against Norway. Although the Allies responded quickly, and even enjoyed initial success, British ground forces were poorly trained and ill-equipped for clashes on snow and ice, and quickly lost their advantage. Britain evacuated the majority of its Expeditionary Force from Norway after fighting for less than two months.

During two days of debate on May 7 and 8, members of Parliament rehashed the campaign and sought to assign blame for Britain's failed attempt to save Norway from the German invaders. Although Neville Chamberlain was the obvious target for the ire of members of the opposition Labour Party, First Lord of the Admiralty Winston Churchill also braced for a harsh cascade of criticism.

Britain's navy sank ten German destroyers and two cruisers, and temporarily impaired Germany's ability to wage war at sea. However,

Germany's successful campaign owed much to the initiative of its navy in the first days of the Norwegian operation, which caught the British by surprise and helped the Germans gain an advantage in Norway that they held to the end of the war.

On Chamberlain's part, the seventy-one-year-old prime minister was confident that his Conservative party's two-hundred-seat majority provided a safe buffer against any degree of discord.

Leo Amery, the member from Birmingham Sparkbrook, was part of Chamberlain's Conservative majority. Amery, who rose to speak late on Tuesday, May 7, was considered brilliant but also a "notorious bore."[15] British journalist Colin Coote wrote, "Perhaps he knew so much that he took a little too long to say it," and, "It was, indeed, remarked of him that he would have been prime minister if he had been half a head taller and his speeches had been half an hour shorter."[16]

On this day, in this speech, however, Amery turned on Chamberlain with concise eloquence: "Somehow or other we must get into the Government men who can match our enemies in fighting spirit, in daring, in resolution and in thirst for victory."[17]

The broadside that followed those early remarks sealed Amery's legacy. His diatribe inspired former prime minister David Lloyd George to observe that "in fifty years he had heard few speeches to match it in sustained power and none with so dramatic a climax."[18]

When Amery entered the House early that afternoon, he was not sure if he would use the closing passage he had drafted. As he wrote in his diary, "I doubted whether this was not too strong meat."[19] He planned to take the temperature of the room while listening to the speakers who preceded him. As he witnessed the fury of his fellow MPs, their vitriol left no doubt in Amery's mind that no meat could be too strong, and no words could be too barbed.

By the time the speaker of the house recognized Amery, it was eight o'clock in the evening, and he briefly considered delaying his speech until the next day. Although fewer than a dozen members lingered in their seats, a large audience gradually formed as other members drifted back into the hall after an ally of Amery recruited them from the smoking room in the Commons and nearby clubs. When Amery reached the climax of his address, he spoke to a packed house.[20]

Amery, who had quoted Oliver Cromwell early in his address, closed with an inspired piece of damnation from a speech Cromwell had directed to the Long Parliament, a body that had served for twenty years, ending in 1660. After a slight hesitation and a quick glance in the direction of Lloyd George, Amery turned Cromwell's diatribe on Neville Chamberlain. "You have sat too long here for any good you have been doing. Depart, I say, and let us have done with you. In the name of God, go!"

Amery's words hit like a thunderbolt and were met with shouts and gasps of surprise and wrath. His broadside continued to reverberate in clubs, bars, restaurants, and at private gatherings through the night. Harold Macmillan, a future prime minister, who observed Amery's address as a fellow Conservative member of Parliament, remarked that Amery "effectively destroyed the Chamberlain Government."[21]

The formal destruction of Chamberlain's government began the following day when the Labour Party demanded a division—effectively a vote of confidence in Chamberlain—preceded by a debate. In a division, members would register their votes by walking to one of two lobbies on either side of the rear of the chamber, and then have their votes counted when they reentered from either the "aye" or the "nay" division lobby. Chamberlain leapt to his feet to accept the challenge, declaring, "I have friends in the House."

In the day-long debate that followed, the Commons Chamber was stirred by the clash of spirited mudslinging and resolute loyalty. While many members directed their ire at Prime Minister Chamberlain and his cabinet, some allies of Winston Churchill singled him out for protection.

During an exchange over the Norway debacle, David Lloyd George interjected, "I do not think that the First Lord was entirely responsible for all the things that happened there."

Churchill stood and declared, "I take complete responsibility for everything that has been done by the Admiralty, and I take my full share of the burden."[22]

Lloyd George responded, "The right honorable Gentleman must not allow himself to be converted into an air-raid shelter to keep the splinters from hitting his colleagues."

Duff Cooper, a former first lord of the admiralty in Neville Chamberlain's cabinet, who had resigned in October 1938 to protest the Munich Agreement, also defended the current First Lord: "He will be defending with his eloquence those who have so long refused to listen to his counsel, who treated his warnings with contempt, and who refused to take him into their own confidence."

Winston Churchill, the final speaker before the division, delivered a late-night oration that ended one hour before midnight on May 8. The First Lord held the floor for forty-nine minutes with Duff Cooper's predicted eloquence, and with loyalty to Chamberlain that surprised many. Churchill termed the Allied campaign in Norway "a ghastly success," noting that "7,000 or 8,000 men have been drowned, and thousands of corpses have been washed up on the rocks at the entrance of Oslo."

In sincere support of Chamberlain, he noted, "He thought he had some friends, and I hope he has some friends. He certainly had a good many when things were going well."

Churchill offered this plea: "I say, let pre-war feuds die; let personal quarrels be forgotten, and let us keep our hatreds for the common enemy."

Although Chamberlain won the majority of the votes in the late-night division, he was humiliated by the underwhelming margin of support that he received. Chamberlain's typical majority of more than two hundred in previous divisions had slipped to just eight-one votes, which was considered well short of an effective majority, especially in time of war. The House of Commons had 615 members in 1940.

When the result was announced, the House erupted in pandemonium, accented by shouts of "Resign!" and "In the name of God, go!" As Neville Chamberlain walked from the chamber, startled and humiliated, Josiah Wedgwood and Harold Macmillan derisively serenaded the P.M. with an off-key chorus of *Rule, Britannia!*[23]

Rule, Britannia! Britannia rule the waves:
Britons never will be slaves.

Chamberlain held on to steadily diminishing strands of hope for an opportunity to form a new government and remain in power. News of the German attack briefly invigorated his vanity and sense of duty. However, when the Labour Party announced their refusal to join Chamberlain in a coalition government, the prime minister resigned late on the afternoon of May 10, 1940.

The German invasion, which had provided an unlikely lifeline for Paul Reynaud, did not spare Neville Chamberlain. Hitler's attack on Britain's allies did, however, solidify confidence in Winston Churchill as the ideal man to lead Great Britain in wartime.

Less than two hours after accepting Neville Chamberlain's resignation, King George VI summoned his first lord of the admiralty to Buckingham Palace and greeted Churchill with a wry question: "I suppose you don't know why I have sent for you?"

"Sir, I simply couldn't imagine why."

And with that, the king and his new prime minister shared a brittle laugh. Britain's monarch asked Churchill to form a government, fulfilling Churchill's life's ambition at the age of sixty-five.

Churchill had not been the king's first choice to succeed Chamberlain. Indeed, he very likely was not the king's second or third choice. King George had hoped Lord Halifax—Britain's foreign secretary—would be proposed as the leader most likely to command the confidence of the House of Commons. Historian Andrew Roberts suggests that "the Cabinet, the Privy Council, the Conservative Party, the House of Lords, . . . the City of London, the BBC, *The Times*, and the Church of England" all would have preferred Lord Halifax.[24] However, as a member of the House of Lords, Halifax acknowledged the challenge of leading the Commons. In addition, Halifax had no interest in heading a wartime government in which Churchill would have been the inevitable—and irrepressible—choice for secretary of state for war.

The greatest day of Winston Churchill's life had dawned with the first furious widespread fighting in a war that had been meekly declared eight months earlier. The long anticipated but still shocking blitzkrieg attacks unleashed by Adolf Hitler on Belgium, Holland, and Luxembourg just before sunrise continued unabated. With everything from glider landings on an "impregnable" Belgian fortress to coordinated assaults by tanks and Stuka dive bombers that had no precedent, the German invaders outraced the Allies' defenses and imagination. The challenge that Winston Churchill accepted at day's end was immense.

And yet, as Churchill wrote in the final paragraph of *The Gathering Storm*, the first volume in his history of World War II,

> as I went to bed at about 3 A.M., I was conscious of a profound sense of relief. At last I had the authority to give directions over the whole scene. I felt as if I were walking with Destiny, and that all my past life had been but a preparation for this hour and for this trial. Eleven years in the political wilderness had freed me from ordinary party antagonisms. My warnings over the last six years had been so numerous, so detailed, and were now so terribly vindicated, that no one could gainsay me. I could not be reproached either for making the war or with want of preparation for it. I thought I knew a good deal about it all, and I was sure I should not fail. Therefore, although impatient for the morning, I slept soundly and had no need for cheering dreams. Facts are better than dreams.[25]

CHAPTER 4

NOT ILLUMINATED BY THE MERCY OF CHRIST

PAUL REYNAUD, ON HIS fiftieth day as prime minister of France, woke to the news of the German blitzkrieg and called off his plan from the previous afternoon to resign and form a new government. He also retained General Maurice Gamelin and sent a supportive message to the commander of France's military: "The battle has begun. Only one thing counts: to win it. We shall work together toward that goal."[1]

From his headquarters in the heavily fortified Château de Vincennes, described by one officer as "a submarine without a periscope,"[2] Gamelin replied, "*Monsieur le Président*, I see only one answer to your message. France alone counts."

Reynaud remarked to Undersecretary of State Paul Baudouin later that morning, "Gamelin has been saved. At last he has got the battle he has been waiting for—indeed hoping for. . . . Well, we'll see what Gamelin is worth."

The clash exploded into France the next day. Holland surrendered within a week. Belgium fought for just eighteen days. German tanks and infantrymen quickly spread across France, some dashing toward Paris, some racing toward the English Channel, all avoiding the faux barrier of the Maginot Line. Mechanized columns crossed dozens of bridges in France without mishap.

Winston Churchill was roused from his sleep on the morning of May 15, 1940, for an urgent telephone call from Paul Reynaud. The French prime minister's first words, which he blurted in English, stunned his counterpart: "We have been defeated . . . we are beaten; we have lost the battle."[3]

May 15 was Churchill's fifth full day as Britain's prime minister and the fifth day since Adolf Hitler's army and air force launched their attacks on Western Europe. The battle had just begun, and Churchill knew that France was far from defeated. But Reynaud was dangerously unnerved. A British admiral had once noted Churchill's knack for making him feel "a little braver and a little more sure of final victory."[4] Churchill promised to fly to Paris the following day to steady and reinforce the bravery of his ally.

Churchill, who had quickly asserted his primacy in Britain's war planning and operations by assuming the self-fashioned role of minister of defence, met with Reynaud and the principal officers of his government and the French military on the evening of May 16. The French leaders' most pressing desire was additional support from Britain's Royal Air Force. The RAF had almost thirty-five squadrons (to be precise, 416 aircraft, with 12 aircraft per squadron) stationed in France.[5] After the meeting, to Reynaud's relief, Churchill sought and received approval from his war cabinet to add six additional squadrons to the four new squadrons he had originally planned to offer to France.[6]

General Maurice Gamelin was given just one week to prove his worth before he was sacked and replaced as commander-in-chief of the French Armed Forces by General Maxime Weygand.

In addition, Reynaud revealed in a May 18 radio address that the most prominent living hero from World War I had joined his government. "The Victor of Verdun, Marshal Pétain, returned this morning from Madrid. He will now be at my side . . . putting all his wisdom and all his force in the service of the country. He will remain there until victory is won."[7]

More than any other living Frenchman, Henri Philippe Benoni Omer Pétain rode a wave of glory from World War I into this new battle. Pétain, who was born in 1856, graduated from the French military academy at St. Cyr in 1878 ranked number 229 out of the 286 cadets who "pledged on bended knee their willingness to die for their country." By the time the first shots were fired in World War I, Pétain, a colonel who had been told he would never be promoted to general, was already within two years of the army's mandatory retirement age.[8]

Battlefield catastrophes, a stunning toll of casualties, and the demotion of incompetent senior officers opened an unexpected path for Pétain, who was promoted to brigadier general in the first month of the war. Pétain earned the eternal crown of "Victor of Verdun" for his decisive role in the Allies' victory in the war's longest and most brutal battle. Each side suffered more than 100,000 fatalities during 299 days of fighting at Verdun in 1916. After a string of mutinies in 1917, during which some soldiers blatantly refused orders to attack or took to the battlefield drunk and without weapons, Pétain's firm but compassionate leadership helped restore the French Army into a cohesive fighting unit.

In the twenty-two years between the world wars, Pétain enjoyed the laurels of a distinguished commander of the winning side. He was an advocate of "battlefields prepared in peacetime," which included 1916-era trenches as well as the static Maginot Line.[9] The marshal scorned tanks, aeroplanes, and mobile attack forces as new, risky, and unproven tools and tactics that went against his experience-born principles.

When Pétain was an assistant professor of infantry tactics at the École de Guerre, he mentored Charles de Gaulle, an officer who was thirty-four years his junior. By 1940 the two men barely spoke, due in large part to their different opinions on how to fight a war. De Gaulle, the champion of aggressive tank warfare, had been promoted to brigadier general shortly before one of their final meetings in June of 1940. The marshal dismissed his former student: "You're a general! I don't congratulate you. What good are ranks in defeat?"[10]

In his eighty-fifth year, Pétain still exhibited the façade of a leader. The wrinkles that framed the octogenarian's icy gray-blue eyes did nothing to diminish their brilliance. His mustache, a bushy flag of flamboyance during the Great War, was now a tight, grave accent. His trim figure and noble countenance evoked an imposing command presence. Pétain projected the haughty mien of a man who expected others to take him as seriously as he took himself. Philippe Pétain had once declared, "They call me only in catastrophes."[11] In the face of catastrophe—just eight days after Germany's invasion—and in desperate need of personal, military, and public inspiration, Paul Reynaud welcomed Pétain home from Spain where he had served as France's ambassador to the government of General

Francisco Franco. Reynaud knew his announcement of the marshal's return would boost morale and inspire hope. More tangibly, even though Reynaud had no specific military responsibilities, Reynaud expected him to miraculously deliver their nation from defeat.

Reynaud was not aware that before Pétain left Spain, he confided to General Franco, "My country has been beaten and they are calling me back to make peace and to sign an armistice."[12]

It did not take long for Reynaud to sour on Pétain. Two weeks after the marshal joined his cabinet, Reynaud mentioned to Anthony Eden, Britain's Secretary of State for War, that he would not be surprised to hear Pétain speak in favor of an armistice if a large part of France were occupied by German forces.[13]

Reynaud's prediction was realized on June 9, 1940, when Pétain presented an argument for France to seek an armistice—with the condition that France accept it only if Germany offered honorable terms. Reynaud dismissed the marshal's suggestion, commenting that no one could expect honorable terms from Adolf Hitler. When he reminded Pétain of their country's commitment to not seek a separate armistice without British consent, the marshal replied, "England put us into this position."

Reynaud had no illusions about how France would fare if it submitted to Germany. In a radio address to his nation, the French prime minister painted a stark picture of life under Adolf Hitler: "It would be the Middle Ages again, but not illuminated by the mercy of Christ."[14]

By the last week of May, less than three weeks into the fighting, the British Expeditionary Force (BEF)—Britain's army—was retreating toward Dunkirk on the Channel coast. By the first week of June, most of the BEF had sailed back across the Channel to England in a miraculous flotilla of Royal Navy ships, civilian cabin cruisers, trawlers, tugboats, barges, and lifeboats manned by fishermen, shopkeepers, bank clerks, retirees, and at least one Dominican monk. In their frantic escape from Dunkirk, British soldiers left almost all of their vehicles and heavy weapons behind.

The Dunkirk evacuation—codenamed Operation Dynamo—was not solely a British affair. The 338,000 rescued troops included more than 100,000 Frenchmen. And while the tale of Dunkirk is best remembered for the storybook heroics of the rescuers and the rescued, the operation was also an underappreciated, if at times contentious, collaboration between the navies of Britain and France. Vice Admiral Jean Abrial led French operations in cooperation with British vice admirals Bertram Ramsay and James Somerville. King George VI expressed his thanks to Abrial in a June 5 audience at Buckingham Palace.[15]

The evacuation of so many men in the face of potential annihilation was understandably celebrated throughout Britain. In his famous "We shall fight them on the beaches" speech, Churchill tempered British jubilation with a note of practical caution: "We must be very careful not to assign to this deliverance the attributes of a victory. Wars are not won by evacuations."[16]

The German propaganda machine responded to Churchill's Dunkirk address with its only compliment for the prime minister during Hitler's reign as chancellor, a flippant salute to his "sober, unvarnished, manly confession of defeat."[17]

No one in France assigned the attributes of victory to the story of Dunkirk. The French version is a tale of abandonment and betrayal. In the eyes of many in France, not only had British forces contributed little on the ground or in the air in their fight against the German invaders, the British had left France to face the full onslaught of Germany's tanks, infantry, and dive bombers on its own when they retreated across the English Channel.

France and Britain had been joined as allies by treaty and common sentiment. British historian Ian Ousby noted that the months of May and June 1940 were "one of the few points in history when the Prime Minister of Britain was a francophile and the Prime Minister of France was an anglophile."[18]

When the two nations declared war on September 3, 1939, they accepted that France's manpower contribution on the ground would dwarf Britain's. France and Britain joined the fray with the tacit understanding that Britain would balance its participation with contributions from the Royal Navy as well as support from Spitfires, Hurricanes, and other aircraft of the Royal Air Force.

Almost all of the fighting in the spring and early summer of 1940 took place on French soil. In the minds of many Frenchmen, their principal ally's commitment to their joint cause was an expression of Britain's willingness to fight to the last French soldier. The allocation of Royal Air Force assets between French and British skies was a thorny challenge for Winston Churchill, and it flared into a continual and contentious point of disagreement between French and British leaders. Paul Reynaud and his generals believed the Royal Air Force could turn the tide in the Battle of France. They wanted nothing less than an absolute commitment of British air power, including the complete relocation of the RAF to French airfields. To the consternation of senior RAF officers, Churchill initially sympathized with French pleas and supported the transfer of greater numbers of air force squadrons to France than his military advisors thought prudent.

That changed after a tense meeting in the cabinet room at 10 Downing Street when Air Chief Marshal Hugh Dowding calmly set a sheet of paper on the table in front of the prime minister. Dowding had drawn a simple graph in pencil that visualized an undeniable trend—the steep decline in the number of Hurricane fighters as a result of aerial battles with the Luftwaffe. Dowding emphatically stated and convincingly showed in his graph, "If the present rate of wastage continues for another fortnight we shall not have a single Hurricane left in France or in this country."[19]

Dowding's compelling argument did not result in the removal of British planes from the skies of France; the Royal Air Force flew sorties for as long as France remained engaged in the war. However, by early June as German bombs routinely cratered French airfields, the majority of British fighters flew across the Channel from their bases in England. The most tangible result of Dowding's hand-drawn data visualization was Churchill's unwavering commitment to maintain a minimum of twenty-five RAF fighter squadrons in Britain.[20] The value of Churchill's and Dowding's resolve in the face of continual French protests was borne out when the Battle of Britain began in the second week of July 1940.

The will of the French to engage in battle was sapped after five weeks of steady losses and a steep toll of military and civilian deaths. The leaders of France had no stomach for a bloodbath in or around their capital. Paul Reynaud, Philippe Pétain, and the French government fled Paris in haste on June 10 for the flimsy safety of the first in a series of temporary capitals, leaving the City of Light conspicuously undefended and wide open to Hitler's rapidly advancing army.

General Maxime Weygand, who had dictated France's armistice terms to a German delegation in 1918, declared Paris an open city. A message from Weygand to the advancing Germans confirmed that "In order that Paris shall preserve its character as an Open City it is my intention to avoid any defensive organization around the city."[21]

A stream of French ministers and mistresses trickled into the city of Tours, many arriving in the predawn hours of Tuesday, June 11, after a journey of 145 miles. As France's leaders found temporary refuge, German wireless broadcasts mocked "the provisional, the very provisional capital of France."[22] Tours would be the first of three very provisional capitals into which France's governing ministers would briefly settle during the next three weeks. Tours would serve as the de facto capital of France for just the next three days. And then the government would move on once again.

While Tours provided the French government with expedient refuge from the German onrush, the city could not readily accommodate a large and sudden influx of visitors. As a result, ministers were scattered across the Loire Valley—as far as Briare, a two-hour drive from Tours.

Churchill flew to Briare on June 11 for two days of meetings. This was his fourth trip to France during his first five weeks as Britain's prime minister. With the risk from Luftwaffe fighters surging by the day, Churchill's de Haviland Flamingo was escorted by twelve Royal Air Force Hurricanes.[23] He met that evening with French political and military leaders, including Paul Reynaud, Marshal Pétain, and General Maxime Weygand, the commander of all of France's armed forces.

In a cablegram sent the previous day, in which he beseeched Franklin Roosevelt "to declare publicly that the United States will give the Allies aid and material support by all means 'short of an expeditionary force' . . . before it is too late," Reynaud vowed, "We shall fight before Paris; we shall fight behind Paris."[24] He said nothing about fighting in Paris, the city he fled hours after writing to the American president.

Although Paris had been abandoned, Winston Churchill continued to voice support for the defense of France's capital. Monuments and museums should be sacrificed if that would save France. The British prime minister "emphasized the enormous absorbing power of the house-to-house defence of a great city upon an invading army."[25] He hoped that an extended period of block-by-block, door-to-door combat would help wear down the resources and the will of the German invaders and perhaps prolong the fight until the United States joined the Allied cause. Churchill challenged his French counterpart to inspire the citizens of France to engage German invaders just as he expected the men and women of Britain to respond when the inevitable German attacks on London and other cities came. "When German tanks enter a town, what can the people do? The crews must be fired at if they get out. Blow down buildings on top of them."[26]

Major General Sir Edward Louis Spears, Churchill's personal liaison to the French prime minister, later reflected, "He wanted the French to fight in Paris, describing how a great city, if stubbornly defended, absorbed immense armies, and the pageant of history, the lurid glow of burning cities, some as beautiful as Paris, collapsing on garrisons who refused to accept defeat, arose before our eyes."[27] Spears added that when Churchill shared this vision with Reynaud, Weygand, and Marshal Pétain, "The French perceptibly froze." They sat "back in their chairs with a tension of a motorist pressing hard on the brakes."

Pétain rebuffed Churchill's arguments. "To make Paris into a city of ruins will not affect the issue."

Churchill persisted and championed tactics that would help the Allies fend off and turn the tables on the German invaders. But it was not his city, not his country, and not his decision to make.

Late on June 12, hours after Churchill arrived back in London from Briare, General Weygand stunned an evening meeting of Paul Reynaud's cabinet when he pronounced his stark expectation for the fall of France. His army was "at its last gasp," and Weygand implored the government's leaders to seek an armistice with Germany to end the bloodbath.[28]

Reynaud was not as doom-ridden as Weygand, but he now felt compelled to broach with Churchill the contingent possibility of a separate peace agreement with Germany. Churchill responded to a new plea from Reynaud and returned to France the following day. General Spears, who served as an interpreter for the discussion between the two prime ministers, later summarized Reynaud's appeal, "The Government has not lost sight of the fact that a solemn pledge had been entered into that no separate peace would be concluded. But what was the British Government's attitude in view of the present situation? France, as General Weygand had said, has been completely sacrificed. She had nothing left."[29]

Churchill weighed his words and replied,

> The British people have not yet felt the German lash, but they do not underestimate its force. This in no way deters them; far from being cowed, they are looking forward to thrashing Hitler. They have but one thought, to win the war and destroy Hitlerism. . . . We must fight, we will fight, and that is why we must ask our friends to fight on. . . . She still has her fine Navy, her great Empire. . . . The war will continue, and can but end in our destruction or our victory. That is my answer to your question.[30]

Reynaud rebounded with assurance that he had never questioned the indomitable "resolution of the British nation." Now, however, Reynaud bluntly asked Churchill, "Would Great Britain not agree that, France having nothing further to contribute to the common cause, she would release her from the agreement concluded three months ago and allow her to conclude a separate peace?"

As Churchill began his reply, Spears noted that "it was evident from his first words that he refused to consider Reynaud's suggestion. Characteristically, his method of avoiding the dilemma was to rise above it." Churchill replied, "Under no circumstances will Great Britain waste time in reproaches and recriminations. But that is a very different matter from becoming a consenting party to a peace made in contravention of the agreement so recently concluded."[31]

Churchill suggested a possible last-ditch lifeline for France. "Before posing ourselves decisive questions, we must appeal to Roosevelt. Let the French Government undertake to do this and we will support them by telegram."

Reynaud agreed to send one final telegram to President Roosevelt, imploring him to provide tangible assistance against Germany. In a June 14 plea to America's president, Reynaud conveyed his desperation and outlined three choices that France now faced in this "most tragic hour." She could "continue to sacrifice her youth into a hopeless struggle," her government could flee to North Africa and thereby leave the rest of the country to "live abandoned abating itself under the shadow of Nazi domination," or France could "ask Hitler for conditions of an armistice." If France fell, the defeat of England appeared "possible if not probable."[32]

Reynaud knew that his urgent request for America to join France and Britain in the war was the longest of longshots. America was officially neutral. The 435 members of America's 76th Congress, who held the power to declare war, were overwhelmingly against the sacrifice of American lives in a new war on foreign soil in which they had no direct stake.

Before departing for his return flight to London, Churchill made a fresh request to Reynaud on behalf of Britain. France held more than four hundred Luftwaffe pilots in captivity, most of whom had been shot down by the Royal Air Force. Churchill requested the transfer of those captured German airmen to British custody to prevent them from reentering the battle. Reynaud promised to set the transfer process in motion.[33] Thus concluded Churchill's third consecutive day of meetings in battle-ravaged France. He had met with Paul Reynaud during all three days of the French government's temporary residency in Tours and Briare. Churchill would not return to French soil until June 12, 1944, six days after the Allies' D-day invasion began the liberation of France.

After a cramped and hectic three-day hiatus in Tours, France's governing ministers moved again, this time to the provisional safety of Bordeaux, 195 miles farther south of Tours and 360 miles away from Paris.

Notwithstanding Winston Churchill's hope to see buildings blown down on top of the invaders of Paris, no one in France took up his plea for a defense of their capital. In the early hours of June 14, 1940, as France's ministers and their families scrambled to find quarters in Bordeaux, German infantrymen trickled and then flooded into the undefended French capital by truck, tank, motorcycle, horseback, and foot. By dinner time flags and banners that bore the odious German swastika flew at Versailles, the Arc de Triomphe, and from the Eiffel Tower as German officers and men in neat, dark-gray uniforms and gleaming black boots filled tables at cafes throughout France's abandoned capital.

Prussian general and military theorist Carl von Clausewitz wrote about the demoralizing impact on public opinion of "great victories, and by the possession of the enemy's capital."[34] With the emotional heart of France now in German possession, it became more apparent by the day that regardless of the military means at their disposal, Maxime Weygand, his army, and the leaders of France lacked the will to take back Paris.

In contrast, as General Hastings "Pug" Ismay wrote, "For all his simulated cheerfulness, Mr. Churchill made it clear that his whole heart went out to his beloved France in her agony, and that we would do all in human power to aid her."[35]

Winston Churchill spent the early part of June 15, 1940, the day after Paris was occupied, dictating telegrams to President Roosevelt and to the premiers of British dominions. After his messages of gratitude and hope and his requests for additional aid were on their way, Churchill traveled to Chequers, the prime minister's country retreat, in the company of several family members as well as John Colville, his private secretary.

Chequers, a manor house built in the mid-1500s, has served as a weekend home for British prime ministers since 1921. This bucolic getaway from No. 10 Downing Street sits forty-five miles northwest of London. Churchill's predecessor, Neville Chamberlain, considered Chequers an oasis for leisurely respites from the burdens of Monday-to-Friday government work. The residence had only one telephone, located in the kitchen, which suited Chamberlain, who preferred not to be disturbed on weekends or evenings. Churchill, on the other hand, had a battery of phones installed and transformed this rustic manor into a bustling hub from which he managed the war on many weekends.

As was the custom, the party's 9:30 dinner on this Saturday in mid-June was fortified with "champagne and brandy and cigars." Later that night, Colville, who had spent much of his time before and after dinner on the telephone, informed Churchill that "fuller information had now been received about the French attitude, which appeared to be slipping."

Churchill suggested, "tell them that if they let us have their fleet we shall never forget, but if they surrender without consulting us we shall never forgive. We shall blacken their name for a thousand years!"

Colville's record of that night mentions that the prime minister was "in high spirits" into the early morning hours, and his account of that conversation ends: "Then, half afraid that I might take him seriously, he added: 'Don't, of course, do that just yet.'"[36]

Reynaud met with General Spears and British ambassador Sir Ronald Campbell just after seven o'clock on the evening of June 15. Mindful that President Roosevelt was likely to reject his telegraphed plea to join the fighting, Reynaud began to draft a formal request for Britain to release France from their joint agreement and thus enable France to seek Armistice terms from Germany, and thereby pause the fighting.

Seventy-nine days had passed since Paul Reynaud and Neville Chamberlain had signed the agreement that neither government would request an armistice without the other's consent. Reynaud's request to sunder that bond was about to set off a round of rancor and confusion. He couched and cushioned his appeal in naive logic. Yes, France desired to learn Hitler's armistice terms, but its "Cabinet Council does not doubt that these conditions will in any event be unacceptable." Nonetheless, the French "have decided that it is indispensable that this should be proved beyond doubt."[37] To assuage a prevailing British concern, Reynaud promised "the surrender of the French Fleet to Germany would be held as an unacceptable condition."

As General Spears later wrote—no doubt with a smirk—France wished to request armistice terms from Adolf Hitler "'on approval' to be returned if not entirely satisfactory."[38]

An aide interrupted the meeting to hand Reynaud a telegram with the anxiously awaited reply from America. Although President Roosevelt expressed admiration for French valor, and promised additional "aeroplanes, artillery and ammunition of all kinds," the American president added, "I know you will understand that these declarations imply no military engagements. Congress alone can undertake such engagements." Spears observed that Reynaud digested Roosevelt's refusal to provide salvation with resigned dignity.[39]

Reynaud now moved to release France from its reciprocal pledge to Britain. In a telegram to Winston Churchill, Reynaud referenced their meeting in Tours where "it was agreed . . . that the question of authorizing a request for an armistice would be reconsidered if President Roosevelt's reply was negative. This eventuality having materialized, I think the question must now be put afresh."

Reynaud, tired and on edge, asked to see Spears and Campbell again early the next morning. Barely enough time had passed for Churchill and his cabinet to review the French prime minister's request, and a reply had not yet arrived. Spears filled that vacuum by reminding Reynaud that the joint agreement signed in March "had not been drawn up as a polite formula. . . . Instead, the agreement had been written as a prescient covenant 'to bind the two countries to each other in the gravest contingencies, so that it would not be possible, whatever the temptation, however attractive the bait offered by the enemy, however terrible the conditions to which each might be subjected, for either country to abandon its ally or shake itself free of its pledge.'"[40]

Spears noted, "We argued, and argued again, that those who drew up the agreement and signed it, and he was one of them, knowing they could not foresee the future, had taken this step intending to bind the two countries to a common fate."

A short time after the morning meeting concluded, Ambassador Campbell received a telegram with Churchill's reply to Reynaud's plea:

> *Mr. Churchill to M. Reynaud*
>
> Our agreement forbidding separate negotiations, whether for armistice or peace, was made with the French Republic, and not with any particular French administration or statesman. It therefore involves the honour of France. Nevertheless, provided, but only provided, that the French Fleet is sailed forthwith for British harbours pending negotiations, His Majesty's Government give their full consent to an inquiry for the French Government to ascertain

> the terms of an armistice for France. His Majesty's Government, being resolved to continue the war, wholly exclude themselves from all part in the above-mentioned inquiry concerning an armistice.[41]

Churchill's response was explicit. Britain extended permission for France to query separate armistice terms provided—"but only provided"—that the French fleet sailed to the safety of British harbors.

When Spears and Campbell brought the telegram to Reynaud, the French prime minister's reaction was defiant and haughty. "What a very silly thing to do, to ask that the French Fleet should go to British harbours when it is in fact at this very moment protecting Algeria and the Western Mediterranean . . . *non, vraiment, c'est trop bete.* [No, really, it is too silly.]" Reynaud added, "For one thing, the French Fleet is relieving the British in the Mediterranean. To send ours away would place a fresh strain on yours."[42]

In a cabinet meeting later that day, Reynaud read President Roosevelt's telegram aloud. Remarkably he did not read the telegram from Churchill. Instead he provided an incomplete and misleading summary: "The British Cabinet had not ratified the position taken at Tours by Mr. Churchill and his two colleagues. Whilst the French Government asked the British Government's assent to enquire of the enemy the conditions for an eventual armistice, the British Government appeared to have adopted an intransigent attitude, which foreshadowed a refusal."[43]

The British sent a second telegram to Ambassador Campbell at four o'clock that afternoon. It instructed him to inform Paul Reynaud:

> We expect to be consulted as soon as any armistice terms are received. This is necessary not merely in virtue of Treaty forbidding separate peace or armistice, but also in view of vital consequences of any armistice to ourselves, having regard especially to the fact that British troops are fighting with the French Army. You should impress on French Government that in stipulating for removal of French Fleet to British ports we have in mind French interests as well as our own, and are convinced that it will strengthen the hands of the French Government in any armistice discussions if they can show that the French Navy is out of reach of the German forces.[44]

Five minutes after receiving this second telegram, Spears and Campbell visited Reynaud once again. Spears recorded that after Campbell translated the text to French as he read the telegram aloud, the French prime minister "reacted as he had done to the first message; he invoked the same arguments and so did we."[45]

Time was running short. Reynaud had scheduled a meeting with his cabinet at 5 o'clock that evening. The primary topic for discussion was whether France should continue the fight or request Germany's armistice terms. Reynaud was still prepared to argue for a prolonged engagement, and he showed no sign that he would order the French fleet to sail for Britain in exchange for permission to query Germany for its terms.

The three men were deep into their contentious discussion when a phone on Reynaud's desk rang. Less than an hour before the scheduled 5 o'clock meeting, at a time when hope was especially flimsy, Reynaud was about to receive a most audacious proposal, a plan for salvation, an offer beyond even his most fantastic dreams.

Winston Churchill and the British government, desperate to keep France and its fleet in the war, were about to offer to unite with their ally to form a single sovereign nation.

CHAPTER 5

AND THUS WE SHALL CONQUER

GENERAL SPEARS CAPTURED Paul Reynaud's astonishment as he raised the phone to his ear. "The next moment his eyebrows went up so far they became indistinguishable from his neatly brushed hair; one eyebrow to either side of the parting."[1]

Reynaud's protégé Charles de Gaulle was on the line, calling from London on behalf of the British government to convey their proposal to unite. Frenchmen and Britons would share common citizenship. There would be one parliament, a joint war cabinet, a united army, a common currency. The monarchy? That was a matter to settle later. Time mattered more than details.

As de Gaulle shared the British proposal, Reynaud grabbed a pencil and scribbled furiously. With a meeting of his cabinet scheduled to begin in less than one hour, Reynaud was desperate to capture every detail of the offer that now provided France with a most improbable lifeline.

> At this most fateful moment in the history of the modern world the Governments of the United Kingdom and the French Republic make this declaration of indissoluble union and unyielding resolution in their common defence of justice and freedom against subjection to a system which reduces mankind to a life of robots and slaves.[2]
>
> The two Governments declare France and Great Britain shall no longer be two nations, but one Franco-British Union.

With the phone to his ear, the prime minister wrote at a frantic pace and, "in a frightful scrawl, getting more excited as the message unfolded." The proposal continued: "The constitution of the Union will provide for joint organs of defence, foreign, financial, and economic policies. Every citizen of France will enjoy immediately citizenship of Great Britain; every British subject will become a citizen of France."

As Reynaud's frenetic transcription filled each page, Spears handed him a clean sheet, pressing down to prevent it from slipping as the French prime minister held the phone in his left hand and wrote with his right. "During the war there shall be a single War Cabinet, and all the forces of Britain and France, whether on land, sea, or in the air, will be placed under its direction. It will govern from wherever it best can. The two Parliaments will be formally associated. . . . The Union will concentrate its whole energy against the power of the enemy, no matter where the battle may be."

Charles de Gaulle read the final words of the British offer twenty minutes before the scheduled start of Reynaud's cabinet meeting.

"And thus we shall conquer."

Reynaud and de Gaulle had conducted their telephone conversation in French. After taking down every word in the British offer, the incredulous Reynaud asked, "Does he agree to this? Did Churchill give this to you personally?" De Gaulle handed the telephone to Churchill, who assured Reynaud that Britain's offer was sincere—an indisputable mark of Britain's commitment to France and to their mutual fate.

Reynaud put down the phone and said to Spears, "I will die defending these proposals." Churchill and Reynaud had agreed to meet the following day. Churchill would travel by warship to Concarneau in southern Brittany. This would be his sixth trip to France in the thirty-six days since the fighting began. No time or momentum was to be lost in sealing the union between the two allies.

After the call ended, the beaming de Gaulle heard a suggestion that he—still a newly minted brigadier general—would be Commander-in-Chief of the joint army. Churchill muttered, "*je l'arrangerai.* [I'll sort it]"[3] Former prime minister Neville Chamberlain, in his current role as Lord President of the Council, was dispatched to Buckingham Palace to brief the King on the planned union.

Churchill and an entourage would ride by train from London to Portsmouth that night and, from there, board a warship and steam to Concarneau on the Bay of Biscay. Churchill called Inspector Walter Thompson, his bodyguard, and told him to arm well for a suddenly conceived, and perhaps risky trip. Churchill assured Thompson that he too would carry a gun.[4]

With so little time and so many details to resolve, Churchill asked de Gaulle to fly ahead to France. His early arrival would allow him to reinforce the plan for the union with Reynaud and his cabinet. De Gaulle, who had assumed an increasingly vital role in the relations between the French and British governments, would also help prepare for the next day's momentous meeting at Concarneau.

Before departing, de Gaulle and Jean Monnet, a French businessman who helped coordinate war supplies between France and Britain, had a brief conversation with Churchill. Monnet asked Churchill if he would reconsider his recent decision to send no more British aircraft to French airfields. To Monnet's and de Gaulle's surprise, Churchill was steadfast in his decision to preserve the core of the Royal Air Force for the inevitable Battle of Britain. Churchill later wrote, "I told him there was no possibility of this being done."[5]

As the two Frenchmen took their leave, just as de Gaulle reached the door, the stoic French general acknowledged the disappointing reality of Churchill's position, saying in English, "I think you are quite right." De Gaulle sped to the airport for his hastily arranged flight to Bordeaux.

Churchill ended a meeting with his war cabinet at six in the evening and was driven to Waterloo Station. Inspector Thompson arrived before Churchill, in time to search and secure the prime minister's compartment on the waiting train. Churchill's wife, Clementine, traveled to the station to bid him adieu. At 9:30 on the evening of June 16, Churchill settled into his seat and closed his eyes, hoping to catch at least a few minutes rest before setting out on his historic and dangerous journey, potentially vulnerable to German submarines and aircraft.[6]

Reynaud, anxious to share Britain's audacious proposal, convened his Council of Ministers at 5 p.m. in a ballroom at the Hotel du Quartier Général in Bordeaux. Twenty-four men, including Marshal Pétain and

Paul Baudouin, joined Reynaud behind closed doors. Spears and Campbell, who waited with increased anxiety and diminishing patience at their nearby hotel while the French ministers met to discuss the Franco-British union, were finally summoned at 7:30 to meet with Paul Reynaud. After a brief conversation, Britain's two advocates rushed back to their hotel to send an urgent message to the foreign office in London.[7]

At Waterloo Station, all of the members of Churchill's party were now seated in the prime minister's rail car, about to make their way to Portsmouth where a battleship was raising steam for the next leg of the long night's journey.

Shortly before the train was about to lurch down the line, a courier dashed into the station carrying a small dispatch case.[8] As the courier approached Churchill's private car, Inspector Thompson held him up briefly, checked his identification, and heard the required password for passage onto the train. After the courier handed the dispatch box to Churchill, the prime minister opened a sealed envelope and read the urgent message that had just arrived from Ambassador Campbell in Bordeaux. "Ministerial crisis has opened. . . . Hope to have news by midnight. Meanwhile meeting arranged for tomorrow impossible."[9]

The prime minister rose, made eye contact with his bodyguard, and jerked his head to motion their way off the train. Thompson saw tears in Churchill's eyes. As a weary and disappointed Churchill returned to the prime minister's residence on Downing Street, Charles de Gaulle's plane approached Bordeaux, landing at the airport in nearby Merignac just before 10 p.m. A military aide, Colonel Jacques Humbert, waited as the general's plane taxied to a halt at the end of the grass landing strip.[10] When de Gaulle stepped down from the plane, the news from Humbert instantly shattered his exhilaration.

Paul Reynaud had resigned, and all hope for a Franco-British union was lost.

Members of Paul Reynaud's cabinet had trudged into the hotel ballroom earlier that evening in an atmosphere of mournful expectation and glum relief. How much longer would they wait to request the inevitable armistice terms from Germany, and how should they respond if the German terms dishonored France?

Instead of discussing the armistice as expected, Reynaud announced a miraculous alternative for them to consider. With a copy of Britain's extraordinary proposal in hand, Reynaud read the details to his assembled colleagues. To Reynaud's dismay, the offer that had so surprised and revitalized him less than an hour before seemed not much of a surprise to some in the room. Reynaud later shared his suspicion that several ministers were aware of the details even before he read them aloud. He suspected a tap on his telephone line.

When his first reading of Britain's offer generated little reaction, the crestfallen prime minister read the proposal a second time. Reynaud described their reaction: "Some were astonished, others taken aback, more were hostile."[11]

Marshal Pétain spat his disdain for the ally that had fallen short of his expectations on the battlefield. "To make a union with Great Britain was fusion with a corpse."[12] Minister of State Jean Ybarnégaray reacted: "Better to be a Nazi province. At least we know what that means."

Georges Mandel, minister of the interior, was one of Reynaud's few vocal supporters. He asked, "Would you rather be a German district than a British Dominion?" However, his question was met with sharp glares and silent contempt.

Reynaud filled the silence. "I prefer to collaborate with my allies rather than my enemies," provoking cries of derision.

Mandel later told Spears that Reynaud read the proposal—as Spears paraphrased in his inimitable fashion—"without heat or fire, like a lawyer defending a cause he did not believe in and for which he had been promised an inadequate fee."[13]

A majority of the ministers saw no reason to continue the war and no reason to extend the carnage on French soil. The prospect of a union with the ally who had contributed less than its fair share of armed men and fighter planes generated no enthusiasm. Rather than fight on, the cabinet was ready to query Hitler for his terms with an implied caveat that they would reject the German armistice if the terms were dishonorable.

After two hours without serious consideration or a formal vote on Britain's proposal to unite, Reynaud called the meeting to a close.

When Spears and Campbell met with Reynaud just after the session ended, they were shattered by the cabinet's de facto rejection of Britain's offer. They were also astonished by Reynaud's relaxed demeanor in the meeting's immediate aftermath. "It was obvious that he was immensely relieved but at some pains not to show it." Spears described the scene as "if, walking into a room to condole with a widower, one was confronted by a bridegroom." Reynaud gave the impression of "a man receiving the condolences of friends of a rich uncle."[14]

Reynaud told Spears that he had mentioned Churchill's intended visit the following day, "but it made no difference, they had made up their minds." At that point in the evening, he had not yet resigned. Campbell and Spears begged Reynaud to stand firm. They would return at ten o'clock that night for another meeting with the French prime minister.

When Spears and Campbell returned, Reynaud informed them that he had resigned, despite their pleas to defer that decision.

Spears wrote that after a brief conversation, "The Ambassador and I stared at Reynaud. There was silence. All words were useless now."[15] Reynaud's vow to "die defending these proposals" was short-lived.

Earlier that evening, after ending his call with Churchill and de Gaulle and just before meeting with his cabinet, the suddenly vitalized Reynaud shared his presumption that Britain's offer of union superseded the two telegrams that demanded French ships sail to British harbors. Spears and Campbell tentatively agreed with the French prime minister. When they returned to their hotel, they found a telegram from the Foreign Office directing them to "Please suspend action." As a result, they sent a message to Reynaud confirming that "the two telegrams should be considered as cancelled."[16]

In his account of that tumultuous day, Churchill reflected that "'suspended' would have been more appropriate. The War Cabinet had not altered its position in any respect. We felt, however, that it would be better to give the Declaration of Union its full chance under the most favourable conditions."[17]

Churchill added, "Our two telegrams about the Fleet were never presented to the Council. The demand that it should sail to British ports as a prelude to the negotiations with the Germans was never considered by the Reynaud Cabinet, which was now in complete decomposition."[18]

Nor was Reynaud's promise that France would transfer their 400 captured Luftwaffe pilots to Britain fulfilled. As Churchill noted in *Their Finest Hour*, "These German pilots all became available for the Battle of Britain, and we had to shoot them down a second time."[19]

In the immediate aftermath of Paul Reynaud's resignation, Marshal Pétain was asked to form a new government. The Marshal, evidently prepared for his summons to power, reached into a jacket pocket and withdrew a list of the ministers he wanted in his cabinet.

One appointment in Pétain's new government particularly concerned Spears. Admiral François Darlan would be France's new Minister of Marine, adding administrative chores to his Admiral of the Fleet responsibilities. Darlan's navy was the one arm of the French military that had not been defeated. Now, however, in Spears' opinion, "Darlan as Pétain's Minister of Marine was identifying himself with defeat."[20]

General Spears encountered one more surprise on the night of Reynaud's resignation when Charles de Gaulle asked for his help to flee to Britain. Spears understood that helping de Gaulle cross the English Channel would be the final signature on his work as Churchill's liaison to Paul Reynaud. The establishment of a French mission led by de Gaulle in London would challenge the government that Marshal Pétain was now expected to lead under German rule.

In Spears' account of their departure the following morning, "Such was de Gaulle's fear of being arrested at the last moment that, for the purpose of deceiving the French airmen, he suggested that we should behave as if he was seeing me off. A little comedy was therefore carried out. Whilst the engine was being revved up I stood at the open door of the plane and bid him goodbye. At the actual moment of departure I hauled him and his A. D. C. [aide de camp] on board."[21]

Charles de Gaulle's fear for his personal safety had been prescient and self-fulfilling. A French military court sentenced him to death in absentia—for desertion—seven weeks later. To his credit, Marshal Pétain quietly planned to commute de Gaulle's sentence if his former protégé returned to France while he governed.[22]

Now that Britain's offer of union had been dismissed without serious consideration, and now that Paul Reynaud had been replaced by Marshal Pétain, Churchill insisted on speaking directly with his new French counterpart. As Churchill sat in a comfortable armchair in the study at 10 Downing Street, operators worked late into the night to get a call through to the new leader of France. The marshal was finally reached at two o'clock in the morning on June 17.

Churchill never shared the specifics of the call in which he implored Pétain not to surrender French ships to Germany. However, General Leslie Hollis, the military secretary to the cabinet, sat with Churchill through the long night, waiting for the two leaders to connect. After listening to Churchill's side of the conversation, Hollis later said, "It was the most violent conversation I ever heard Churchill conduct. He only spoke so roughly because he felt that anger might sway the old Marshal when nothing would."[23]

Churchill sent a more conciliatory telegram to Pétain and General Weygand later that day. A copy was sent to Ambassador Campbell with a request that he share the message with Admiral Darlan.

In a report to the Foreign Office, Sir Ronald Campbell mentioned, he "was informed that the Council of Ministers had taken the attitude that it was a point of honour for France to receive the armistice terms with her armies and fleet still fighting."[24]

Darlan responded to Campbell's request for personal assurance that his ships would not fall into German hands with the promise, "As long as I can issue orders you have nothing to fear."[25]

To ensure the reliability of his orders, Darlan implemented a communications protocol to address a matter of personal concern. He informed his senior commanders that all future communications should be considered genuine only if they concluded with his "XAVIER 377" authentication signature. This concern would be validated just two days later when

French ships received a signal that ordered them to "cease all war operations" and "immediately go to the nearest French port." The message was signed, "Vive la France. DARLAN," but was missing the XAVIER 377 authenticator. Not only was this message ignored by all French officers, it also alerted both the French and British navies to the duplicitous use of the French communications network by the German navy.[26]

Less than twenty-four hours after Paul Reynaud's wildest dream died in Bordeaux, his successor signaled France's willingness to bow to Germany. Before sunrise on the morning of June 17, the French Foreign Office asked the Spanish ambassador to request the peace terms that Germany was willing to propose.

On the following day, as a violent thunderstorm rattled and drenched Bordeaux, Marshal Pétain made his first radio address to the country he now led.[27] "The Victor of Verdun," the living icon who had failed to inspire France to victory, closed his speech by saying, "With a heavy heart, I tell you today that it is necessary to stop the fighting."

Pétain did not expect French soldiers to lay down their arms—the Germans still battled ferociously after all—but that was the most expedient interpretation by men who were under fire in the fields for what was now an officially hopeless cause. Within hours, General Alphonse Georges complained to General Weygand that while Germany had not relented on the battlefield, the marshal's message had "broken the last resistance of the French army." Soldiers across France unshouldered their weapons, removed their uniforms, and headed home. In the forty-three days days after Germany invaded Western Europe, 90,000 French soldiers died, 200,000 were wounded, and 1.9 million men were declared missing or taken prisoner.[28]

Marshal Pétain, General Weygand, and other French leaders assumed that an armistice would soon bring a temporary pause in the fighting. They also believed that France and Germany would settle accounts with a peace treaty several months later—after Britain's defeat—and that French prisoners of war would then be freed. Of course, the conquest of Churchill's Britain never occurred, and Germany never signed a peace treaty with France. Most of those French prisoners remained captive until the war's end in 1945.

In his champagne-, brandy-, and cigar-fortified conversation with John Colville at Chequers two days earlier, Churchill jested that Colville should let the French know that he would "blacken their name for a thousand years" if they handed their fleet over to Germany before instructing Colville not to send the message. Now, in a cable to the new leaders of France, Churchill conveyed this threat with a more distinctive Churchillian turn of phrase: "I wish to repeat to you my profound conviction that the illustrious Marshal Pétain and the famous General Weygand, our comrades in two great wars against the Germans, will not injure their ally by delivering over to the enemy the fine French Fleet. Such an act would scarify their names for a thousand years of history."[29]

Churchill broadcast a message across Britain with a conciliatory tone on the evening of June 17, 1940: "The news from France is very bad, and I grieve for the gallant French people who have fallen into this terrible misfortune. Nothing will alter our feelings towards them or our faith that the genius of France will rise again."[30]

His words conveyed Churchill's lifelong affection for France. What was left unsaid was that in order to ensure that the genius of France would rise again, Churchill would not hesitate to apply harsh measures. As the world would soon learn, Churchill was willing to destroy the French fleet rather than permit Germany to take it into its possession and sail it against the Royal Navy.

General Spears later described the relaxed conversation that he and Ambassador Campbell enjoyed as they waited for the French cabinet's response to Britain's proposal to unite. The two men agreed that "the picture evoked by an Anglo-French Parliament was irresistibly funny, for their only common denominator would be abysmal ignorance of each other's language."[31]

Spears was a member of parliament, and his attachment to France was so widely recognized in London that some journalists dubbed him "the member for Paris." Spears now joked to Campbell, "Under this scheme this might come true."[32]

It is inconceivable that the British royal family would have accepted a change in their station, and no more likely that the anti-monarchy majority in France would have accepted the rule of a king and queen. And there was no possibility that either army would have accepted Charles de Gaulle—the youngest brigadier general in the French Army—as commander-in-chief of a combined force.[33]

The union of Britain and France was a fragile dream born of desperation. A union with Britain this far into the fight would not have undone the toll of battered towns and downed bridges in France. The mere matter of a Franco-British union would not have unshackled the open and now conspicuously occupied city of Paris.

Churchill's refusal to sacrifice additional planes and pilots in the Battle of France is testament to the shallow depth of his support for the proposed union. There was no comparison between Churchill's fondness for France and his love and devotion to Britain. Churchill's consideration of a Franco-British union was less an indication of his affection for the French than a sign of his willingness to accept an upheaval of such consequence to preserve the safety and secure the future of Great Britain.

PART 2

SUNDERED

CHAPTER 6

YOU DO NOT NEGOTIATE AN ARMISTICE

BUT FOR AN OCCASIONAL disturbance for the installation and ceremonial unveiling of new monuments, the glade of the Armistice in Compiègne, a town fifty-five miles northeast of Paris, sat in hushed repose in the two decades after France and Germany signed an armistice agreement there at the end of World War I. On Friday, June 21, 1940, a crew of German Army engineers disrupted the site's tranquility.

The glade would serve as the stage for a production by Adolf Hitler. Wehrmacht engineers worked with jackhammers and pick axes to transform the quiet memorial to the end of the previous world war into a set where Hitler's greatest triumph would soon be celebrated and captured on film.

A statue of Marshal Ferdinand Foch looked down from the eastern edge of the glade—a broad lawn, half-ringed by towering beech trees. Foch, the Supreme Allied Commander in the final year of World War I, had imposed the Allies' armistice terms on Germany at this site at the end of that war. The German set decorators left the marshal's statue untouched—as if to let him witness the undoing of his victory—but the desecration of other artifacts signaled the Germans' disdain for Compiègne's significance to France.

At the far end of Marshal Foch's gaze, the site's armistice museum was newly scarred: A large hole had been carefully punched through the building's front wall with pneumatic drills, just barely wide enough and just barely tall enough to drag a railway carriage through. Foch's hallowed rolling office, a converted dining car, was pulled out of the museum and rolled to the center of the glade—to the precise spot where it stood when Foch pressed German delegates to accept the Allies' armistice terms while seated at a long rectangular table on November 11, 1918. Now, in this same car, roles and fates would be reversed.

The scene and the afternoon's events had been carefully staged to maximize their propaganda value as well as to ensure the humiliation of the French. German newsreel cameras rolled to capture the day's activities for posterity, as well as to incite the emotions of French and German citizenry in precisely opposite directions.

At a quarter past three in the afternoon, a German party led by Adolf Hitler pulled up to the curve in the road where the wide path that leads into the park began. A large corps of uniformed extras—a Wehrmacht honor battalion—stood at attention, three-deep, along that path.[1]

Eight malevolent men paraded down the minced stone and dirt pathway toward the rail carriage: Hitler, Goering, Raeder, Keitel, Hess, Ribbentrop, Brauchitsch, and Jodl. Hitler proffered the stiff-armed Nazi salute as he strode past the hundreds of German soldiers who stood in rapt attention as their Führer marched past.

American correspondent William L. Shirer was among a group of foreign journalists invited by German leaders to accompany the Wehrmacht on its advance through France. Shirer made his own way to Compiègne after a German officer tipped him off to the upcoming armistice ceremony.

Across the Atlantic Ocean that morning, radio listeners could hear over their crackling sets, "Hello America. . . . This is William L. Shirer. . . . We've got our microphone at the edge of a little clearing in the Forest of Compiègne."[2] Reporting from the site, Shirer remarked that Hitler walked with "a certain spring in his step" and noted his solemn and grave countenance.

When Hitler reached the center of the glade, he stood alone as he paused to absorb the scene. For a moment he stood, arms folded, in front of a broad, flat granite block that rose knee-high in the center of the clearing. Hitler glared at the inscription that read in French, "Here on 11 November 1918 succumbed the criminal pride of the German empire vanquished by the free peoples which it tried to enslave." The Germans would dynamite that massive slab the following day.

Hitler's expression, clear through Shirer's binoculars, made a deep and lasting impression on the American journalist who stood fifty yards off to the side. The führer was "afire with scorn, anger, hate, revenge and triumph."[3] Shirer wrote of Hitler's "burning contempt for this place now and all that it has stood for in the twenty-two years since it witnessed the humbling of the German Empire."

The German party walked a few steps over to Foch's railcar. After a brief pause, Hitler was the first to climb the three steps into the carriage, with the rest of his party close behind. The name cards at each seat showed where each negotiator sat in 1918. Hitler took his place in Marshal Foch's wooden chair at the center of the green-baize draped table.

After the Germans settled into their places at the table, a French contingent marched toward the railcar with an escort of three German officers. General Charles Huntziger, the leader of the French delegation, acknowledged the German honor guard that still lined the path into the glade with a stiff salute. Huntziger's party included Vice Admiral Maurice Le Luc, Admiral Darlan's chief of staff, who would play an important role in the Franco-British naval drama in the weeks ahead.

Huntziger and the French delegation walked haltingly into the railcar, their faces a tableau of dejection and crushing humility. The Germans rose to their feet as the French entered, the men on each side saluting their counterparts according to their national custom, the Germans thrusting their right arms in their "Heil Hitler!" salute, the French wearily touching their foreheads in the more traditional sign of respect.

With everyone seated, Adolf Hitler peered down at the table in silence as General Wilhelm Keitel rose and opened with a statement on behalf of the Führer in which he recounted in German the grievances that had simmered since the last war ended.[4] The Germans had selected Compiègne as the perfect site for "an act of reparative justice." Their aim was "to efface once and for all . . . a memory that was a far from glorious page in the history of France and that was felt by the German people to be the greatest dishonor of all time."[5]

After Keitel finished, Paul Schmidt, the German leaders' favored interpreter, repeated the preamble in French. At that point, Hitler, Goering, and all of the Germans except Keitel left the railcar. Keitel, who would be hanged at Nuremberg five years later, handed Huntziger a printed copy of the twenty-four articles in the German agreement. A team of translators under the supervision of Schmidt had worked by candlelight in a nearby church the night before to translate the German armistice terms into French.[6] After scanning the document, Huntziger remarked that its terms were "hard and merciless."[7]

At 8:15 that night—five hours after the French negotiators entered the glade and thirty hours after they left the temporary French capital of Bordeaux—General Huntziger was permitted to telephone his anxious military and government leaders who were in the dark as to the negotiators' whereabouts.

As soon as General Weygand joined the call, Huntziger said, "I am telephoning from the coach . . . the coach you know." As Paul Schmidt listened to the call via a wiretap, Weygand's impatience was apparent. "Have you got the conditions?" he asked. "What are they like?"[8]

Huntziger shared his impression that the German terms, "although harsh, contained nothing which directly offended against honor."[9] Huntziger added that "a great deal of cordiality was hardly to be expected."[10] And, "We have simply been given an armistice convention of twenty-four articles and told that it cannot be modified. I am only permitted to ask questions to clear up various points. I've done so."

Weygand was furious that Huntziger was not permitted to send a messenger with a copy of the terms. "The text should be sent by air. You don't bind the fate of a country to text dictated over the telephone."[11]

Despite Weygand's plea, the fate of France *was* dictated over the telephone. Huntziger slowly read each of the twenty-four articles to Weygand, who repeated each word aloud to an aide who wrote them down in longhand. This crude transmission of the armistice took more than one hour. That passage of time was significant because the French were also squeezed by a deadline for acceptance. The Germans demanded France's acquiescence to their terms by nine o'clock the next morning.

Hitler's armistice terms included severe constraints to the French military and citizenry, along with several surprising and devious measures of restraint to ensure France would not reject the armistice and elect to continue the war on the side of Britain.

Once General Weygand, Marshal Pétain, and other leaders of the new French government had an opportunity to review the terms and consider their significance, they discussed the modifications and concessions they would request—notwithstanding General Huntziger's statement that "it cannot be modified." As Camille Chautemps, France's deputy prime minister, noted, "It did not take us long to learn that you do not negotiate an armistice."[12]

The armistice document spelled out Adolf Hitler's scheme for the subjugation and humiliation of France. The sanctions imposed by the German victors ranged in severity from punitive to draconian.

Article 2 defined a new map of France. The country was divided into a German-occupied zone and a separate free zone—or *zone libre*—which would be governed by Marshal Pétain. The three-fifths of French soil under German occupation included Paris, as well as the coastlines of the Atlantic Ocean and the English Channel. France's Mediterranean coastline fell into the free zone.

Article 18 required France to "bear the costs of maintenance of German occupation troops on French soil," a levy that amounted to 400 million French francs, the equivalent of 8.9 million U.S. dollars—currently valued at just over 200 million U.S. dollars—per day.[13]

The primary focus of British concern was Article 8, which addressed the fate of the French fleet. During his initial call to General Weygand from Compiègne, General Huntziger stated that Germany's conditions for the fleet were "better than expected."[14] Although the French government requested several modifications to Article 8, General Weygand, Marshal Pétain, and even Admiral Darlan concurred that Germany's stipulations for the immobilization of French ships did not conflict with French honor.

Article 8 was a finely calculated and surprisingly measured product of Adolf Hitler's imagination. The "naval clause" implied a level of freedom for the French fleet, but it did so with enough ambiguity that Britain and France reached significantly different interpretations. Its conditions were restrictive, but not unduly oppressive. Hitler tempered his constraints on the fleet to minimize the likelihood that his demands would provoke François Darlan to sail his ships to British harbors. At the same time,

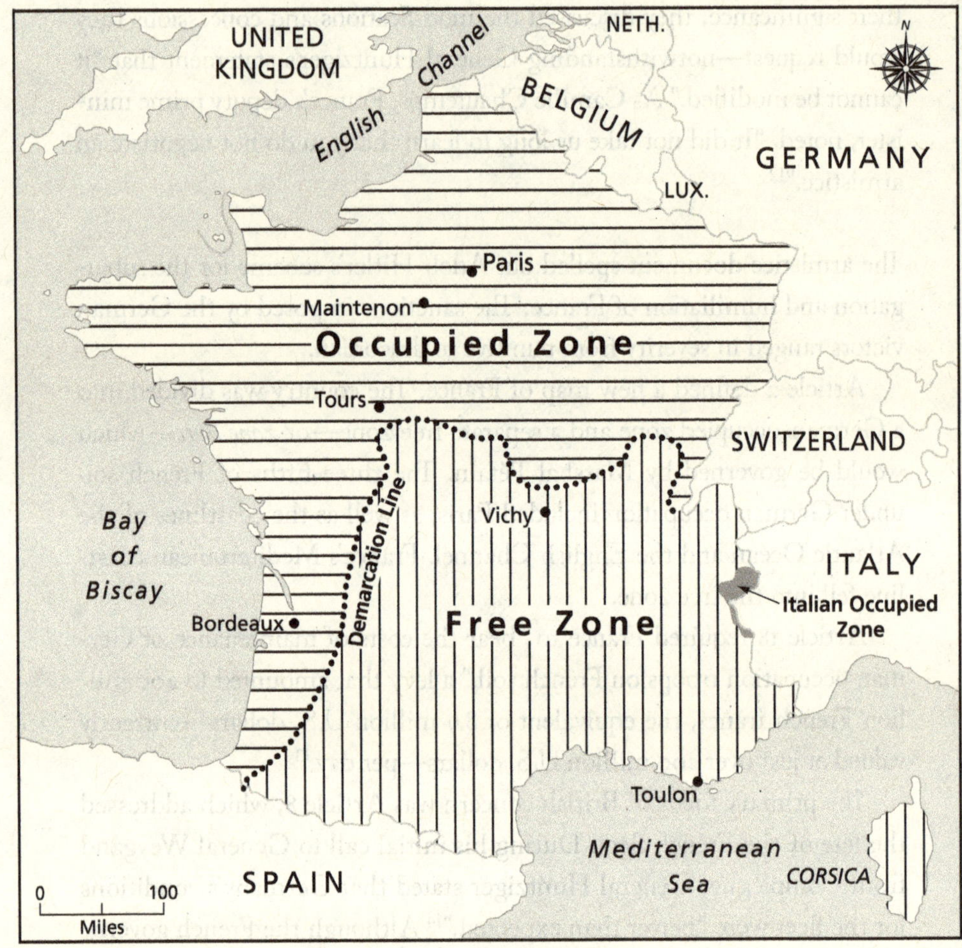

MAP 1. France: Occupied Zone and Free Zone

Article 8 offered no comfort to Britain that Germany would not eventually grab French ships and turn them against the Royal Navy:[15]

> The French war fleet, with the exception of the part permitted to the French Government for the protection of French interests in its colonial empire, is to be assembled in ports to be specified and is to be demobilized and disarmed under German or Italian supervision. The choice of these ports will be determined by the peacetime stations of the ships.

> The German Government solemnly declares to the French Government that it does not intend to use for its own purposes in the war the French fleet which is in ports under German supervision, with the exception of those units needed for coastal patrol and for mine sweeping.
>
> Furthermore they solemnly and expressly declare that they have no intention of raising any claim to the French War Fleet at time of the conclusion of peace.
>
> With the exception of that part of the French war fleet, still to be determined, which is to represent French interests in the colonial empire, all war vessels which are outside French territorial waters are to be recalled to France.

As the French interpreted Article 8, they would retain their fleet. The honor and dignity of France would not be stained by the loss of a single ship to Hitler's Germany. The British, once they learned the details of Article 8—and that took some time—formed a very different opinion.

Shortly before midnight on Friday, June 21, while the French and German delegations camped at Compiègne, still at odds over fine points of the armistice, Sir Ronald Campbell learned that the armistice terms were now in the hands of the French government. Ambassador Campbell, who had been told a broad outline of the main conditions of the agreement, tried desperately to reach Marshal Pétain or Foreign Minister Paul Baudouin to learn the precise impact of the armistice on the French fleet.[16]

Pétain and Baudouin were locked in a post-midnight cabinet discussion of how France should respond to the German terms. The meeting, which began at 1 a.m. on Saturday, June 22, ran for two hours. Campbell had previously reminded Baudouin that Britain expected France to share the terms as soon as they were in hand. "Naturally," replied Baudouin, who was on his first full day as foreign minister in Marshal Pétain's new government. "We have every intention of doing so."[17]

Undeterred by the late hour, Campbell waited, quite impatiently, outside the meeting room while the ministers deliberated. After just thirty minutes, although he had not yet seen the full agreement, the British ambassador dashed off a speculative note to Baudouin: "I have no doubt that the cabinet will recognize the insidious character of the condition concerning the fleet. No confidence can be given to the word of the Germans. They always break it."[18]

When the meeting adjourned at 3 a.m., Baudouin rebuffed Campbell's plea to discuss the armistice, the ambassador that he had to draft the official French reply before the Germans' 9 a.m. deadline. Campbell next confronted Marshal Pétain, who assured him, "Your government need have no fear."[19] The marshal added, "We hope the fleet can go to North Africa. The Germans won't touch it there. If they try, it will be scuttled."

Campbell would not rest until he learned the specific details of the armistice and their implications for Britain. He found Baudouin's foreign office secretary, François Charles-Roux, who agreed to discuss the terms. On the mistaken assumption that Campbell knew the details of the agreement, Charles-Roux jumped into an explanation of the amendments France would propose. When he realized Campbell did not follow what he was talking about, Charles-Roux handed Campbell a copy of the agreement. When Campbell read the naval terms, he "stammered and stumbled, forgetting in his agitation how to express himself in French, which he normally spoke fluently."[20]

The French-speaking British ambassador exploded in English, "But you're delivering your fleet!" Charles-Roux disputed Campbell's interpretation and assured him that the fleet would be disarmed in French ports. Sir Ronald, not at all reassured, replied, "But a disarmed ship with only an anchor watch, in an occupied port, would be at the mercy of a sudden seizure by the occupying force." (An anchor watch is a light security presence on a ship at anchor). Charles-Roux assured Campbell that French officers would scuttle their ships rather than see them fall into German hands.

Charles-Roux permitted Campbell to write out a copy of the entire agreement and begged him to consider France's dire lack of leverage. "The knife is at our throats." As Campbell finished and prepared to leave, he declared, "Poor France. She will never rise from this fall."

Campbell wired the armistice terms to the British Foreign Office. Although France had not yet signed the agreement, and the French government still hoped to negotiate more lenient terms, Campbell received a quick and definitive response: "French government apparently hopeless. Our only hope is Admiral Darlan. Proposed terms put Fleet entirely at German command. No reliance possible on German promises. Campbell must insist to Admiral Darlan that if Fleet cannot be surrendered to Great Britain or United States, it must be scuttled."[21]

Admiral Jean Louis Xavier François Darlan, Britain's "only hope," was the absolute leader of the French Navy, admired and unequivocally obeyed by his men—in effect, an "admiralissimo."[22]

Darlan was the son of a lawyer—an outlier in a family of seagoing men. The admiral's grandfather, Sabin Darlan, sailed on a French man-of-war, as did his great-grandfather, Antoine Darlan. The Darlan family's ties to the sea were so long and so encrusted with barnacles that some in their hometown of Nérac whispered with a wink that a Darlan had manned the helm of Noah's Ark.[23]

The five-foot, four-inch admiral, an avid pipe-smoker who was rarely seen with his bald head bared, led the reemergence of the French Navy as a vital fighting force. In doing so, he surrounded himself with a fiercely loyal group of subordinate officers who became known as "les A. D. D.," the *Amis de Darlan*.

Darlan had expressed his defiance toward the German threat on multiple occasions. On May 28, 1940, the day Belgium surrendered and three weeks before France requested Germany's armistice terms, Darlan passed a handwritten memorandum to his aide, Vice Admiral Maurice Le Luc: "In case military events lead to an armistice, the conditions of which would be set by the Germans, and if these conditions include the surrender of the Fleet, I have no intention of carrying out that order." Darlan added that if those conditions came to pass, all French naval vessels "must proceed to the British port that is easiest to reach."[24] On June 3 at Maintenon, he made a remarkable declaration to Jules Moch, another naval aide: "If one day an armistice is sought, I shall finish my career by an act of splendid indiscipline. I shall leave with the Fleet."[25] Later that month, shortly before Le Luc's departure on the day-long journey that would lead to Compiègne, Darlan assured his aide, "Courage, my friend. They will not get our ships. I will sink them, or, perhaps, get away with them. I repeat, they will not get them."[26] On the day that Britain proposed the union with France, Charles de Gaulle assured Winston Churchill, "Whatever happens, the French fleet will not be willingly surrendered. . . . the fleet is Darlan's fief. A feudal lord does not surrender his fief."[27]

Despite his projected self-assurance, Darlan's skin was perpetually thin. When King George VI was crowned at Westminster Abbey in 1937, Darlan resented his placement "behind a pillar and after the Chinese admiral."[28] Although he was the highest-ranking officer in the French Navy, his vice admiral rank placed him at a middling level in the global pecking order of military officers. Darlan carped until he was promoted to admiral of the fleet, a newly created rank in the French Navy. Darlan triggered an "awful scrap" in January 1940 when he refused Britain's award of the Grand Cross of the British Empire, outraged that his recognition was inferior to the awards bestowed upon French generals Georges and Gamelin. Britain upgraded Darlan's award to the Knight Grand Cross.[29] A French ambassador remarked, "I have never met a man with greater pride, nor with greater vanity."[30]

When King George VI reviewed the Royal Navy's Reserve Fleet in Weymouth Bay in August 1939, Admiral of the Fleet François Darlan, now in the top ranks of the naval hierarchy and a valued ally to Britain, joined the king for the inspection of 130 British warships. Admiral Dudley Pound, who was known to be cold and remote,[31] warmly suggested that Darlan consider himself a member of the royal yacht's crew.[32]

Despite the respect he received from the king, the prime minister, and the first sea lord, Darlan's attitude toward the British was, at best, haughty. He belittled Britain's management of their navy. "The English maneuvere their warships in London, like pawns on the chessboard . . . The naval lords can thus point out on a map the positions of all their ships at any time. . . . I probably don't know at all times where all my ships are. What do I care? I know that they will arrive at the fixed point at the desired time."[33]

He referred to an early Franco-British naval treaty as "a vast fabric of stupidities."[34] After the evacuation of British—and French—forces from the beaches of Dunkirk, Darlan wrote to his wife, "The prospect of getting out suddenly make the crawling British grow wings."[35] He once dismissed Admiral Dudley Pound as "le demi-kilo."[36] Churchill humored Darlan as "one of those good Frenchmen who hate England."[37] Although this story was later dispelled by his two primary biographers, Darlan manufactured and freely shared a basis for his grudge—a claim that his great-grandfather Antoine was killed by a Royal Navy shell during the Battle of Trafalgar in 1805.[38]

After adjourning their meeting at three o'clock on the morning of June 22, 1940, Marshal Pétain and his ministers regrouped five hours later to resume their discussion of the armistice terms. General Weygand telephoned General Huntziger in Compiègne at 10 a.m. with the cabinet's requested revisions. The original 9 a.m. deadline had passed, but General Keitel allowed additional time for the cabinet to provide their comments and requests. Those requests included a remapping of the French-controlled free zone to include Paris, noting that "an occupation of this kind represented an abominable humiliation."[39]

Although there was little likelihood that the Germans would negotiate any part of the agreement, the ministers refused to accept the German terms without dissent. At minimum they wished to register their fight for better terms for posterity. Ultimately almost all of the French requests, including their plea to redraw the free zone to include Paris, were rejected. Article 8 required French ships to return to "the peacetime stations of the ships," which, for the most part were ports in France. The French requested the following amendment, in part to ensure that their ships could not easily be bombed by Britain—who, quite suddenly, was a potential foe: "After demobilization and landing of ammunition under German or Italian supervision, the French warships will be taken to French African ports with half their peacetime complement."

Although this request was also rejected, its refusal was couched to imply it would receive additional consideration. The official German response read, "The modification proposed is not accepted for insertion in the agreement. The Germans do not refuse to contemplate the acceptance of the proposal made, but they consider that it is a measure of application coming within the competence of the Armistice Commission."[40]

At 4 p.m. a German listener on the tapped line heard Huntziger request from Weygand "not merely an authorization to sign, but an order from the French government to do so."[41] At 6:30 p.m. General Keitel sent a note to General Huntziger demanding that the French either accept or reject Germany's armistice terms within one hour. If France did not sign the agreement by 7:30 p.m., Germany would end the negotiations, and the war would continue. At 6:50 p.m. on June 22, with forty minutes to spare, General Huntziger struggled to hold back tears as he signed the armistice agreement that paused the fighting between France and Germany.

And yet the armistice was not yet official.

Article 23 stipulated that the Franco-German armistice would not be final until six hours after France signed a similar agreement with Italy. This requirement was particularly grating to General Huntziger. Italy had waited until June 10 to declare war and then had barely fought. Huntziger told Keitel, "Although Italy has declared war on France, she has not waged war. France in fact does not have to ask Italy for an armistice, because the armistice has actually existed since the day of the declaration of war."[42]

But Huntziger had no choice. The French delegation flew to Rome on June 23 and signed the Italian armistice agreement at 7:35 p.m. on June 24.[43]

In accordance with Hitler's instructions to Benito Mussolini, the German and Italian armistice agreements were virtually identical, including the articles that dealt with the French fleet (Article 8 in the German agreement and Article 12 in the Italian agreement).

At 1:35 a.m. on June 25, 1940—six hours after Huntziger signed the Italian armistice agreement, and forty-six days after the first German tanks roared across the borders of its western neighbors—a ceasefire between France, Germany, and Italy went into effect.

Great Britain, with support from its Dominion nations, now faced Germany alone, a prospect that stirred as much relief as consternation. Some welcomed the prospect, including a sports-minded Londoner who proudly declared, "we're in the Final, and it's to be played on the Home Ground."[44]

Winston Churchill had acknowledged Britain's peril and expressed his bravado the week before. In a speech to the House of Commons, Churchill remarked that "in casting up this dread balance-sheet, contemplating our dangers with a disillusioned eye, I see great reason for intense vigilance and exertion, but none whatever for panic or despair."[45]

Churchill continued in the speech that helped define his legacy as an orator and a leader:

> What General Weygand called the "Battle of France" is over. I expect that the battle of Britain is about to begin. Upon this battle depends the survival of Christian civilisation. Upon it depends our own British life and the long continuity of our institutions and our Empire. . . . Let us therefore brace ourselves to our duty and so bear ourselves that if the British Commonwealth and Empire lasts for a thousand years men will still say, "This was their finest hour."

CHAPTER 7

TWO ESCAPES

THE FIRST HIGH-LEVEL discussion of British concerns about the French fleet took place during a June 7, 1940, meeting between Admiral Dudley Pound and two officials from Britain's foreign office. The participants were true to stereotyped form, with the naval officer anticipating a military clash and diplomats Alexander Cadogan and Maurice Hankey hoping for a negotiated solution.

The three men agreed on their desire to avoid a nightmarish prospect that was barely conceivable. When discussing the possibility that Admiral Darlan might order his ships to sail to British harbors, Cadogan expressed his anxiety about "how awkward it would be . . . if the Germans . . . threatened to destroy Paris unless we handed over the French Fleet."

Dudley Pound predicted that Admiral Darlan was more likely to scuttle his ships before the Germans could grab them. In any case Pound was adamant that "the only solution was to sink the French Fleet." The first sea lord added, "If necessary, we would torpedo the French ships ourselves."[1]

Winston Churchill first expressed his concern about the fleet directly to Admiral Darlan on June 12, five days before France queried Germany for its armistice terms. At the end of two days of meetings in Briare, Churchill encountered Darlan just before heading to an aerodrome for his flight back to London. The prime minister pulled the French admiral aside and demanded, "Darlan, I hope that you will never surrender the Fleet." Admiral Darlan assured Churchill, "There is no question of doing so," and added, "It would be contrary to our naval traditions and our honor."[2]

On the morning of June 18, U.S. Secretary of State Cordell Hull conveyed a message to Admiral Darlan on behalf of President Roosevelt in which he declared that if the French fleet was "surrendered to Germany, the French government will permanently lose the friendship and goodwill of the government of the United States."[3] According to the expansive *British Foreign Policy in the Second World War*, "The French Government considered this message an 'intolerable interference' on the part of a neutral country and especially on the part of a country which had 'failed to come up to their expectations.'"[4]

Admiral Darlan's reaction was less diplomatic. "The chief of the French Navy needs no advice from the United States about what to do to defend its honor." He also snarled to an aide, "And now Roosevelt is shitting on me."[5]

The professional and political heads of Britain's Navy—First Sea Lord Dudley Pound and First Lord of the Admiralty A. V. Alexander—traveled to Bordeaux on June 18 for a meeting with Admiral Darlan. Alexander's participation provided peer-to-peer recognition of Darlan's recently added minister of marine portfolio.

Germany's conquest of France was practically complete by the time of their meeting. Wehrmacht soldiers had been sampling petits fours and mille-feuilles in cafes and boulangeries in the open city of Paris for five days. The French government had requested Germany's terms for an armistice but was still in the dark about where the two sides would meet to negotiate.

Darlan proactively addressed two of the ships of greatest concern to Britain, the battleships *Richelieu* and *Jean Bart*. Although both vessels were, at best, months away from completion, their potential to bolster the French, British, or German fleets provoked alternating sentiments of desire and concern. Although neither ship would be the largest nor the fastest on the seas, both would be capable of engaging any ship in battle when fully fitted out and commissioned. In hostile hands, the *Richelieu* and *Jean Bart* would magnify the peril to Britain. The Royal Navy had worthy equals—her *King George V*-class of battleships—under construction, but the first ship of that class would not be commissioned until later in the year.

In his meeting with Pound and Alexander, Darlan mused that he might send the *Richelieu* to a navy yard in either the United States or Canada for completion. He had ruled out British yards due to the risk of German bombing. The *Jean Bart* presented a unique challenge. Even partially constructed, she was so massive that she could only set sail from her berth in Saint-Nazaire on the one night each month when the tides were at their highest. If she missed her next window, Darlan indicated that the French would destroy her in port to keep her out of German hands.[6]

Darlan also offered an intriguing suggestion. France expected the *Clemenceau*, a battleship in the same class as the *Richelieu*, to be commissioned in 1943. As of June 1940, she was only 10 percent complete.[7] To ensure that Germany did not commandeer her hull and complete her construction, Darlan suggested that the British bomb her in the shipyard at Brest.[8]

French Rear Admiral Gabriel Auphan, who participated in the meeting, wrote that Darlan gave the British "his word of honour that . . . our ships would be used by none but ourselves. They would remain French or would be destroyed." No one knew at the time that the safety of the *Richelieu* and the *Jean Bart*—as well as the pluck of their commanders—would be tested before day's end.

By the end of the meeting, Auphan believed Darlan had convinced the British of his resolve. "The British left us, moved, friendly and apparently satisfied."

The British might have been moved, and they might have seemed friendly, but according to an account from author Alec de Montmorency, they were hardly satisfied. Dudley Pound dismissed Darlan's assurance, telling an aide, "We have no use for words."[9]

The meeting also left Darlan with a cynical taste. In a letter to his wife the following day, he reflected that his British visitors had left the impression of "heirs who had come to make sure the dying man had decided in their favor."[10]

At a time when Winston Churchill, Dudley Pound, and A. V. Alexander questioned the French Navy's ability to control the destiny of its fleet, the commanding officers of two of the ships most coveted by Churchill, the *Richelieu* and the *Jean Bart*, executed heroic escapes to avoid seizure by approaching German forces.

Auphan, coauthor of *The French Navy in World War II*, wrote that France was prepared early in the war to sail key ships to Britain or to

French colonial ports in the event that France was overrun or was forced to submit to a dishonorable armistice.[11] Auphan claimed that orders for the ships' departures had been encrypted in advance and only awaited final approval from the government for the ships to cast off.

On June 15, the day after German forces swept into Paris, the French admiralty alerted the commanding officers at each French naval base to prepare their ships to sail on short notice. A separate message detailed specific plans for the *Richelieu* and the *Jean Bart*, both of which were still under construction in the yards at Brest and Saint-Nazaire respectively.

Although the *Richelieu* had not completed its sea trials and the *Jean Bart*'s had not yet begun, their captains had orders to sail for England if a German advance threatened their security. In a June 15 meeting with a British naval attaché, Admiral Auphan, who evidently was not aware of Admiral Darlan's misgivings about potential German attacks on French warships in British ports, stated "as regards *Richelieu* and *Jean Bart*, they will go to England if danger from air attack is too great or if grave eventuality should arise."[12]

As French resistance crumbled on the ground, the rapid advance of German troops did indeed threaten the two battleships. The *Richelieu* and the *Jean Bart* both sailed in haste. Neither ship sailed for Britain, however.

Vice Admiral Marcel Traub, in Brest where the partially finished *Richelieu* was anchored, received an urgent telephone call at 11 a.m. on June 18. A German detachment had taken Lieutenant General René Altmayer prisoner in Rennes just moments before. His captors had neglected to cut the telephone wire to the room where Altmayer was confined, and he had the presence of mind to call with a warning that a German motorized division was advancing toward Brest, with no reliable French forces in their 150-mile path.[13]

It would take the Germans roughly ten hours to reach Brest, where eighty-three French warships waited at their berths. Vice Admiral Traub initiated a whirlwind evacuation.

The battleship *Paris*, damaged by a German bomb at Le Havre the week before, was eased out of drydock and sailed to the safety of the British base at Plymouth with her repair work barely begun. The *Surcouf*, the largest submarine in the world, was at Brest for an overhaul. Although she was "unable to dive or go any faster than 4 knots," the *Surcouf* also made her way to Plymouth.[14]

Newly delivered equipment sat dockside near the *Richelieu*. Not only was the equipment embarked in haste, so were the contractors who would oversee its installation during *Richelieu*'s maiden voyage.[15] To prevent the next generation of naval officers from falling into German captivity, the *Richelieu* also carried away all 250 midshipmen from the École Navale—the French naval academy. Instead of sailing for Britain, the *Richelieu* headed to Dakar in French West Africa, where she arrived on the evening of June 23, 1940. As a result of her hasty departure, the *Richelieu* was short on cooking supplies, tropical uniforms, and even ammunition, which, until the last minute, the French had assumed they would requisition from a British naval yard. By the time a German detachment arrived in the early evening to take control of the port in Brest, only a handful of old, obsolete, and toothless ships remained.

The *Jean Bart* and the *Richelieu* were France's two largest warships, each displacing 37,850 tons, with a 32.5-foot draft (the depth below the waterline), 813-foot length, and 108-foot beam (or width). By mid-June, the *Richelieu*'s sister ship, the *Jean Bart*, was not remotely battle-worthy. In fact, she was barely seaworthy, still under construction in a drydock, her decks cluttered with scaffolding. Although size can be an asset for a warship, the *Jean Bart* was constructed in a naval yard that was constrained by a narrow, shallow channel. Even with the channel specially dredged to accommodate the massive battleship, she could only depart during the very narrow, one-night window in June when tides were at their absolute highest levels. With German forces closing on Saint-Nazaire, her sole opportunity to escape would be at high tide late on the night of June 18/19. The French expected German forces to storm their port the following day.

HMS *Vanquisher*, a British destroyer, was anchored in Saint-Nazaire during those final days of amity between the French and British navies. Vice Admiral T. J. Hallett carried orders to assist with the sailing of the *Jean Bart* as needed or, if necessary, to see that she was destroyed. French dockyard workers were prepared to wreck the *Jean Bart* themselves if she was unable to make a timely getaway.[16]

The shallow harbor at Saint-Nazaire was the most significant obstacle to the escape of the immense warship. Concerns about the draft and beam of *Jean Bart* were so acute that dredging continued until two o'clock in the morning on June 19. Engineers had dredged all the way through the mud to the very bottom of the channel and then began blasting more deeply through solid rock. The channel was finally deepened to a bit more than 26 feet, which was 6.5 feet less than *Jean Bart*'s draft with a full complement of supplies, men, and armament. To lighten her load and reduce her draft, after her dry dock was flooded, *Jean Bart* was towed into the channel with "no water, no provisions, no fuel oil, and only one of the 380-mm turrets in place."[17]

Tugboats maneuvered *Jean Bart* out of the port and into the Loire River at 3:30 a.m. The Loire's ship channel was almost as narrow as it was shallow, and the battleship ran aground several minutes after setting off. Six tugs worked to free her.

At 4:40 in the morning, just as the *Jean Bart* was about to get under way in the Loire under the command of Captain Pierre-Jean Ronarc'h, three Heinkel bombers attacked the almost defenseless ship. One German bomb grazed the *Jean Bart*, causing only minor damage.

While at sea, the *Jean Bart* once again encountered Vice Admiral Hallett and the *Vanquisher*, accompanied by two British tugboats. Captain Ronarc'h tactfully declined Hallett's offer to tow his ship to Britain. For a short time, the *Vanquisher* joined *Jean Bart*'s convoy to Casablanca, where she arrived early on the evening of June 22, the same day France signed its armistice with Germany.

As Admiral George Hamilton D'Oyly Lyon of the Royal Navy approached the French colonial port of Dakar for a friendly visit on June 25, he was shocked to see the *Richelieu* making her way out of the harbor. The British had assumed that the *Richelieu*'s refuge at Dakar would last significantly longer than one week.

Admiral D'Oyly Lyon commanded the seaplane tender *Albatross*, which was no match for the *Richelieu*, and so he did not engage her. Instead First

Sea Lord Dudley Pound dispatched a small but potent squadron from Gibraltar that included the aircraft carrier *Ark Royal*, the battlecruiser HMS *Hood*, and five destroyers in the direction of the Canary Islands. The Canaries were approximately midway between Dakar and Gibraltar and would put them on the most likely course to intercept the French battleship on her mystery-cloaked voyage.

The British were not alone in their concern about the *Richelieu*. Remarkably, when the French admiralty first learned of *Richelieu*'s departure from Dakar, they had no idea of her bearing nor the intent behind her sailing. It appeared to both sides that the *Richelieu* was under the command of a rogue skipper.

Before the *Richelieu* departed Dakar, Captain Richard Onslow of the Royal Navy had called on her commander, Captain Paul Marzin. Onslow tried to convince Marzin to sail his ship to a British-controlled port. Marzin "felt that he was being treated as an enemy and that, furthermore, the atmosphere at Dakar was one of betrayal." When Marzin learned that additional British ships, including the heavy cruiser HMS *Dorsetshire*, were planning to stop at Dakar, he decided on his own to depart for Casablanca where he would anchor near the *Jean Bart*.

Since Captain Marzin had not shared his intentions with the French admiralty, his sudden action triggered fears in Bordeaux that his battleship might be on her way to a neutral port or, much worse, to a British harbor. French Vice Admiral Emmanuel Ollive broadcast an order to Marzin on the evening of June 25, demanding an immediate return to Dakar. Marzin, suspicious that the order had been sent by either the Germans or the British, ignored it. Marzin did, however, react to a cable from François Darlan, authenticated by the admiral's XAVIER 377 signature. Darlan, who considered Marzin a member of his small A.D.D. circle, candidly scolded his subordinate *ami*:

> I am amazed to learn of your departure from Dakar. You do not have the right to dispose of your ship at your discretion or for the benefit of a power other than France. All the English news is false and of a nature to cause a civil war to break out for their own benefit,

> which would definitively ruin our country. Stay in Dakar until further orders from your leaders.
>
> DARLAN—XAVIER 377[18]

The *Richelieu* reversed course and returned to Dakar a short time after Marzin received Darlan's message. Although her escape from Brest and Marzin's impulsive two-day excursion would not be the last of the *Richelieu*'s uniquely independent adventures in the war, the actions of Captain Marzin and Captain Ronarc'h reinforced François Darlan's vow that his ships would not fall meekly into German, or British, hands.

CHAPTER 8

ANY ENEMY OR EX-ALLY

THE STAGING OF FRENCH warships in multiple ports on multiple continents complicated Winston Churchill's plan to ensure they did not fall into German control. French battleships, cruisers, and destroyers were anchored in ports that included Mers-el-Kébir, Algeria; Alexandria, Egypt; Toulon on the French Mediterranean coast; Bizerte, Tunisia; Sfax, Tunisia; Dakar, Senegal; Casablanca, Morocco; Martinique in the West Indies; and in multiple British ports, including Plymouth and Portsmouth.

On June 21, 1940, Admiral Darlan ordered "all warships or merchant ships present in British territory to put to sea and make for a French port." When Britain's war cabinet met the next day in the absence of Winston Churchill, they agreed that it was "undesirable to risk upsetting Admiral Darlan by making difficulties about French warships leaving British ports."[1] When, later that same day, German radio broadcasts announced the signing of the armistice agreement at Compiègne, the cabinet reversed its decision and denied the departure of French ships from British harbors.

Churchill was back at the table for a second meeting of the war cabinet that evening. The prime minister and his war cabinet agreed that in addition to securing French ships in British ports, under no circumstances should the *Richelieu* and *Jean Bart* escape their new harbors and fall into German hands. Churchill, of course, had no qualms about upsetting Admiral Darlan.

> However good his intentions might be, he [Darlan] might be forced to resign and his place taken by another Minister who would not shrink from betraying us. The most important thing is to make certain of the two modern battleships *Richelieu* and *Jean Bart*. If these two fell into the hands of the Germans, they would have a very formidable line of battle when the *Bismarck* was commissioned next August.[2]

Sir Ronald Campbell made plans to return to England even before French negotiators signed the German armistice agreement. As the British ambassador told a French diplomat, he was accredited to a free government that had been allied with Britain. He did not believe his king or prime minister would approve of him working with a government that would soon be under German control.[3] In addition, the British foreign office had warned Campbell to avoid capture—which was not an idle concern. Sir Lancelot Oliphant, Britain's ambassador to Belgium and Luxembourg, had been taken prisoner in early June. He would remain in German captivity until late September the following year.

During a hasty round of farewells near midnight on June 22, Paul Baudouin implored Campbell to remain in France to continue representing British interests. Baudouin assured Campbell that Admiral Darlan had requested permission to anchor French ships in North African colonial ports, which did nothing to alleviate the British ambassador's concerns. As Campbell wrote in an early-morning telegram to the British foreign office:

> Diabolically clever German terms have evidently destroyed the last remnants of French courage. If, as I presume to be certain, Germans reject counter-proposal as regards their fleet, I do not believe for a moment that the French, in their present state of collapse, would hold out against original German condition to recall the fleet to French ports, and might even reverse scuttling order. They could still square their conscience by saying ships could not be used against us. We are thus thrown back on Darlan's pathetic assurances to First Lord of the Admiralty [a reference to Darlan's June 18 meeting with A. V. Alexander].[4]

Despite instructions from the foreign office to Ambassador Campbell that he inform Admiral Darlan of Britain's insistence that he scuttle his fleet if it was not sailed to Britain or the United States, Campbell departed in such haste that he did not speak with Darlan. Instead, Britain's concerns were indirectly conveyed to Darlan in a cable from Vice Admiral Jean-Ernest Odend'hal from the French Naval Mission in London: "British Government still unfamiliar with wording of naval clauses signed. Fully familiar only with original German wording communicated by its

Ambassador. Is afraid of seeing our fleet, once disarmed, fall into enemy hands and used against us. Can you instruct me?"[5]

Darlan replied with the guidance that Odend'hal had requested, along with a plea to the British: "All provisions accepted are conditioned by the fact that the French Fleet will definitely remain French, under the French flag, in French ports with French skeleton crews. These conditions do not endanger British interests. On the other hand the attitude of the British authorities that you report can only be viewed as unfriendly. Insist that measures contemplated are hastily called off."

As Admiral Darlan continued his efforts to protect his ships from German seizure, he conceived a new concern—that France's recent ally might attempt to grab or sink his fleet. On June 23, he radioed a message to all French warships with a warning that the British were trying "to get their hands on the French fleet and French colonies."

Darlan provided additional perspective on his distrust of the British in a separate cable: "Given the unfriendly attitude of the British authorities and their undisguised spite at not being able to intern our Fleet in England, I ask you to keep your relationships with the Royal Navy to an essential minimum."[6]

Early on the morning of Sunday June 23, after the British had finally digested the full text of the German armistice agreement, Admiral Dudley Pound sent an urgent cable to Admiral Darlan. Pound's message included a personal plea based on his skeptical interpretation of Article 8. Pound was especially concerned about the fate of France's battleships, and he placed no trust in Hitler's promise not to incorporate them into the German fleet. Pound reminded the French admiral of Britain's conditional agreement for France to discuss armistice terms with Germany. "This condition was that the French Fleet shall be sent to British ports so that we may be able to make certain that they will not fall into the hands of our enemies."[7]

Two hours after sending his cable to Darlan, Pound, acting on behalf of the war cabinet, conveyed an even more impassioned plea to another French admiral. The British had intercepted a cable from Darlan in which he designated four admirals as potential "heirs"—Jean de Laborde,

Jean-Pierre Esteva, Jean-Marie Charles Abrial, and Marcel-Bruno Gensoul—to succeed him in the event that Darlan was removed from command or incapacitated in any way.[8]

In a message to Vice Admiral Esteva, commander of French naval forces in the Mediterranean, Pound assured his friend of long standing of his belief in Darlan's "intention to continue the fight," but,

> If the Germans gain some control over ships such as *Richelieu, Jean Bart, Dunkerque* and *Strasbourg*, they will most certainly use some excuse to delay their demilitarisation, in order to incorporate them in their fleet at some later date. You will understand, I am sure, that such a thing must not (I repeat must not) occur.
>
> If it was decided not to continue to fight, may we have your assurance that the condition under which His Majesty's Government agreed to the request for an armistice will be fulfilled?
>
> That condition was that the French Fleet should be sent to British ports, thus providing the certainty that it will not (I repeat will not) fall into the hands of the enemy. This is an agonising period for us, as you will surely understand, as long as we cannot be certain of this. I would be very grateful if you would reassure me on this point.[9]

In reply, Esteva reiterated the French Navy's blanket commitment that they would never surrender their ships to Germany. He also reinforced his specific loyalty to Admiral Darlan by stating that if the French government, and not Darlan, ordered him to surrender his ships, he would disobey that order.[10] A less prominent French admiral employed a less diplomatic turn of phrase when he saluted Darlan's refusal to "deposit his ships at the English pawnshop."[11]

Winston Churchill lashed out vehemently in a June 23 statement, the day after France signed the German armistice agreement. "His Majesty's Government have heard with grief and amazement that the terms dictated by the Germans have been accepted by the French Government at Bordeaux." He called for "all Frenchmen outside the power of the enemy to aid [the British] in their task and thereby render its accomplishment more sure and more swift."[12]

Paul Baudouin responded to Churchill with a cable in which he mentioned his "saddened amazement" at Churchill's denouncement and implored the prime minister to appreciate that "the French are showing more grandeur by admitting defeat than in trying to avoid it by vain and illusory efforts."[13]

Although he no longer had a role in the French government, Paul Reynaud sent a personal plea to Churchill. "I appeal to your friendship and to the confidence which you have always accorded me. Nothing would make Hitler happier than a falling out, public and permanent, between our two countries."[14] He tried to defuse Churchill's concerns about the French fleet. "The stipulations of the Armistice agreement on this subject are, it is true, of a nature to make you uneasy. But I have just questioned Admiral Darlan in the presence of Marshal Pétain. Darlan stated to me that . . . steps will be taken so that, under no circumstances will the enemy be able to make use of our fleet against Britain."

Finally, Reynaud reminded Churchill, "You were good enough to tell me at Briare and at Tours that, if a Government other than my own, adopted a different policy and asked for an armistice, Britain would not waste her time in useless recriminations."

Reynaud's reminder was misleading since it included only the first half of Churchill's statement from their June 13 meeting at Tours. General Spears, who participated in both the Briare and Tours meetings, captured Churchill's conditional vow. "Under no circumstances will Great Britain waste time in reproaches and recriminations. But that is a very different matter from being a consenting party to a peace made in contravention of the agreement so recently concluded."[15]

Marshal Pétain and Foreign Minister Paul Baudouin provisionally selected Paul Reynaud as the new government's ambassador to the United States. His appointment was abruptly reversed after two of his aides were arrested at the Spanish border, on their way to America in advance of Reynaud, with two million dollars of undeclared gold in what they assumed was diplomatically secure luggage.[16]

Two weeks later, after lunch with his mistress Hélène de Portes at a café near the coastal city of Sète, Reynaud's Renault Juvaquatre veered off the road and smashed into a tree. Reynaud was partially scalped and seriously injured.[17] Madame de Portes was killed instantly by heavily laden trunks that tumbled from the back seat.

Marshal Pétain had Reynaud arrested a short time after he left the hospital. Reynaud spent the remainder of the war in French and German prisons. General Maxime Weygand, General Maurice Gamelin, and Reynaud's rival Édouard Daladier were imprisoned for much of the war as well.

With the German and Italian armistice agreements now in place, Darlan left no doubt that the French fleet was not to fall into *any* foreign hands. With the German agreement's ban on wireless communications about to go into effect, the admiral of the fleet sent his final encrypted order, in which he dictated the future disposition of the French fleet, to his principal commanders on June 24:[18]

> First—The demobilizing warships are to stay French, under French flag, with reduced French crews, remaining in French metropolitan or colonial ports.
>
> Second—Secret precautions for sabotage are to be made in order that any enemy or ex-ally seizing a vessel by force may not be able to make use of it.
>
> Third—Should the Armistice Commission charged with interpreting the text come to a decision different from that in paragraph one, warships are, without further orders, to be dispatched to the United States, or, alternatively, scuttled, provided that no other action is possible to preserve them from the enemy. Under no circumstances are they to fall intact into enemy hands.
>
> Fourth—Ships that seek refuge abroad are not to be used in operations against Germany or Italy without prior orders from the Commander in Chief.
>
> Fifth—In no case obey the orders of a foreign admiralty.

When Vice Admiral Odend'hal shared Darlan's message with the British admiralty the next day, he delivered an altered version. Just a few words had been deleted, but their impact significantly affected Britain's interpretation of Darlan's intent. The word "ex-ally" had been omitted from paragraph two, and paragraph five had been removed in its entirety.

With France no longer fighting at Britain's side, Winston Churchill was more determined than ever to gain control of his former ally's most valuable military asset before Adolf Hitler could grab it. All the while, Darlan, still nominally in command of that asset, was equally resolute that none of his ships would fall into Hitler's hands. Although they shared the objective of protecting French ships from German seizure, Churchill and Darlan diverged sharply on how to achieve their common goal.

Churchill demanded that France release her ships to the protection of Great Britain or the United States. Darlan was confident in his ability to control the destiny of his fiefdom, and he trusted his commanding officers to scuttle their ships if Hitler broke his vow that Germany did "not intend to use the French Fleet . . . for its purposes in war."

What Churchill did not realize at the time was that Darlan was every bit as determined to keep his ships out of British hands.

Marshal Pétain spoke to reassure the French public in a June 25 radio broadcast: "At least our honor is saved. No one will make use of our planes or our fleet. . . . The government remains free. France will be administered only by the French."

Winston Churchill emphatically disagreed and continued to dispute French claims of independent authority and action. In a speech to the House of Commons on the day of Pétain's broadcast, Churchill spoke of his sorrow for the fate of France, "to whom we have been joined so long in war and peace." He expressed his skepticism about the new French government which had "delivered themselves over to the enemy and lie wholly in his power."[19]

Churchill shared his partisan interpretation of Article 8: "From this text it is clear that the French war vessels under this Armistice pass into German and Italian control while fully armed. We note, of course, in the same Article the solemn declaration of the German Government that they have no intention of using them for their own purposes during the war.

What is the value of that? Ask half a dozen countries what is the value of such solemn assurance."

As for Britain's future actions, Churchill promised that "neither patience nor resolution will be lacking in the measures they [His Majesty's government and military] may think it right to take for the safety of the Empire."[20] Churchill would manifest his resolution through action. Patience, on the other hand, as John Colville observed, was "a virtue with which he was totally unfamiliar."[21]

The British granted Charles de Gaulle access to BBC microphones for several broadcasts, hoping that his perspective on Pétain's acceptance of Germany's armistice terms would resonate on both sides of the Channel.

Taking to the airwaves on the evening of June 25, de Gaulle brutally rebutted Pétain's claim that "at least our honor is saved" and delivered a denunciation that approached the level of Leo Amery's rebuke of Neville Chamberlain:

> You were led to believe, Marshal, that an armistice . . . would be honorable. . . . This armistice is dishonorable. Two thirds of our territory occupied by the enemy—and what an enemy! Our entire Army demobilized, our officers and men prisoners. Our fleet, our planes, our tanks, our arms, handed over intact so that the enemy may use them against our own Allies. The country, the government, you yourself, reduced to servitude.
>
> Ah! To obtain and accept such an enslavement, we do not need the Conqueror of Verdun. Anyone else would have sufficed.[22]

François Darlan shared his perspective on the German and Italian armistice agreements in a June 26 cable to his senior officers. The message was not encrypted, but it carried his XAVIER 377 signature for authenticity:

> I have the terms of the two armistices in my hand; neither one is dishonorable. Our navy and our air force can be seen by their

exceptional treatment to be paid homage for their conduct and recognition of their valor. . . .

We keep all our ships and all our aircraft of naval aviation, our effective seamen on active service are not limited, and our adversaries have undertaken a solemn engagement not to touch our navy in the peace treaty. What more could we hope, being defeated? It now remains to accept the signed conventions with dignity. To do otherwise would bring about the definitive ruin of our country, gravely wounded by a defeat. To respond to outside interests would lead our territory into becoming a German province.[23]

Darlan, along with Marshal Pétain and General Weygand, continued to believe that Germany would soon vanquish Britain. In addition to his warning against "outside interests," Darlan declared, "Our former allies are not to be listened to: let us think French and act French."

By this early point in the war, London was already home to the governments-in-exile of Czechoslovakia, the Netherlands, Norway, and Poland. Churchill hoped a leader with the prestige of Paul Reynaud—or perhaps even François Darlan—would flee to London to lead one additional government-in-exile from British soil. Charles de Gaulle's biographer Jean Lacouture quoted Churchill saying years later, "If Darlan had chosen to fight in June 1940, he would have been a de Gaulle raised to the tenth power."[24]

In his war memoirs, Churchill wrote that Darlan

would not have come like General de Gaulle with only an unconquerable heart and a few kindred spirits. He would have carried with him outside the German reach the fourth Navy in the world, whose officers and men were personally devoted to him. Acting thus, Darlan would have become the chief of the French Resistance with a mighty weapon in his hand. British and American dockyards and arsenals would have been at his disposal for the maintenance of his fleet. The French gold reserve in the United States would have assured him, once recognised, of ample resources. The whole French Empire would have rallied to him. Nothing could have prevented him from being the Liberator of France.[25]

But Darlan now had no intention of sailing to Britain. Two weeks after Darlan teased Jules Moch with a vow of "splendid indiscipline" by means of a naval exodus across the English Channel, Darlan told Moch that "England is finished," and "we have no right to separate the fleet from the country."[26]

Darlan wrote in his diary that if he had allowed the fleet to sail to England, "either the English would have used it against the Germans, and France would have suffered, or they would have disarmed it and left it to rot."[27]

As for the French pledge to not seek German armistice terms without British approval, an aide to Darlan wrote that "in our eyes" the agreement had "only the authority of a press release."[28]

On June 27 Churchill told Charles de Gaulle, "You are alone—well I . . . I shall recognize you alone."[29] The British government officially acknowledged de Gaulle as the leader of Free France on the following day. Most other nations, including the United States, accepted the legitimacy of Marshal Pétain's French government in Vichy. With his recognition of de Gaulle and Free France, Churchill unequivocally turned his back on the nation to which he had extended the offer of a union just twelve days before.

PART 3

ADVERSARIES

CHAPTER 9

A STATE OF STUPEFIED MISERY

MARCEL-BRUNO GENSOUL, the rare French admiral to have sailed with British warships under his command, now led the French Navy's most prominent squadron. France's *Force de Raid*—with the battleships *Dunkerque* and *Strasbourg*, the two newest and most lethal battle-ready ships in the French fleet, at its core—was anchored at Mers-el-Kébir, a small Mediterranean port on the coast of the French colony of Algeria.

When François Darlan named four potential heirs, he listed Gensoul fourth in his rank-ordered list, after Admirals de Laborde ("the best sailor of his generation"), Esteva, and Abrial. Darlan recognized that Gensoul "would carry out my orders with intelligence and precision," in contrast with Jean de Laborde who "would have exceeded my orders . . . driven by his need for action."[1]

Cedric Holland described Gensoul to fellow British officers much as Darlan perceived him: "In my opinion he's correct—completely service. He'll never step out of line. He's also, perhaps, somewhat pigheaded." In addition, although he had sailed under Gensoul's command in a joint operation at the end of 1939, "I don't know him well. He was described to me as a little overfull of his own importance—something of a small man in a big position."[2] Dudley Pound believed that Gensoul "was not a man of original or bold ideas."[3] As Gensoul would soon prove, no French admiral was less likely to stray from his orders.

Gensoul was unsettled by the arrival of an unexpected British visitor when Admiral Dudley North sailed into Mers-el-Kébir on June 23, 1940, uninvited and unannounced. The two admirals met for twenty minutes on Gensoul's flagship, the *Dunkerque*. North reported afterward that the French admiral "appeared to be in a state of stupefied misery." He sensed that Gensoul was on the brink of tears as he declared his intention to "obey the orders of a legally constituted French government while it existed," and to continue the fight under Darlan's orders if the government was dissolved.[4]

Gensoul bluntly rejected North's suggestion to either join with the British navy or turn his ships over to British control. He gave his word of honor that, in accordance with Admiral Darlan's mandate, under no circumstances would he surrender his ships to either German or Italian forces. North noted that Gensoul "repeated his assurance several times and I must say that I believed him." Gensoul also conveyed his candid expectation that Britain would fall to Germany in a matter of weeks, and so, to relinquish command of his ships to the British would be "silly."

North added that after meeting for only twenty minutes, he and Gensoul

> parted on quite friendly terms. He looked utterly dejected, and I felt keenly for him. We shook hands on the quarter deck. . . . the [*Dunkerque*'s] band played *Aux Champs* to a British admiral for the last time. At the quay, where my destroyer, *Douglas*, was berthed, the captain of the dockyard told me in perfect English that he was ashamed of his Government and that he wished to apologize. He wished me the best of luck.[5]

Britain's war cabinet met three separate times on Monday, June 24—at noon, 6 p.m. and 10:30 p.m.—to discuss the full range of options for British action against the French Navy.

Churchill feared that Marshal Pétain lacked the mettle to protect the French fleet from German seizure. During the first meeting of that long day, Churchill remarked, "In the near future we shall have to solve the problem of future relations with the present French Government," and declared that "no trust could be put in the German word. No limit existed as to the danger which Germany would thrust upon France. It is not a question of recrimination, but of things which are to us matters of life and death."[6]

Dudley North cabled a summary of his conversation with Admiral Gensoul for the cabinet's benefit, reinforcing Gensoul's rigid loyalty to Admiral Darlan. He expected Gensoul to resist British pleas to relinquish control of his ships and was certain Gensoul would defend himself against hostile action if confronted by the Royal Navy.

The noon session ended with the war cabinet still shy of an agreement on how to achieve their goal to gain control of the French fleet, or even the specific message they would send to the French government. Churchill and his ministers planned to regroup in the evening.

The most significant outcome of the noon meeting was a consensus that if they achieved nothing else, Britain must gain control over France's four largest ships—the *Dunkerque*, the *Strasbourg*, the *Jean Bart*, and the *Richelieu*. If possession was not feasible, Britain would pressure France to scuttle those ships. If the French Navy refused to sink their own ships, Britain would destroy them.

The war cabinet opened their 6 p.m. meeting with a discussion of Mers-el-Kébir. The small Algerian port where the battleships *Dunkerque* and *Strasbourg* sat at anchor was framed by a mountainous backdrop, a fort that overlooked the harbor, additional shore batteries, and a massive stone breakwater, or "mole," all of which served as barriers against attack.

In the opinion of the war cabinet, the risks presented by a battle in this well-defended harbor outweighed the potential benefits of securing or sinking the *Dunkerque* and *Strasbourg*. To avoid that danger, the cabinet elected to have the Royal Navy shadow French ships as they proceeded to French ports as mandated by the armistice terms.[7] This—quite notably—was the one very brief moment in time when the consensus of Britain's war cabinet was to allow the peaceful repositioning of the French fleet in general accordance with the German armistice terms. That consensus evaporated before the meeting ended.

A messenger interrupted the cabinet's evening session with news that France had signed its armistice agreement with Italy. Cabinet members had expected Benito Mussolini to assert claims on the French Navy that were even more egregious than those made by Adolf Hitler. In relative terms, they were pleasantly surprised to learn that the Italian agreement largely mirrored the terms of the German armistice agreement. Hitler had not permitted his Italian minion to demand exorbitant concessions that would have ruptured the armistice and disrupted his carefully crafted plan for the subjugation of France. The British would learn after the war that Mussolini's original aspirations included a joint Italo-German occupation of France, possession of all French colonies in North Africa, and a significant share of the French fleet.[8] A tripartite German-Italian-French armistice commission, with the French represented by General Charles Huntziger, was established to enable the three sides to resolve differences in translation, semantics, and intent.

The completion of the Italian armistice agreement was Germany's final condition for the cessation of fighting. Article 23 in the German agreement stated, "Hostilities will be stopped six hours after the moment at which Italian Government has notified the German Government of conclusion of its agreement." Now more than ever, the actions of the leaders of France meant more than their words.

To this point Britain had sputtered objections and warnings in the direction of France but had not yet served their former ally with an ultimatum for the specific disposition of its fleet. The cabinet agreed to "make a formal communication to the French Government" that Britain would not tolerate the risk of French ships falling into German hands. The repositioning of the French fleet in accordance with either German or Italian directives was not acceptable. Churchill and Halifax agreed to collaborate on the wording of an ultimatum for France to scuttle its ships before a specific deadline, "otherwise Britain would take action by force against them."[9]

With France now conclusively lost as an ally, the cabinet moved closer—but not all the way—to a final plan to resolve Britain's concerns about the French fleet during their third meeting of the day, which began at 10:30 p.m.

As the cabinet reconsidered the relative threats to Britain from the *Dunkerque* and the *Strasbourg* on one hand, and the *Richelieu* and the *Jean Bart* on the other, the masters of Britain's war strategy ricocheted between several tentative conclusions not only during the meeting but in the days that followed.

After a brief digression over the relative advantages of subduing France's submarines or its surface ships, the cabinet agreed to focus on their surface ships. As for which specific surface ships to target, the cabinet changed direction multiple times. Churchill and the admiralty were loath to spread the Royal Navy's finite assets in pursuit of all four ships of concern in their three current ports. After tabling their worries about the partially completed *Richelieu* and *Jean Bart*, they decided to focus on the two most lethal seagoing French warships, the battleships *Dunkerque* and *Strasbourg*, anchored at Mers-el-Kébir, despite Admiral Gensoul's ability and intent to defend that small port.

The ministers reasoned that the *Richelieu* and *Jean Bart*, neither fully seaworthy or battleworthy, posed less of a threat to Britain from their remote berths in Casablanca and Dakar respectively.[10] But then again, although the *Dunkerque* and *Strasbourg* posed the greatest immediate risk to Britain if integrated into the German fleet, an attack on those ships at Mers-el-Kébir would also pose the greatest potential risk to Royal Navy vessels.

First Sea Lord Dudley Pound sparked second (or perhaps third or fourth) thoughts when he expressed concerns about the danger involved in a confrontation at Mers-el-Kébir: "the probable loss of our two ships [thought to be HMS *Hood* and HMS *Resolution*[11]] seemed a heavy price to pay for the elimination or partial elimination of the *Force de Raid*. Admiral Darlan and other French Admirals had maintained the consistent attitude that in no circumstances would the French Fleet be surrendered, and it would seem more likely that we should achieve our object by trusting in these assurances, rather than by attempting to eliminate units of the French Fleet by force."[12]

The cabinet also discussed the somber reality that a decision "to order the destruction of people who had only 48 hours before been Allies would be hard to make." In the ongoing debate about the acceptable balance between the threat of losing control of French ships versus the risk of losing British ships in battle, Dudley Pound's argument won through. He convinced Churchill—at least momentarily—that an attack at Mers-el-Kébir would be unwise and would be a risk not worth taking. As a result, Churchill, normally the most steadfast of men, reversed course once again and rationalized that "the ships which mattered most were the *Jean Bart* and *Richelieu* which were at present unarmed and should prove easy to secure once they left the shelter of the French [West African] port."

And yet the third meeting of that long day ended with a decision to remain indecisive. The cabinet delayed a commitment to any specific action against the French fleet, aside from a decision to prevent French warships currently in British ports from departing for as long as possible. While the cabinet leaned toward a plan to gain control of the *Richelieu* and the *Jean Bart*, their commitment to this action was brittle. So brittle, in fact, that they continued to seriously evaluate the possibility of a confrontation at Mers-el-Kébir.

Dudley Pound sought additional clarity the following day. He telegraphed Dudley North at Gibraltar to confirm North's impressions from his meeting with Admiral Gensoul on the *Dunkerque* the previous week: "Do you consider that there would be any prospect of French ships at Oran surrendering to us if British force arrived off port and summoned them to surrender?"

North repeated his assertion that Gensoul would not surrender his ships. If the British hoped to subdue the *Dunkerque* and *Strasbourg*, they would have to resort to forceful measures.

CHAPTER 10

IT IS EVENTS THAT MOVE THE WORLD

NOTWITHSTANDING GENERAL WILHELM Keitel's declaration that Germany's armistice agreement was "unalterable and must be accepted or rejected" in its original form, several of its twenty-four articles were sufficiently imprecise to allow room for debate.

François Darlan hoped to use the first meeting of the German Armistice Commission—scheduled for Saturday, June 29, 1940, in Wiesbaden—to win approval to settle his ships in colonial ports on the coast of Africa, in part to protect his fleet from British bombardment or seizure. Darlan also hoped the possibility of German concessions would dampen the steady increase in tension between Britain and France. In advance of the armistice commission meeting, Darlan instructed Vice Admiral Odend'hal to implore the British to withhold judgment until France and Germany finalized the fine points of their agreement.

Winston Churchill not only declined to withhold judgment, he also pressed for an immediate determination whether French warships would be interned in French metropolitan ports or in North Africa.[1]

After the Germans booted the decision on the stations of French ships to its under-commission for naval affairs, a separate Italian armistice commission accepted France's request to intern its ships in either the French port of Toulon on the Mediterranean—and, notably, in the free zone—or in North African ports. This was a significant concession. None of the French ships would be forced to return to ports within the German occupied zone.[2]

Darlan tacked on an urgent appeal to the update he conveyed to the British through Vice Admiral Odend'hal: "Italian Government authorizes the stationing of the Fleet, with half crews, at Toulon and in North Africa.

I have firm hopes that it will be likewise with the German Government, whose reply we are now awaiting. Under these conditions all British pretexts for detaining our forces are without foundation, and I beg of you to insist on our men-of-war and merchantmen being released."

Churchill was unconvinced and remained resolute that no matter how the Germans and Italians modified their respective terms, Britain must gain physical control of the newest and largest ships in the French fleet. What remained unresolved was how best to gain that control.

During a war cabinet meeting on June 28, Lord Halifax shared the gist of a report from American under-secretary of state Sumner Welles, who suggested that "in the view of the American Government the surrender of the French naval fleet was the most degrading surrender in history." Halifax added, "It seems safe to assume that any action which we might do in respect of the French Fleet would be applauded in the United States."[3]

Although the United States was not yet engaged in the war, Churchill was alert to American opinion. While it is unlikely that any degree of opposition from the United States would have altered his intended action against the French Navy, the prime minister welcomed American approval. An indirect signal that America would not oppose the use of force against French warships reinforced his resolve.

Winston and Clementine Churchill were joined at Chequers on Friday, June 28, by a coterie of friends, advisors, diplomats, and military officers who could be counted on to share opinions, advice, wit, cigars, cocktails, and stimulating conversation throughout the weekend. After the women retired from the dining room that first night, Churchill settled into a solemn post-dinner discussion with Robert Vansittart and Alexis Leger, who had worked respectively in the British and French foreign offices.

The prime minister termed their conversation a *cercle sacré* and asked how Britain might be able to—as John Colville paraphrased—"maintain the goodwill of the French people for whose salvation we were the last hope, while we were obliged to starve them by blockade and destroy their towns by bombs. How could we convince them that we were being cruel in order to be kind?"[4]

Churchill asked Leger for his frank insights on the collapse of France. Leger, a future Nobel Prize–winning poet, a fervent anti-Nazi, and a consistent anti-appeaser, endorsed a light touch. He counseled Churchill to maintain contact with France's meandering government. Britain should avoid confrontation and should embrace the use of propaganda. He recommended that Britain attempt to *influence* France rather than *challenge* its recent ally. Vansittart, who was one of Britain's most ardent opponents of appeasement with Hitler, agreed with Leger on the wisdom of appeasing France. Both men suggested that a cautious approach to relations with France would have the most significant impact on American opinion as well.

Churchill was unmoved and bluntly rejected their recommendations, replying, "Propaganda is all very well, but it is events that move the world."

He continued, "If we smash the Huns here we shall need no propaganda in the United States." Churchill added that it was "the night before the battle. It may be long: now we must live; next year we shall be winning; the year after that we shall triumph."[5]

One of the first in a series of events that would soon move the world was the formation of a new Royal Navy squadron at Gibraltar. Vice Admiral James Somerville sailed from Portsmouth on Thursday, June 27, to take command of the new squadron: an assemblage of warships with the mass and the might to mount an attack on key elements of Admiral Darlan's fleet. This newly scratched-together squadron bore the nondescript name "Force H." Its centerpiece was the battlecruiser HMS *Hood*. Other ships in Force H ranged from the aircraft carrier *Ark Royal*—commissioned just two years before—and, at the other extreme, the battleship *Valiant*, which had traded salvoes with the German High Seas Fleet at Jutland in the summer of 1916.

HMS *Hood* was named after Vice Admiral Lord Samuel Hood, an ancestor of James Somerville, who battled the French Navy in the 1700s, and who, most notably, set fire to the French dockyard at Toulon in 1793.[6] The *Hood* was, in the view of a British admiral, "the grandest looking man-of-war in the world . . . the most beautiful ship built since the days of sail."[7] She was also the most massive (44,600-ton displacement) and yet

MAP 2. Theater of Battle

one of the fastest (with a top speed of 32 knots) armored ship on the seas.[8] Service on board the "mighty 'ood" was a cherished honor.

Churchill and his war cabinet had by now determined that the loss of the *Dunkerque* and the *Strasbourg* into German control represented the greatest threat to Britain. And so, despite the potential risk to HMS *Hood* and other British ships, the initial assignment of Force H was "to secure the transfer, surrender or destruction of the French warships at Oran and Mers-el-Kébir."[9] A secondary priority was to keep the Italian fleet bottled up in the Mediterranean.

The command structure of the Royal Navy was delineated in part by bodies of water. Gibraltar, a small but vitally important slice of British territory on the southern tip of Spain, served as an important dividing point. The Mediterranean (to the east of Gibraltar) and the Atlantic (to the west of Gibraltar) were each under the command of different admirals. Andrew Cunningham—commander-in-chief, Mediterranean—led British naval forces in the Mediterranean. Dudley North—Admiral, Gibraltar—filled the same role in the North Atlantic.

Force H would operate in both the Mediterranean and the Atlantic. While the British admiralty in Whitehall held the ultimate operational authority over Force H, they directed Vice Admiral Somerville to cooperate with Admiral Cunningham and Admiral North, two like-minded colleagues as well as longtime friends.

(A note about geographical references: Oran and Mers-el-Kébir are often referred to interchangeably in historical accounts and, by necessity, in this book. Oran is roughly two hundred times larger than Mers-el-Kébir in land mass and is a significant city in Algeria. The two ports are separated by just four miles. Mers-el-Kébir's significance was as a naval port, particularly during World War II, when it was home to key elements of the French fleet. The clash between the British and French navies at Mers-el-Kébir is a focus of this book, and the majority of the references here are to Mers-el-Kébir. The verbatim accounts quoted in this book retain the specific geographic reference from the source material. This can be confusing at times, as even naval officers sometimes refer to Oran in their descriptions of events at Mers-el-Kébir. Oran and Mers-el-Kébir can be thought of as a single general area, with the knowledge that Mers-el-Kébir was the focal point of British interest and controversy.)

Vice Admiral Sir James Fownes Somerville joined the Navy at the age of fourteen in January 1897. Forty-plus years of handwritten Royal Navy service records paint a striking picture of Somerville's character and competence. These records attest to his ability to inspire his men with "the keenness & enthusiasm that he himself possesses." His confident personality included "a gift for turning away wrath by tactful jest." He was a paragon of fitness who "has proved himself to be nearly the ideal Commodore as any human being could hope or wish to attain . . . He nearly approaches perfection as an Officer and a Man."[10]

Somerville was blessed with an unbounded sense of curiosity, and he enjoyed taking part in the activities of the men he led. His fascinations included naval aviation, and he was the rare commander who took the opportunity to sit in the observer's seat in open-cockpit biplanes that either flew from carrier decks or were launched with gut-wrenching velocity from deck-mounted catapults on smaller warships. Somerville's men were accustomed to the sight of the admiral rowing his personal skiff around his flagship, rippling by other ships in the harbor most mornings before breakfast. When he was ashore, they watched him walk the steep paths of the Rock of Gibraltar at a brisk pace. Somerville was candid, quick-witted, and fearless in speaking his mind to higher authority. He led "with a calculated lack of formality,"[11] but he "did not suffer fools or inefficiency."[12]

His son, Lieutenant Commander John Somerville, considered his father a pragmatic leader who always "measured the risk against the dividend."[13] Somerville had an impish sense of humor and a situationally scatological vocabulary.[14] A fellow officer claimed "he could pour forth the language of a fisherman."[15] Despite the occasional reference to "naughty James," his men more commonly expressed their admiration for "Uncle James."

In the summer of 1939, at a time when James Somerville was clearly destined for a significant role in the war that appeared inevitable, his career was derailed. A mere five weeks before Britain and France declared war on Germany, an entry in his service record on July 31, 1939, simply reads, "Placed on Retired List—medically unfit." At the age of fifty-seven, James Somerville was forced out of uniform and cast ashore.

A deep and persistent cough had prompted a physical exam that indicated a case of pulmonary tuberculosis. Somerville argued—and earlier x-rays supported—that the scars on his lungs were relics of a long dormant encounter with the disease. Although trace amounts of tuberculosis bacilli were evident in his sputum, his active symptoms vanished during Somerville's forced passage from the East Indies back to Britain in isolation on board a passenger liner. Despite less than conclusive evidence and Somerville's strenuous objections, the surgeon rear admiral of the Royal Navy claimed he had no choice other than to mandate Somerville's removal from the service to prevent a highly transmittable disease from ravaging its way through the confines of a ship.

Somerville, who had once criticized men who "have to go down each stair carefully instead of sliding down the banisters when the house is on fire," was not a man to embrace a forced retirement.[16] He vigorously contested the doctor's opinions and the admiralty's decision, and he revived his career by means of his personal initiative. With "only vague authority behind him," he worked his way back into naval operations.

Somerville had demonstrated an early interest in radar. On the day after war was declared, five weeks after he was proclaimed unfit for duty, he "was instructed by the Third Sea Lord to supervise the development and fitting of R.D/F [radio direction finding—i.e., radar] apparatus for naval purposes."[17] The rollout was so effective that Somerville is considered "the foster father of naval radar."[18]

Although he longed for an assignment at sea, Somerville embraced his new, if vaguely defined, responsibilities. As he shared in a letter to a fellow admiral, "My job lets me butt in everywhere so like a bloody bee I carry somebody's problem on my backside and fertilise some other bloke's idea."[19]

Somerville was also drafted for an unlikely stint to describe and explain developments in the war to the men and women sitting in front of their radio sets across Britain. A file packed with enthusiastic letters from his audience members in the early months of 1940 indicates the popularity of this charismatic admiral's broadcasts over the BBC's airwaves. One listener saluted "a thundering good discourse," while another declared Somerville's broadcasts "grand stuff, and just what one wants to hear." A writer shared, "Your talks have been a Tonic, a breath of the Seas." And another added, "I felt that you were talking to me last night over the air."

Despite the occasional criticism—"Our general advice to you is to keep off the air. Many others are more competent. You are only wasting everybody's time & patience"—the publisher of C. S. Forester's Horatio Hornblower novels was so captivated by Somerville's broadcasts that he encouraged Somerville to write a book of his own, claiming it would be "not only successful but exceedingly valuable." Despite that encouragement, James Somerville never wrote a book.[20]

Another ad hoc assignment during Somerville's not-quite-a-wilderness year was "Inspector of Anti-aircraft Weapons and Devices." Unofficially known as the "Department of Wheezers and Dodgers," Somerville's outfit developed and tested a variety of devices—ranging from kites to rockets—to defend against low-flying German aircraft.

This assignment took a critical turn in May 1940 after British forces began their retreat toward Dunkirk and other channel ports in France. Brigadier Claude Nicholson, whose 30th Infantry Brigade was ordered to defend the vital British garrison at Calais, issued an urgent plea for additional firepower to defend against German tanks. Winston Churchill suggested that twelve-pound antiaircraft guns could be mounted on lorries and employed as anti-tank guns. Since this would be an innovative application of antiaircraft weapons and devices, Somerville crossed the Channel to expedite the implementation of this ad hoc weaponry at Calais.[21]

When Somerville arrived at Nicholson's much beleaguered command post, hours after midnight on May 25, Nicholson assumed he and his men were about to be evacuated. Somerville instead shared the grim message that Churchill expected him to "fight to the last in order to hold up the advance of the Germans." Nicholson accepted his fate with a hero's nonchalance. He was captured by German forces after his garrison's gallant defense bought invaluable time for the men on Dunkirk's beaches. Nicholson survived the battle at Calais but died—presumably by suicide—in a German prisoner of war camp in 1943.

When Somerville returned from Dunkirk, he found that Vice Admiral Bertram Ramsay was working day and night to coordinate the evacuation of British and French forces from the chaos and carnage of the besieged town's beaches. Somerville volunteered to alternate twelve-hour shifts with Ramsay.[22] The two admirals coordinated evacuation activities until the last man was taken off the beach on June 4.

In a May 30 letter to his wife, Somerville shared an interesting aside from the daily updates he provided to the prime minister: "Winston and I usually hold light converse on the telephone at 6.30 a.m. As he always has his teeth out then it's not so easy."[23]

In a June 18, 1940, report Vice Admiral Ramsay shared his appreciation for Somerville's assistance in the near miraculous rescue of more than a third-of-a-million men, including more than 100,000 Frenchmen, from the beaches of Dunkirk: "The attributes of this officer for initiative and resource are well known throughout the Service but I venture to express the opinion that never in the course of his long and distinguished career have they been put to better use than during the operations for the evacuation of the Allied Armies from Dunkirk."[24]

James Somerville reconfirmed his fitness for duty, and First Sea Lord Dudley Pound summoned him to lead Force H—the Royal Navy squadron that was assembled to confront the French ships at Mers-el-Kébir.

CHAPTER 11

TRANSFORM A DEFEATED ALLY INTO AN ACTIVE ENEMY

ON TUESDAY, JUNE 25, 1940, the day after France signed its armistice agreement with Italy, François Darlan ordered his senior officers to "Disembark immediately all British liaison officers and personnel. . . . Watch out for possible British attacks."[1] With that order, Darlan brought the Franco-British naval liaison program to an abrupt end.

British commander George Kempthorne Collett, who had been quartered on Admiral Gensoul's flagship at Mers-el-Kébir, had a wistful departure, much along the lines of Admiral Dudley North's sendoff two days earlier. "As I left the quarter deck of *Dunkerque*, I think almost all of the officers were on deck to see me off, and they all insisted on shaking me by the hand, wishing me good luck and saying how much they wished they were coming with me." Collett thought highly of Gensoul, whom he considered "a cool-headed man" who was intensely loyal to Admiral Darlan.[2]

After Collett returned to the British base at Gibraltar on a French destroyer provided by Gensoul, he shared his assessment of the morale of the French Navy's lower ranks: "To them the war is over and they want to return to their wives and families." He recommended caution: "When I left the Fleet I was convinced that the ships would never be turned over intact to the Germans, and even more definitely not to the Italians. The orders for scuttling and/or wrecking the ships had been issued. . . . I am convinced that we shall gain nothing by threats or attempts at coercion."

Cedric Holland, who had commanded a heavy cruiser and a battleship prior to his liaison posting to Paris, returned to sea in April with a prominent assignment: the command of the Navy's newest and largest aircraft carrier, the HMS *Ark Royal*.

On the eve of Holland's departure, French and British officers at Maintenon raised an evening full of toasts to the fortunes of the British captain. French naval officer and historian Henri Ballande wrote, "Each of us regarded him as a personal friend, and regretted his leaving."[3]

In his written evaluation of Holland's service in France, British ambassador Sir Ronald Campbell remarked that Holland "enjoyed the confidence and esteem of all the French Officers with whom he was in contact, in particular of Admiral Darlan, who has spoken of Captain Holland and his work in terms of the highest praise." Darlan expressed his respect and esteem by naming Holland a Commander of the Legion of Honor, a significant honor that France more typically bestowed upon admirals.[4]

Holland, the British officer with the most extensive connections in the French Navy and the best insights into the character of its leaders, received a short leave from his carrier duties to fly to Casablanca to assess the mindsets of senior French officers. Holland provided an illuminating assessment of French morale in his report on the meetings that spanned June 24 and 25. Holland returned convinced that the loyalty of senior French officers to Marshal Petain's new government was solid, and he had no doubt they would continue to follow Admiral Darlan's orders. Holland reported that his contacts in the French Navy, Admiral Darlan in particular, resented Winston Churchill's verbal broadsides against their government. News of the armistice commission's willingness to allow the French Navy to position its ships in ports outside the German occupied zone further reduced the likelihood of any elements of the French Navy sailing off with their British counterparts.[5] Admiral Jean de Laborde, Darlan's principal heir-designate, assured Holland that he and other French officers would continue to follow Admiral Darlan's orders.

The British captain, who had grown close to Darlan in Paris and at Maintenon, was taken aback by his current read on the leader of the French Navy, however. "Admiral Darlan is a fighting man with character, determination and energy. What appears to be his present conduct is completely at variance with what one would expect of him and the only plausible explanation appears to be that he is not a free agent."

In addition to his impression that Darlan resented Churchill's recent denunciations of his government, Holland believed Darlan's new ministerial assignment had affected his outlook, and speculated that perhaps Darlan "has found his hands more and more tied until he is virtually a prisoner of the German Directorate." Holland concluded, "The present feelings amongst the officers are those of bewilderment, humiliation and disparagement [*sic*].

After François Darlan ordered British liaison officers to debark from French ships, the British admiralty surprisingly welcomed French Vice Admiral Jean-Ernest Odend'hal to remain in London, but only after placing limits on his freedom of action. Although Odend'hal was admired, respected, and generally considered "a nice old cup of tea," both the French and British navies constrained his initiative in the wake of the armistice. Darlan "gave him practically no latitude and used him as little more than a post office."[6]

After Admiral Pound demanded that he turn over "ciphers, plans of minefields and secret information in his possession," Odend'hal registered a protest and stressed that all Royal Navy materials had been returned or destroyed by burning. His demand to retain French cipher material and signals logs was subsequently granted.[7]

Although both admiralties now hobbled his potential effectiveness, Odend'hal remained an important conduit for information; post offices do serve a purpose, after all. To the misfortune of both the French and British navies, however, as Odend'hal had already demonstrated, his most significant impact would result from presumably well-intentioned manipulations of important communications.

James Somerville disembarked at Gibraltar on the evening of June 30 after a fifty-hour voyage from Portsmouth. Dudley North greeted Somerville and briefed him on his visit to Mers-el-Kébir the previous week. North told Somerville—as he had previously indicated to the admiralty—that he trusted Admiral Marcel-Bruno Gensoul's pledge that he would never allow his ships to fall into German or Italian hands. Admiral North cautioned Somerville about the collateral effects of a violent clash, suggesting that the death of a single French sailor would unite the French Navy against Britain.

Somerville's discussion with Admiral North reinforced his belief that French officers would not betray their loyalty to François Darlan and Marshal Petain's government. Somerville empathized with his former counterparts who now risked severe personal reprisals for contravention of the German armistice terms.

Several hours after he arrived at Gibraltar and hoisted his flag on HMS *Hood*, Somerville met with his senior officers in Force H to discuss the opposition they were likely to face in a confrontation at Mers-el-Kébir. Somerville also wanted to hear their views on the possible use of force against their former allies.

The officers first discussed the physical obstacles they expected to encounter. These included two steel-mesh submarine nets (often called "booms") that blocked the harbor's entrance, an armed fort at the mouth of the harbor, and a twenty-foot-tall breakwater behind which the French ships sat at anchor. When the discussion turned to the probable French response to hostile action, the officers unanimously agreed that the use of force would rebound poorly against Britain. Their worst fear was a fatal misstep that would result in war between Britain and France.

The officers were apprehensive at the prospect of presenting an ultimatum that the French were sure to reject. With the knowledge that they would then be ordered to mount an assault on their recent allies, the men conceived of an "attack" that would begin as little more than a bluff: "a round or two (aimed not to hit) should be fired to show that we were in earnest, and if this failed to bring acceptance of our terms, a limited period of gunfire and/or bombing should be used to cause evacuation of the ships, final sinking being effected by torpedo-bomber attack or demolition, according to circumstance."[8]

Somerville met with Cedric Holland and two other recently reassigned liaison officers the following morning, July 1, 1940. Holland, who was now under Somerville's command, had participated in Somerville's meeting with his commanding officers the previous night. In the first meeting,

Holland shared his impressions of Admiral Darlan and also replied to a question about why Darlan had not sailed off with the French Navy:

> I know Darlan reasonably well. He's ambitious. He could certainly do it. If he did, I've no doubt he would spring into the limelight of history as a great leader. He hates the Germans personally. He's very proud of his unique position as Admiral of the Fleet. The centralisation of command of all sea forces in the person of the Chief of the Naval Staff has always been very marked, although Darlan has often been at pains to assure me otherwise. I imagine, therefore, that all senior officers are awaiting orders from their Chief.[9]

Much in keeping with the opinions Somerville had absorbed the previous night, Holland and his two colleagues—Lieutenant Commander George Davies and Lieutenant Commander Alexander Spearman—shared their belief that their brothers in the French Navy would not betray the trust they had earned by their actions to this point in the war, and would never allow Germany or Italy to assume control of their ships. They argued against the use of force and warned of its repercussions.

The three former liaisons to the French Navy believed nonbelligerent dialogue would be the most effective tack with their former colleagues. They also advised Somerville to spread Britain's message throughout the ranks on Admiral Gensoul's ships, given the likelihood that most French sailors would not otherwise be aware of the details of the quarrel between the British and French navies. Finally, Spearman and Davies recommended that if the French declined to submit to a British ultimatum, Force H should depart Mers-el-Kébir without firing a shot, which they hoped the French would interpret as a noble gesture.

Holland and his team believed they could avoid bloodshed and perhaps even prevent a war between Britain and France with a calculated, noncombative plan that would minimize the potential for a volatile encounter in the harbor at Mers-el-Kébir. They surmised that instead of attempting to pound the French into submission with broadsides of two-thousand-pound shells, a demonstration of goodwill would be more likely to secure their allegiance.

The views of Holland, Spearman, and Davies helped shape Somerville's strategy. The leader of Force H distilled his officers' input into an idealistic plan to coax the French into either joining forces with the Royal Navy or scuttling their ships. Regardless of the French reaction to British proposals, Somerville decided to recommend that Force H withdraw without opening fire.

A senior colleague helped reinforce Somerville's beliefs. On the evening of June 30, Admiral Andrew Cunningham, who currently had French ships under his watch in the British-controlled port at Alexandria, Egypt, cabled a prescient expression of his "strong opposition to the proposal that ships at Alexandria should be seized forcibly, and to the use of force at Oran," which he considered might have serious repercussions.[10]

As Somerville weighed the input from his men, including their recommendation for a velvet-gloved approach, he received a signal from the Admiralty with the iron-fisted options he was to present to Admiral Gensoul at Mers-el-Kébir:[11]

First. To bring their ships to British harbours and fight for us.

Second. To steam their ships to a British port in which case crews would be repatriated whenever desired. The ships would be handed over at the peace and would not be used against Germans or Italians unless they break the terms of the Armistice. Full compensation paid to France for any loss or damage during the war.

Third. To demilitarise immediately their ships to our satisfaction.

Fourth. To sink their ships.

Somerville replied to the admiralty with a cable in which he detailed his recommendations for an alternate course of action:

I have had further opportunity to discuss situation with Holland, Spearman and Davies and I am impressed by their view that use of force should be avoided at all costs.

They consider now that armistice terms are known there is distinct possibility of French accepting first alternative, [i.e., "To bring their ships to British harbours and fight for us"]. To achieve this and, in accordance with their experience of the French, they propose—Holland arrives at 0800 and signals in P/L [plain language].

"The British Admiralty have sent Captain Holland to confer with you. The British Navy hopes their proposals will enable you and your glorious French Navy once more to range yourself side-by-side with them. In these circumstances the ships would remain yours and no-one need have anxiety for the future. A British Fleet is off Oran waiting to welcome you."

One hour after Holland enters harbour Force "H" arrives off Oran and repeats same message addressed to French Admiral using signal projectors trained on as many ships as possible. This is to ensure purport of message is received by officers and men other than the French Admiral.

If French refuse first alternative they consider second alternative be amended as follows: French to proceed to sea with a minimum steaming party, i.e., demilitarised, and allowing themselves to be captured by Force "H", strictly ensuring ships being returned intact to France on completion of hostilities. French can plead they acted under force and that unable to contest British action. . . .

They [i.e., Holland and co.] hold strongly that offensive action on our part would immediately alienate all French wherever they are and transform a defeated ally into an active enemy. They believe our prestige would be enhanced if we withdrew from Oran without taking offensive action.

These views based on very recent contact with French naval authorities. Unless Their Lordships have more definite and contrary information I consider proposals merit very careful consideration.

Very early reply requested as possible acceptance of first or second alternative depends on immediate action.[12]

Somerville and his officers at Gibraltar were in complete agreement that the use of force should—and could—be avoided.

The admiralty took just six hours to respond with a blunt rejection of Somerville's recommendation for a low-caliber initial attack. "It is the firm intention of His Majesty's Government that if French will not accept any of the alternatives which are being sent to you, their ships must be destroyed. The proposals in your [signal] are therefore not acceptable." Unwritten naval custom allowed one protest. Now that his had been rejected, Somerville understood that his only recourse was to faithfully execute his orders.[13] Although disappointed that his views and those of his men held so little influence with the admiralty, Somerville believed that a nonlethal resolution was still within reach. He was confident that Cedric Holland was the perfect delegate to engage in sensitive negotiations with Admiral Marcel-Bruno Gensoul, his one-time commander at sea, and he assigned Holland to lead those negotiations. Somerville also sensed that the intimidating specter of the *Hood*, *Ark Royal*, and fifteen other ships of Force H on the near horizon would help persuade Gensoul and his men to accept one of the four British proposals before their options were winnowed down to a shelling by the Royal Navy.

With their hope for a nonbelligerent overture denied, Vice Admiral Somerville, Captain Holland, and their colleagues began their preparations for violent action, which they felt was unnecessary, to prevent a possible outcome, which they considered unthinkable.

CHAPTER 12

THE CHIEF CONQUERED PROVINCE OF GERMANY

ALTHOUGH THE GUNS had been silenced and the fighting had stopped, the French government was on the move once again. Their three most recent capitals—Paris, Tours, and Bordeaux—were now under German control in the occupied zone. After landing for a single day in the too-small city of Clermont-Ferrand, the wandering French ministers settled for good in the resort town of Vichy on the first of July 1940.

The population of the city of Vichy routinely flexed as tourists ebbed and flowed with the weather. With a base of 30,000 year-round residents, Vichy had the hotel capacity and infrastructure to comfortably accommodate as many as 100,000 people during its peak summer season. By the time the governing ministers settled in, trailed by aides, military leaders, and foreign diplomats, the population bulged to 130,000 men, women, and children. Vichy, 225 miles to the south of Paris, fabled for the restorative powers of its thermal baths, would remain the capital of France for the next four years. During that time, "Vichy" would grow into common use as the generic name for the free zone, its government, and the very notion of France.

When the leaders of France fled Paris on their way to Tours, Bordeaux, Clermont-Ferrand, and then finally to Vichy, the diplomatic corps of every major nation followed—with one exception. American ambassador William Bullitt remained in Paris, ignoring pointed suggestions—but not orders—from Secretary of State Cordell Hull and President Roosevelt to join the French government caravan as it meandered from one temporary haven to another. Bullitt's actions in Paris were very much in keeping with his reputation as a free-wheeling diplomat. A garrulous friend of President

Roosevelt, he often bypassed the state department with a steady stream of chatty calls and cables to FDR.

Bullitt had developed an extraordinary affection for France and the French during his four years as U.S. ambassador. He spoke the language fluently and spent weekends at a centuries-old château that he rented in Chantilly. He nurtured warm relationships with all of the leaders in the continually rotating French government—to the extent that one joked that he wished Bullitt would one day become France's ambassador to the United States.[1]

Bullitt helped mitigate the impact of German occupation and helped manage the transition of Paris to German rule. He also helped concerned American and frantic British citizens make their way out of France during the last two weeks of June. He was so completely ingrained into French society by the summer of 1940 that he was asked to fill the governing void and serve as provisional mayor of Paris.

Beginning on June 14, Bullitt developed amicable relationships with the German military leaders in the occupied city. With America still officially neutral, the Germans candidly shared their intent to attack Britain just as soon as they completed their conquest of France in the weeks to follow.[2] With the German army's saturation of Paris complete, Bullitt prepared to head home to America in early July.

Before flying back to Washington, Ambassador Bullitt traveled to France's momentary capital, Clermont-Ferrand, on July 1, 1940. There he shared postmortem conversations with the men who surrendered France to Germany, the same men who now led France under German control. William H. Shirer later wrote that "Bullitt's report gives better than any contemporary record I've seen the state of mind and heart and soul of the tattered men who controlled the French Government at this hour of adversity and trial."[3]

In his discussion with Bullitt, François Darlan did not hold back his bitter impressions and utter hostility toward the British. Darlan shared his scorn for the Royal Navy and its command structure, telling Bullitt that it "had proved to be as great a surprise as the French Army. It was not directed by a man, but by a Board of Directors who could never make up their minds about anything until it was too late."[4]

Darlan told Bullitt that "he had given absolute orders to the officers of his fleet to immediately sink any ship that the Germans should attempt to seize." Bullitt was surprised by Darlan's statement that he planned to order the *Dunkerque* and the *Strasbourg* to sail from Mers-el-Kébir to the French naval base at Toulon, and noted, "this means that the two most valuable units of the French fleet would soon be in German hands since the Germans could always say that one term of the Armistice or another had not been carried out, and that they were justified in disregarding the other terms of the Armistice." Bullitt wrote that Darlan was not blind to this concern, and the French admiral "had just as little confidence as I had in the German promise. But Darlan counted on France becoming Germany's 'leading vassal state.'"

Bullitt detected a rare moment of glee in Darlan's demeanor as he predicted that Britain would be conquered by Germany within five weeks—that is, if she did not surrender before then. Darlan believed that the British government and citizenry lacked the courage to endure the inevitable onslaught of German bombs.

When Bullitt called attention to Darlan's evident pleasure, the commander of the French Navy did not deny his satisfaction and smiled again. Darlan's disdain for the British was matched by distrust. He could not conceive of any conditions under which he would sail his fleet to England because he was certain Britain would never return a single French ship. Also, if by some chance Britain won the war, Darlan expected their treatment of France to be no more generous than the treatment they would receive from Germany.

Darlan was incensed that French warships had been denied permission to depart Alexandria, and he intended to order those ships to shoot their way out to freedom.

Darlan declared that "the French army had not only been defeated," it was "completely disintegrated." On the other hand, "the French fleet had not been defeated and its spirit remained intact." He expected "that the officer corps of the French navy would play a great role in rebuilding France."[5]

Finally, Darlan expressed his belief that he did not foresee "that German domination of the earth would be permanent, although it might be long."

Darlan told Bullitt that President Roosevelt's criticism of the armistice and its impact on the fleet had stung. Darlan claimed to Bullitt that even before terms had been received from Germany, he had conveyed orders to his captains that if Germany required a transfer of the French fleet, they were to "leave at once for Martinique and Guantanamo to place the fleet in the hands of the United States."

Bullitt enjoyed a relaxed three-hour lunch with Marshal Pétain, whom he described as "calm, serious and altogether dignified."[6] The marshal echoed Admiral Darlan's bitterness toward Britain's contribution in the Battle of France: "The truth was that the British had scarcely participated in the decisive battle of the war. Their troops had run, and although they had 40 squadrons of pursuit planes in England, they had sent only 5 to participate in the battle." Pétain's assertion was untrue. A minimum of twelve RAF squadrons joined the action in French skies on a daily basis until France signed the German armistice agreement.[7]

The marshal added his assurance to Bullitt that France would never surrender its fleet to Germany, and shared that all French commanders had received orders to sink their ships rather than let them fall into German hands.

Pétain expected France to become "the chief conquered province of Germany," and foresaw that Germany would bomb and assault Britain into submission in the near future.

The somber assessments of Philippe Pétain and François Darlan were not just the bitter outbursts of jilted former allies. There were grains of reality in their premonitions for the downfall of Britain. The outlook for Britain in the summer of 1940 was more dire than at any other point in the war. There was a genuine possibility that Churchill's island nation was vulnerable to an attack or to sea-based strangulation by Hitler's Germany.

The near miraculous evacuation of 338,000 men—including 225,000 British soldiers—from the beaches of Dunkirk was justifiably celebrated. However, 40,000 British soldiers were left behind and taken prisoner. Of the 445 tanks shipped to France between September 1939 and June 1940, only 22 returned to Britain. Only 322 out of 2,794 artillery pieces made it back.[8]

The British Army was undermanned and perilously underequipped. The Royal Air Force's inventory of fighter planes had been depleted to the absolute minimum required for the defense of British skies. Notwithstanding their bravado, with France removed from the fighting, all of Britain anticipated Germany's next action—an attack by air or an invasion by sea—with apprehension.

The chiefs of staff of Britain's army, navy, and air force drafted a report on "British Strategy in a Certain Eventuality"—that "eventuality" being Britain having to carry on the war without France at its side. Their report, which Churchill termed "grave and grim," noted,

> Britain's "Navy and Air Force together should be able to prevent Germany carrying out a serious seaborne invasion of this country . . ."
>
> If "Germany gained complete air superiority, we consider that the Navy could hold up an invasion for a time, but not for an indefinite period . . ."
>
> "If, with our Navy unable to prevent it, and our Air Force gone, Germany attempted an invasion, our coast and beach defences could not prevent German tanks and infantry getting a firm footing on our shores. In the circumstances envisioned above our land forces would be insufficient to deal with a serious invasion."[9]

Churchill was under pressure—no more so than from his foreign minister, Lord Halifax—to forestall an attack by, at the very minimum, requesting the peace terms that Hitler might be willing to offer. Although he never wavered in the slightest degree, the prime minister had not completely ignored the possibility of a settlement with Germany.

Churchill, who met with his five-man war cabinet each day, invited cabinet members who were not in his war cabinet to his room at the House of Commons in late May to share their perspective on the war. Hugh Dalton, Churchill's minister of economic warfare and one of the meeting's roughly twenty-five participants, provides the most detailed account of that session, including this message from Churchill: "I have thought carefully in these last days whether it was part of my duty to consider entering into negotiations with 'That Man.' But it was idle to think that, if we tried to make peace now, we should get better terms than if we fought it out. The Germans would demand our fleet—that would be called 'disarmament'—our naval bases, and much else. We should become a slave state. . . ."

Churchill concluded, "I am convinced that every man of you would rise up and tear me down from my place if I were for one moment to contemplate parley or surrender. If this long island story of ours is to end at last, let it end only when each one of us lies choking in his own blood upon the ground."[10]

The reaction to this declaration was so striking that Churchill shared it in his history of the war: "There occurred a demonstration which, considering the character of the gathering—twenty-five experienced politicians and Parliament men, who represented all the different points of view, whether right or wrong, before the war—surprised me. Quite a number seemed to jump up from the table and come running to my chair, shouting and patting me on the back."[11]

At a time when many in the world had invested all their hope in Winston Churchill, at a time when the pressure on Churchill to submit to Hitler's might was at its peak, the team of disparate personalities that he had drawn together in his cabinet spontaneously reinvigorated him every bit as much as he inspired them.

CHAPTER 13

ALMOST INEPT IN ITS UNWISDOM

ANDREW CUNNINGHAM FORETOLD his destiny at the age of ten when he told his father, "I should like to be an admiral." When Cunningham boarded the Royal Navy's training ship HMS *Britannia* four years later, James Somerville was a fellow cadet.[1] They would remain friends for life.

As Cunningham wrote in his memoirs, "Though born in Ireland, I am a Scot," with Scottish family lines that he traced to the early 1600s.[2] A fellow admiral praised this proud Scotsman as a "bonnie fechter"—an intrepid fighter.[3] Like most men who cast their lot to the sea, Cunningham detested his periodic assignments on shore. "He was a deck sailor rather than a desk sailor."[4] On deck he was a skilled navigator who "could cut an egg in half with a battleship."[5]

One writer labeled Cunningham "The Great Insubordinate."[6] This bonnie fechter's written and personal contacts with Winston Churchill bore signs of mutual friction, which resulted more from misunderstanding than objective animus. Churchill's private secretary John Colville wrote that Cunningham "nursed hurt feeling engendered by signals he had received from Churchill when he was Commander-in-Chief, Mediterranean, signals which had seemed to cast doubt on his ardour for battle. He had not lacked that ardour, nor had Churchill thought he did."[7]

And despite their chilly relationship, Cunningham and Churchill shared a stony perspective on ships as tools of war. General Dwight Eisenhower praised Cunningham as a "Nelsonian type of admiral" who "believed that ships went to sea in order to find and destroy the enemy."[8] Cunningham would later state, "It takes the navy three years to build a ship but three hundred years to build a tradition."[9]

Known widely as "ABC," Admiral Sir Andrew Browne Cunningham had served a quarter of his forty seagoing years in the Mediterranean. Cunningham hoisted his flag in Britain's naval base at Alexandria in June 1939 after his predecessor—Admiral of the Fleet Sir Dudley Pound—was named first sea lord.[10] A treaty with Egypt, Britain's former protectorate, enabled the Royal Navy to maintain its base in Alexandria. Cunningham considered his posting "the finest appointment the Royal Navy has to offer," and wrote, "I probably knew the Mediterranean as well as any naval officer of my generation."[11]

For the time being, Cunningham was responsible for Royal Navy activity in a relatively calm body of water. After war was declared in September 1939, the initial chases and sea battles took place in the Atlantic. By the spring of 1940, the Mediterranean was about to become an important theater of war more quickly and under different circumstances than Cunningham could have imagined.

A misunderstanding over Royal Navy ship movements in the Mediterranean prompted Cunningham to write a letter of explanation to Admiral Darlan in May 1940. Cunningham concluded his letter by writing, "I am quite sure that the close touch which has now been established between our Naval forces will lead to the most effective and cordial cooperation in the future."[12] A tangible sign of that cooperation was the May 4 arrival in Alexandria of Force X, a French squadron under the command of Vice Admiral René-Émile Godfroy.[13] Force X included three battleships, four cruisers, three destroyers, and one submarine.

Cunningham considered Godfroy "one of the best type of French naval officers."[14] He admired Godfroy's character and intelligence and appreciated that Godfroy was fluent in English. Godfroy's reputation as an Anglophile was no doubt enhanced—to his proud Scottish counterpart in particular—by his marriage to his late wife, a Scotswoman.[15] As Godfroy would soon prove, Andrew Cunningham and the Royal Navy could not have wished for a more perfect ally.

Cunningham assigned a Royal Navy captain to liaise with the captain of each French ship. In turn, Vice Admiral Godfroy posted Commander Philippe Auboyneau—an *ami de Darlan*—as his liaison to Admiral

Cunningham. Auboyneau moved on board Cunningham's flagship HMS *Warspite.*[16]

Cunningham was now in command of a combined fleet that he felt was larger than necessary in a suddenly crowded harbor. He persuaded Godfroy to allow two of his battleships, the *Bretagne* and the *Provence*, to depart for Mers-el-Kébir in the western Mediterranean. The eventual fates of these two ships would turn out to be very different than if they had remained in Alexandria.

Although some in the French government already debated the inevitability of an armistice, their navy was still fully engaged in the war. When Italy raised the stakes by declaring war on the Allies on June 10, 1940, "the fleet at once went to two hours' notice for steam."[17] Now that a confrontation with Italy was certain, Cunningham's and Godfroy's ships joined for a day of maneuvers in the Mediterranean. Cunningham planned to follow up with a joint offensive against Italian targets.

Italy lost little time in taking advantage of its short striking distance from the British Crown Colony of Malta, sixty miles from the coast of Sicily, launching airborne bombing attacks against this vulnerable target. Although the Royal Navy had recently withdrawn all of its ships from Malta, the families of a number of British officers remained, including Admiral Cunningham's wife and two of his nieces.

The Allied navies executed their first combined offensive operation from Alexandria on the morning of June 21 under the command of Vice Admiral John Tovey. France's *Lorraine* joined four British destroyers and two cruisers in a shelling of Bardia on the coast of the Italian colony of Libya. Cunningham planned to lead additional strikes two days later to reinforce the Allies' dominance of the eastern Mediterranean as well as the bonds between French and British seamen. While Cunningham finalized preparations for his combined squadron to sail, French and German negotiators met in Compiègne, where they argued the fine points of the armistice agreement that Germany had imposed earlier that day, but which France had not yet signed.

Even before the armistice agreement was finally signed on the evening of Saturday, June 22, Admiral Darlan issued provisional orders to preserve the independence of his fleet—including orders to ensure no French ships would be constrained in British ports. Darlan provided blunt instructions to French ships currently anchored in Plymouth, Portsmouth, Alexandria, and other British or British-controlled ports to make preparations to sail for French harbors in the Mediterranean or North Africa when so ordered.

French and British crews were scheduled to steam from Alexandria early on Sunday, June 23, for a joint foray against the Italian Navy. Late on the eve of the combined fleet's planned departure, concerned that Force X might break away and continue on to France or to a French colonial port once the ships hit open water, the British admiralty ordered Cunningham to cancel the operation.

Like all Royal Navy officers, Cunningham was well versed in the legacy of Admiral Horatio Nelson. In 1801, as Nelson sailed into a battle that raged in the harbor at Copenhagen, a flurry of signal flags ordered him to withdraw. Nelson, who was blind in one eye, lifted his telescope to that eye, and declared, "I have a right to be blind sometimes. I really do not see the signal."

Cunningham had already turned in for the night by the time Alexandria's master of the fleet delivered a copy of the admiralty's signal to his cabin. The Great Insubordinate read the message and blithely dismissed it, saying, "Nelson is not the only Admiral with a blind eye. Show it to me in the morning."

Three hours later, after French and British ships had raised steam and were soon to leave the harbor, Cunningham strolled to the bridge and cancelled the operation, telling the master of the fleet, "That was a political decision. Return to Alex."[18]

Vice Admiral Godfroy's definitive orders from Admiral Darlan arrived in the early hours of June 25. With France now bound by the terms of its armistice agreements with Germany and Italy, Darlan directed Godfroy to "cease all operations or hostile acts" and immediately sail his ships to Bizerte in the French protectorate of Tunisia.

In keeping with their congenial relationship, Godfroy shared his orders for immediate departure with Cunningham and formally requested permission to sail his ships away from Alexandria.

The British admiral's reply was equally cordial but quite a bit more ominous: "Deeply regret to inform you that I yesterday received orders not to allow your squadron to leave Alexandria."

In the face of conflicting demands from their respective admiralties—one ordering French ships to flee without hesitation, the other instructing a British admiral to prevent the flight of those ships—René-Émile Godfroy and Andrew Cunningham temporarily resolved this literal tug of war on their own.

Although Godfroy and Cunningham had been ordered to take sharply divergent actions, they reached a gentlemen's agreement late on Tuesday, June 25. The admirals concurred that neither would fully comply with his orders, nor would they take the other by surprise with their future actions. Godfroy vowed not to attempt to sail his ships from Alexandria without providing Cunningham with advance notice. For his part, Cunningham promised not to seize Godfroy's ships.

Cunningham summarized the atmosphere in Alexandria in a report to his admiralty. "Our relations are exceptionally friendly and I rather feel he and many of his officers are very glad to have to bow to force majeure. I anticipate no difficulty."[19]

As Admiral Cunningham and Admiral Godfroy honed their compromise, they seasoned their negotiations with extraordinary displays of empathy—on the part of Vice Admiral Godfroy in particular.

Godfroy was alert to Cunningham's trepidation about leaving French ships unguarded. On June 27, in a remarkable indication of good faith, Godfroy "offered to discharge all fuel oil from his ships, to save the British the 'embarrassment' of having to keep a large force in harbour to look after them." In return, Godfroy requested one concession: assurance that Britain would not seize his ships by force.

Cunningham relayed the French admiral's request to his admiralty, and was irritated by the quick denial he received:

> Discharge of oil fuel would be welcomed. Assurance that ships will not be seized should not, repeat not, be given. If discharge of oil fuel is coupled with this assurance you should not press it.

> We have no intention that French ships at Alex. should pass out of our hands into those of the enemy. We should naturally prefer to use them with British crews but if that is not possible, they must be sunk outside the harbour. Do you consider that Godfroy would sink his ships at their moorings if you demanded that they should be handed over to us intact?

François Darlan was irate when he learned of Vice Admiral Godfroy's compromise. The agreement that temporarily defused the tensions in Alexandria put France's compliance with Germany's armistice terms at risk.

Darlan ordered Vice Admiral Odend'hal to express his concern to the British. In a meeting with Dudley Pound on the evening of June 27, Odend'hal handed the First Sea Lord a letter in which he paraphrased Darlan's displeasure. Odend'hal stated that by allowing Force X to sail in cooperation with the Royal Navy until the armistice was finalized, Admiral Darlan had demonstrated "his will to fight up to the last." In the letter in which he summarized Darlan's concern about Britain's posture, Odend'hal included Darlan's "very pressing request":[20]

> It is his foremost desire not to widen the gap between Great Britain and France. The French Admiralty understand the disappointment which the British felt when they saw France compelled to come to terms. They eagerly wish for a British victory . . .
>
> But crippled France ["murdered France" in Darlan's original text] asks to be treated not as an enemy but as a neutral power. Admiral Darlan states that there never was any question of such unfriendly treatment in the conversation with you in Bordeaux.
>
> I have therefore been instructed to ask you pressingly for instructions from the British Admiralty to allow the sailing of Force X from Alexandria . . .

Pound was unmoved by Darlan's plea. The first sea lord shared his blunt perspective on the two countries' changed relationship. As Pound later recapped, he lectured Odend'hal, "The one object we had in view was winning the war, and that it was as essential for them as for us as that we should do so." He added, "Though there was not the slightest doubt that we should win the war, it is essential that we should prevent, as far as possible, the scales being weighted against us at the present time."[21]

In his report on the meeting, Odend'hal recorded a comment from Pound "that Darlan had been the one man whom, had he gone to North Africa and continued the fight, would have been able to save the French colonial empire."[22]

Shortly after midnight on 28 June, Pound sent a personal signal to Andrew Cunningham. Pound's message provided Cunningham with the admiralty's current uncertainty about the implications of the naval clause in the German armistice document. He also included a casual remark that "As soon as an adequate force has been collected at Gibraltar drastic action against ships at Oran will probably be taken if they are still there."[23]

Pound summarized his meeting with Odend'hal and alerted Cunningham to Darlan's protest against Britain's retention of Force X in Alexandria. Pound informed Cunningham, "I replied that we had got to win the war not only for ourselves but for them and all trivialities and sob stuff about friendship and feelings must be swept aside. He asked if the ships would be fired on if they attempted to leave Alexandria and I replied 'yes'; and now they knew it the responsibility will be theirs."[24]

Cunningham sent a pointed reply to Pound's message in which he underscored the merit of the relationship he had established with Godfroy:

> Admiral Godfroy has given me his word and that of his captains that no attempt will be made to leave Alexandria. I, therefore, do not intend to ask for discharge of oil fuel unless it appears that the Admiral is losing control. There is no sign of that at present. . . .
>
> I would emphasize frank and cordial relations existing here and feel more can be done by friendly negotiations than by threatening forcible measures. In any case the ships will not go to sea.[25]

Just as Andrew Cunningham employed a selective blind eye, René-Émile Godfroy chose to present an occasional deaf ear to his admiralty. Godfroy ignored the fury of Admiral Darlan as he worked with Cunningham on a peaceful resolution. Godfroy assured Cunningham that if he received an order to break out while Cunningham's fleet was at sea, he would delay action until the British ships returned to port. Godfroy also reiterated that "nothing could induce him to fire a shot at the British Fleet."

In a June 29 cable to the British admiralty, Cunningham provided insights that Godfroy had shared with him about Darlan's perspective on their cooperation.

> 1. Darlan informed him [Godfroy] that he had given way far too quickly and had made things far too easy for us. Godfroy very angry and has low opinion of Darlan.
> 2. Darlan stated further orders will be coming. If these order French to break out, Godfroy will ask permission to withdraw his present parole not to leave harbour and then ask to sail with a British unit in company in order to scuttle all his ships outside.[26]

Cunningham shared his revised opinion of Darlan in a separate letter to Dudley Pound: "Darlan appears to have let us down badly. I never trusted him. Too political."[27]

At this critical time in the relations between the French and British navies, the French admiralty found itself compelled to relocate its headquarters with impractical haste. Paris, of course, was now saturated with German soldiers, and the once provisional capital of Bordeaux was inside the occupied zone on the new map of France.

Maintenon, which was also in the occupied zone, had been overrun. Hundreds of French Navy officers who had been "on board" were now prisoners of war. The French admiralty scrambled to find a new home in the *zone libre*.

After brief layovers in Montbazon and Dulamont, Darlan and his remaining admiralty staff moved seventy-five miles southeast of Bordeaux to the small commune of Nérac. The prevailing logic of the move was that Nérac was François Darlan's birthplace. His wife and daughter had recently returned to the area. Instead of the advanced communications facilities available in Maintenon, Darlan now relied on a radio truck and the local post office, which, in 1940, provided a telephone exchange, as his communications nerve center.

The degradation of the French Navy's communication capabilities, which manifested in delays of six hours or more in the transmission of cables between the French admiralty and its fleet, and even longer delays in transmissions to and from the British admiralty, would become especially problematic in the days that followed. In that communications vacuum, a French officer pined for "an adroit liaison officer like [Cedric] Holland and a good telephone."[28]

On June 29, the British admiralty confirmed to Admiral Cunningham that he would be required to seize the French ships in Alexandria at the same time Vice Admiral Somerville confronted the French fleet at Mers-el-Kébir. Cunningham was exasperated by the admiralty's refusal to permit him to resolve the stalemate with diplomacy, and expressed his strong opposition.

In Cunningham's mind, there was no danger of the French ships at Alexandria falling into German hands. He was also convinced that if the Royal Navy attempted to take the French ships by force, the French would scuttle them at their berths, "causing unnecessary casualties and fouling the harbour with wrecks."

Cunningham later wrote,

> That I had strong views on the whole operation goes without saying. To me the idea was repugnant. The officers and men in the French squadron were our friends. We had had many most cordial social contacts with them, and they had fought alongside us. Vice-Admiral Godfroy, moreover, was a man of honour in whom we could place implicit faith. Suddenly and without warning to attack and board his ships, and in the course of it probably to inflict many casualties on his sailors, appeared to me to be an act of sheer treachery which was as injudicious as it was unnecessary.[29]

Furthermore Cunningham knew he had leverage over the French: "The French could not go to sea without our consent. The pressure of lack of supplies, pay for the ships' companies, and the urgent wish of his men, particularly the reservists, to go home to France to protect their families, was bound to bring the French Admiral to terms in a short time."

Cunningham shared his assessment of the admiralty's stance in his postwar memoirs: "It was my considered opinion at the time that it was almost inept in its unwisdom."

Cunningham continued to press for permission to sustain his gentlemen's agreement with Vice Admiral Godfroy. In a June 30 cable to Dudley Pound, Cunningham requested "urgent consideration" of his argument, in which he asked, "If ships are to be seized, what is the object? If it is to prevent ships falling into enemy hands, that has already been achieved."

Cunningham also expressed his concern about "repercussions consequent on forcible action at Oran," to which he was "very much against . . . if it can possibly be avoided."[30]

The admiralty was equally unrelenting in its insistence that Cunningham gain undisputed control of the French ships. If Vice Admiral Godfroy refused to voluntarily relinquish control, Cunningham was ordered to present two options at seven o'clock on the morning of July 3. While Winston Churchill and A. V. Alexander focused on the fine details of the impending confrontation at Mers-el-Kébir, Dudley Pound drafted a less stringent set of guidelines for Andrew Cunningham to follow at Alexandria. Those orders took into consideration the advanced state of Cunningham's dialogue with Vice Admiral Godfroy and recognized the Royal Navy's upper hand in the British-controlled harbor. Cunningham's orders, conveyed in a personal signal from Admiral Pound late on July 1, stated that if the French ships could not be obtained for use by the Royal Navy, "they must be dealt with in one of the following ways, which are in order of merit from our point of view":

1. Retained at Alexandria with a skeleton crew, but immediately put in a non-sea-going condition, on the understanding that we would only use them if the Germans or Italians broke the terms of the Armistice. Responsibility for the pay and maintenance of the

personnel and ships would be undertaken by HM Government. Should Admiral Godfroy insist that ships must be demilitarized before he leaves them you may accept this.

2. Sunk at sea.

Pound also informed Cunningham that "An action at Oran will be taken early on Wednesday, 3rd," and instructed him to present the British alternatives to Godfroy at seven o'clock that morning.[31] The tenor of these instructions was quite different from the rigid structure of the finely drawn scripts that would be presented to Vice Admiral Somerville. In addition, given the advantage held by Cunningham, his instructions did not mention an attack on Godfroy's ships.

Captain Cedric "Hooky" Holland, who served as Britain's naval attaché to the French Navy in 1939 and 1940, was selected to negotiate with French Admiral Marcel-Bruno Gensoul at Mers-el-Kébir on July 3, 1940. Holland was promoted to rear admiral before war's end. *National Portrait Gallery, London*

First Lord of the Admiralty Winston Churchill and France's Admiral of the Fleet François Darlan in November 1939. As allies, both men were intent on keeping the French fleet out of German hands. Seven months later, as Prime Minister Churchill's adversary, Darlan was equally resolute on keeping his ships out of British hands. *The Granger Collection*

Leaders of France in June 1940: General Maxime Weygand, Under-Secretary of State for Foreign Affairs Paul Baudouin, Prime Minister Paul Reynaud, and Marshal Philippe Pétain. *Getty Images*

Vice Admiral Sir James Somerville commanded Britain's Force H during its clash with the French fleet at Mers-el-Kébir. *Associated Press*

Anchorage at Mers-el-Kébir in early July 1940. From left to right: the *Dunkerque*, *Provence*, *Strasbourg*, *Bretagne*, and the seaplane tender *Commandante Teste* sit with their bows facing the shore, and their sterns at the breakwater. The destroyers *Mogador*, *Volta*, *Tigre*, *Lynx*, *Kersaint*, and *Le Terrible* are in the foreground. Cedric Holland's route to the *Dunkerque* required him to travel around to the innermost end of the breakwater. *Amicale des Anciens Marins de Mers-el-Kébir*

HMS *Hood*, the pride of the Royal Navy, was considered "the grandest looking man-of-war in the world . . . the most beautiful ship built since the days of sail." *State Library Victoria*

Admiral Marcel-Bruno Gensoul at a memorial service after the deaths of 1,257 seamen at Mers-el-Kébir. *Getty Images*

French Vice Admiral René-Émile Godfroy, the commander of Force X at Alexandria. Godfroy and Britain's Admiral Andrew B. Cunningham selectively deflected orders from their respective admiralties in hopes of reaching a peaceful compromise in their harbor. *Associated Press*

Admiral Andrew B. Cunningham, General Mark W. Clark, Admiral François Darlan (with ubiquitous pipe in hand), and General Dwight D. Eisenhower in Algeria on December 10, 1942, fifteen days before Cunningham, Clark, and Eisenhower attended Darlan's funeral. *Associated Press*

France's *Richelieu* after passing under the Brooklyn Bridge on her way to the Brooklyn naval yard for repairs and modernization in February 1944. *Getty Images*

CHAPTER 14

ONE OF THE MOST DISAGREEABLE AND DIFFICULT TASKS

Winston Churchill had strong opinions about code names that were assigned to military operations, especially those "in which large numbers of men may lose their lives." He directed Britain's armed services to avoid names that were "boastful," "overconfident," or "frivolous." He did not wish to compound the suffering of a widow or a mother with a message that her husband or son was lost "in an operation called 'Bunnyhug' or 'Ballyhoo.'"[1]

"Operation Catapult," the name assigned to the Royal Navy's confrontation with the French fleet at Mers-el-Kébir and other ports, was deemed appropriate for an operation in which British sailors would risk their lives, and French seamen would almost certainly lose theirs.

In the 6:00 p.m. war cabinet meeting on Monday, July 1, 1940, the chiefs of staff, the senior commanders of Britain's three armed services, including Admiral Dudley Pound, recommended "that, from the military point of view, 'Catapult' should be carried out as soon as possible."[2]

The driving force for the acceleration of this potentially combustible engagement was the chiefs' perception of the "likelihood of the French ships falling into the hands of the Germans" and the resulting shift in the "balance of capital ship strength." As for German promises not to use the French ships, "we are under no illusions as to the certainty that, sooner or later, the Germans will employ them against us."

The chiefs of staff reached this recommendation, which Churchill and his war cabinet embraced, after rejecting a more conciliatory recommendation from the subcommittee of planners that reported to them. In the report rejected by the chiefs of staff, the more junior officers "made no bones about their dislike of any intent to destroy the French ships."

Members of the war cabinet were then updated on Vice Admiral Odend'hal's request that Britain resist taking action until Germany and Italy ruled on the final stations of French ships. Winston Churchill, who would not be swayed by the hopes and expectations of French admirals, declared, "Discussions as to the armistice conditions could not affect the real facts of the situation."[3]

The most significant real fact, of course, was that unless the French ships were in British hands or beneath the sea, they remained vulnerable to German seizure. The war cabinet discussed a range of possible options to offer Admiral Gensoul at Mers-el-Kébir. The least practical was a proposal that he simply hand over his ships without crews. In the unimaginable likelihood that Gensoul would accept this offer, the British would then have to draw replacement crews from the already undermanned ships of Force H. This suggestion, unfeasible from every perspective, was quickly abandoned.

In addition to the extremes of surrender and scuttle, Churchill raised a possibility that the war cabinet had not previously discussed: demilitarization of French ships at their berths. Churchill stressed that the French ships would have to be so disabled that they could not be repaired and returned to battle for at least one year.

Dudley Pound enthusiastically supported demilitarization, which would broadly include the thorough disabling of engines, boilers, navigation equipment, communications devices, and all large weapons, as a course that Admiral Gensoul might accept. Demilitarization not only represented a conciliatory option, it also provided some assurance to the French that they would retain possession of their ships, albeit severely wrecked.

In what turned out to be the most consequential product of this meeting, the cabinet elected not to include demilitarization in the initial options that Vice Admiral Somerville would present upon his arrival at Mers-el-Kébir. Instead they authorized Somerville to accept demilitarization if Admiral Gensoul suggested that option and if incapacitation could be achieved by nightfall.

The cabinet also discussed how best to communicate the British ultimatum to Gensoul and his men. Although they had rejected the recommendations of Somerville and Holland for a diplomatic confrontation, the admiralty adopted their suggestion to extend their communications to the ships' companies in the hope of building a groundswell of support to avoid a mortal confrontation.

Suggestions to either blare an audio message to sailors in the harbor or drop leaflets from the *Ark Royal*'s planes were struck down as impractical. In the end British signalmen sowed the Royal Navy's message through the French squadron in Morse code by signal lamp.

The cabinet continued work on their instructions to Vice Admiral Somerville and the precise message he would deliver to Admiral Gensoul. Churchill and First Lord A. V. Alexander agreed to draft the final versions of these communications before night's end. In addition, to ensure that every potential reaction by the French had a well-considered counter-reaction, the cabinet members developed a list of the French Admiral's likely rebuttals and provided suggested responses to Somerville.

The war cabinet had previously discussed a tentative plan to seize the French warships in the British ports of Portsmouth and Plymouth. The local commanders-in-chief had expressed their preference for diplomatic tactics in line with what so far appeared to be a successful tack by Admiral Cunningham in Alexandria. They believed their French counterparts would not open fire and could be blocked from breaking for open seas.

Dudley Pound was unmoved by their arguments and refused to extend the tenuous status of French ships in British harbors or risk their potential flight. He ordered the two commanders-in-chief to prepare for the coordinated seizures of the French ships in their respective ports with "the surprise use of boarding parties, arriving in overwhelming force" in the predawn hours of July 3, in concert with the operations at Mers-el-Kébir and Alexandria.

John Colville recognized that although A. V. Alexander, whom Churchill had selected to succeed him as first lord of the admiralty, "had many virtues," those virtues "did not include modesty. Alexander annoyed Dudley Pound and others by talking about 'my navy', until one day the King pointed out that it was his."[4] Britain's monarch nominally owned every ship in the Royal Navy.

Alexander's one modest trait—his subservience to the prime minister—earned him widespread scorn throughout his navy. James Somerville remarked, "Alexander is completely in [Churchill's] pocket and says 'OK Chief' to everything."[5] Churchill bypassed his first lord to deal directly with top admirals with enough frequency that one noted, "in practice on real issues [Churchill] remained First Lord himself."[6] Such were Churchill's reservations about Alexander that the most sensitive decrypted signals from the German Navy were stamped "Not to be shown to 1st Lord."[7]

On this occasion, however, the prime minister sat with Alexander at 10:00 p.m. on July 1 to collaborate on the final set of guidelines for Vice Admiral Somerville's mission to Mers-el-Kébir. The current and previous first lords of the admiralty crafted the precise wording of each message that Somerville would present to his French counterpart upon arrival.

Somerville's instructions, which the admiralty cabled several minutes after one o'clock on the morning of July 2, began,

> His Majesty's Government have decided that the course to be adopted is as follows:
>
> (a) French [Fleet] at Oran and Mers-el-kabir [*sic*] is to be given four alternatives:
>
> i. To sail their ships to British harbours and to continue to fight with us.
>
> ii. To sail their ships with reduced crews to a British port from which their crews would be repatriated whenever desired [or] in the case of alternative (i) or (ii) being adopted, their ships would be restored to France at the conclusion of the war or full compensation would be paid if they are damaged meanwhile. If the French Admiral accepts alternative (ii), but asks that their ships should not repetition not be used by [British] during war, say we accept this condition for so long as Germany and Italy observe the armistice terms but we particularly do not repetition not wish to raise point ourselves.

iii. To sail their ships with reduced crews to some French port in West Indies such as Martinique. After arrival at this [port] they would either be demilitarised, to our satisfaction, if so desired, or be entrusted to the USA jurisdiction for the duration of the war. The crews would be repatriated.
iv. To sink repetition sink their ships.[8]

This new—and final—list of options varied in two significant ways from the initial list sent to Somerville just the day before. This final list did not include the option to "demilitarise immediately their ships to our satisfaction," and it included the newly added option to "sail their ships with reduced crews to some French port."

These options were unambiguous and ominous. Three of the four placed the French ships under British control, the fourth eliminated the ships altogether. None were likely to receive ready acceptance.

At this point in the instructions, Churchill and Alexander inserted their conditional approval for demilitarization in the ship's berths at Mers-el-Kébir: "Should French Admiral refuse to accept all above alternatives and should he suggest he should demilitarise his ships to our satisfaction at their present berths, you are authorized to accept this further alternative provided you are satisfied that measures taken for demilitarization can be carried out under your supervision within six hours and prevent ships being brought into [service] for at least one year, even at a fully [equipped] dockyard port."

In the event that Admiral Gensoul would not accept any of the British options, the directions to Somerville were dire: "If none of these alternatives are accepted by the French you are to endeavour to destroy repetition destroy ships in Mers-el-kabir [particularly] DUNKERQUE and STRASBOURG using all means at your disposal."

After noting that the admiralty's directions for a "Communication to the French Admiral" would follow, Churchill and Alexander reinforced the importance of the element of surprise, and reiterated their previous denial of Somerville's suggested early arrival by Captain Holland: "It is most undesirable that you should have to deal with the French Fleet at sea and consequently about twelve hours warning, as suggested in your 0812

[Somerville's cable, sent at 8:12 a.m.] of 1st July is not repetition not acceptable. Hence, you should arrive in the vicinity of Oran with your force at whatever time you select, and send your emissary ashore, subsequently taking such action you consider fit with your force in period before time limit given expires."

The formal "Communication to the French Government" that Churchill and Lord Halifax had discussed on June 24 was never sent. As British plans evolved through the final days of June, Churchill and his war cabinet reasoned that British interests would be better served with a surprise confrontation as opposed to providing the French with time to prepare their reaction against the terms of an ultimatum.

Alexander and Churchill expected Somerville, or his designated negotiator Cedric Holland, to use their "Communication to the French Admiral" document to guide a face-to-face meeting with Admiral Gensoul on board his flagship, the *Dunkerque*, the French warship most closely allied with the Royal Navy.

Very few things would go according to plan at Mers-el-Kébir, including the delivery of the message so carefully scripted by Churchill and Alexander.

General Hastings "Pug" Ismay, Churchill's chief staff officer and military advisor, who participated in the July 1 war cabinet meeting, reflected on the British ultimatum to their recent ally: "All who were present when that message was drafted could not but feel sad and, in a sense, guilty. To kick a man when he is down is unattractive at any time; but when the man is a friend who has already suffered grievously, it seems almost to border on infamy."[9] Ismay recognized Churchill's personal torment: "To Churchill, with his deep love of France it must have been an agonizing moment. But he never flinched." Ismay could also envision Somerville's reaction when his final orders arrived in the early morning hours of July 2. "I pictured the horror on the face of James Somerville, a typical British sailor and the soul of chivalry, as he read those instructions."

James Somerville convened the final meeting of his officers in Gibraltar on the morning of July 2, twenty-four hours before their anticipated showdown at Mers-el-Kébir. Somerville and his men hoped to find a balance between the peaceful resolution they still believed was possible and the severe tactics that Churchill and the admiralty insisted were necessary.

Although the admiralty had dashed Somerville's plan for a benign initial approach to Admiral Gensoul, and although Somerville had been ordered to "destroy . . . DUNKERQUE and STRASBOURG using all means at your disposal," Somerville was confident that he and Cedric Holland could persuade Gensoul to accept a nonlethal British option through a combination of "persuasion and threats."

Somerville had distilled the orders from the admiralty into a rebellious scheme of his own design that included an escalating sequence of menacing actions. His tactics began with a diluted version of the admiralty's demands, followed—if necessary—by a symbolic show of force. Only if Gensoul remained defiant would Somerville resort to deadly action.

Phase 1 of Somerville's plan was a rehash of the admiralty's directive with one significant change. In addition to providing Gensoul with options to unite his fleet with Britain's, to steam his *Force de Raid* to British or West Indian ports, or to sink his own ships, Somerville included an alternative for the French "to demilitarise their ships immediately to our satisfaction," a possibility that had been expressly prohibited by Churchill and the admiralty—unless the French raised this suggestion.[10]

If Gensoul rejected all of the options presented in Phase 1, Somerville's Phase 2 would "[s]how that we are in earnest by offensive action without endangering French ships," which violated both the spirit and the letter of the orders he had received.

The specific tactics Somerville had in mind for "offensive action without endangering French ships" included

> "show the French that we are in earnest by the firing of a few rounds or by the dropping of bombs close to, but not actually hitting, French ships."
>
> "HOOD is to be prepared to fire a few salvoes just clear of MERS EL KEBIR harbour."
>
> "ARK ROYAL is to be prepared to carry out a bombing attack on MERS EL KEBIR harbour, taking care to avoid hitting the ships."[11]

Somerville would attack and attempt to destroy the French ships only after every peaceful option was exhausted. In that case, "The priority (in order of importance, though not necessarily in order of sequence) in regard to the destruction of the French Fleet is to be: a. STRASBOURG and DUNKERQUE; b. BRETAGNE and PROVENCE; c. OTHER fighting units in order of size."[12]

In keeping with Winston Churchill's partiality to virile names, Somerville announced that if Gensoul persisted in his resistance to British demands: "the code word 'ANVIL' will be signalled to all our forces. Senior officers are then to take all necessary action to crush the resistance, ceasing fire as soon as it becomes apparent that the French have ceased to resist."[13]

To summarize: If Admiral Gensoul rejected the four British options for peaceful compliance, Vice Admiral Somerville, on his own initiative, intended to begin with a nonlethal show of force in which shells and bombs would be aimed near—but not directly at—the French ships at Mers-el-Kébir. If Admiral Gensoul remained defiant, Somerville's ships would attack Gensoul's *Force de Raid* with the *Dunkerque*, the *Strasbourg*, the *Bretagne*, and the *Provence* as their primary targets.

The level of ferocity of the Royal Navy attack would depend on the degree of compliance or defiance demonstrated by Admiral Gensoul.

Major General Sir Edward Louis Spears was seated in a dentist's chair at midday on July 2, when his procedure was interrupted by a summons from the Prime Minister. When Spears arrived at 10 Downing Street, Churchill shared a copy of the ultimatum that Vice Admiral Somerville would present to Admiral Gensoul the following morning.[14]

Spears considered the message as "painful . . . to read as it had undoubtedly been for the Prime Minister to draft."

Churchill asked Spears if he thought Gensoul would bow to Britain's ultimatum. Spears did not know Gensoul, but from the perspective of his rapport with dozens of senior French military and government leaders, he predicted, "I think he is bound to if he is made to realize we mean what we say."

Shortly after his return from France in mid-June, Spears had taken on a new assignment: head of the British government's mission to General

Charles de Gaulle. Spears asked, "When can I tell de Gaulle? He must be informed before the ultimatum is delivered." Churchill agreed but cautioned, "Not today."

With the expectation that the stalemate in Alexandria would one way or another conclude the following day, Andrew Cunningham described Tuesday, July 2, as "a day of tense anxiety."[15] He briefed his senior officers on the status of negotiations and shared the admiralty's orders for their actions the following morning.

On the evening of July 2, Cunningham had a letter delivered to Vice Admiral Godfroy that read, "My dear Admiral. I have been instructed by the British Admiralty to submit certain proposals to you. Would you be so kind as to come and see me on board the Warspite at 7 a.m. tomorrow, Wednesday. Bring a staff-officer or your flag-officer with you if you like . . ."

It was not lost on Cunningham that the meeting he had requested was at "an unusual hour which must have caused him to realize that something momentous was about to happen."

The men on board the *Dunkerque* enjoyed a relaxed evening respite from the North African sun. The posted activities for the next day included a match against a squad from the *Commandant Teste* for the Fleet water polo championship. The *Dunkerque*'s basketball team was scheduled to take on the team from *Le Terrible*.[16] Crew members planned excursions to nearby Oran. Others looked forward to hiking up the mountain that shadowed their harbor.

Before retiring for the night Lieutenant Bernard Dufay, Gensoul's aide-de-camp, completed his nightly decoding of signals from the admiralty. With no French warships currently at sea, there was little to decipher, and Dufay turned in early.

Winston Churchill spent the afternoon and the early evening of Tuesday, July 2, with Bernard Montgomery, who was then a major general in command of the British Army's 3rd Division. This was the first meeting between Churchill and "Monty." The mercurial British general was wary of politicians. "I considered that they were largely responsible for our troubles." But he sensed that Churchill was not like most other men in politics. Montgomery was aware of, and had admired, Churchill's warnings during the 1930s about the danger of Adolf Hitler's virulent interference in European affairs. He also appreciated Churchill's frequent criticism of Britain's lackadaisical preparation for the war that seemed inevitable.

The prime minister and the general met at Steyning in West Sussex. Montgomery's men enacted an exercise at a small airfield to demonstrate how they would counterattack if German forces had captured the base. Montgomery noted, "He was delighted, especially by the action of the Bren-gun carrier platoon of the battalion." The open, tread-driven vehicles appealed to Churchill's enthusiasm for mobility and speed.

Churchill was invigorated by the day's events and the distraction from the weight of the next day's anticipated clashes in multiple harbors. He invited Montgomery to join him, his wife Clementine, and other members of his party for dinner at the Royal Albion Hotel in Brighton.

Churchill was astonished when drinks were ordered and Montgomery asked only for water. When Churchill suggested he might enjoy a stronger beverage, Montgomery told the prime minister (as Monty later recounted), "I neither drank nor smoked and was 100 percent fit." Churchill replied that "he both drank and smoked and was 200 percent fit."

At the end of the day Montgomery wondered, "I have never discovered what Churchill thought of me that day; I know I was immensely impressed by him."[17]

If fortune held, Force H would encounter Admiral Gensoul's ships moored stern-on to the breakwater with their main guns pointed toward the shore. There was a chance, however slight, that the British would encounter the French ships at sea. No matter the circumstances, the admiralty's instructions to James Somerville emphasized that "the *Dunkerque* and *Strasbourg* should not (R) NOT get into enemy control. Other modern units are important but less so."[18]

Shortly before the British ships sailed from Gibraltar, the admiralty added to Somerville's communications burden with a list of talking points that were "merely intended to be a guide for your consideration" in his discussions with Admiral Gensoul.[19] These guidelines provide a neat summary of the British rationale for taking control of French ships. They also explain Britain's reluctance to rely on French captains to take independent action to scuttle their ships. The talking points included

> On 18 June Darlan gave a personal promise to First Lord and First Sea Lord that French Fleet would never surrender to enemy. . . .
>
> The French may argue that they will scuttle if Germans and Italians attempt to seize ships even in French metropolitan ports. But with French Army disarmed and Fleet laid up with reduced crews under German and Italian surveillance, there can be no (R) no certainty, that, however resolute the attempt to destroy or sink any particular ship, it would possible to forestall seizure by the enemy. . . .
>
> If French Admiral replies to first overture by saying we have no (R) no need to worry since all arrangements have been made, you should reply: How can you be sure that this will be effective? You may be relieved from your command, pressure may be put on [your] ships' companies and so on. The ships' companies may in any case be unwilling to scuttle in a French port for fear of immediate sentence by enemy.
>
> Therefore you must put your intentions into effect now and at this port, when blame will fall on us and not (R) not on your ships' companies.

Force H—two battleships, one battlecruiser, eleven destroyers, two light cruisers, and one aircraft carrier—had assembled at Gibraltar over the last few days of June and the first two days in July. The passage of Force H from Gibraltar to Mers-el-Kébir, which would cover 230 nautical miles, began on the afternoon of Tuesday, July 2. Destroyers from Force H were the first to sail at 3:00 p.m. They completed their first assignment—an anti-submarine sweep of the approaches to the harbor—without incident.

By 5:00 p.m. the seventeen ships in Force H—the battlecruiser *HMS Hood* (Vice Admiral Somerville's flagship), the aircraft carrier *Ark Royal*, the battleships *Valiant* and *Resolution*, the light cruisers *Arethusa* and *Enterprise*, and the destroyers *Active*, *Escort*, *Faulknor*, *Fearless*, *Forester*,

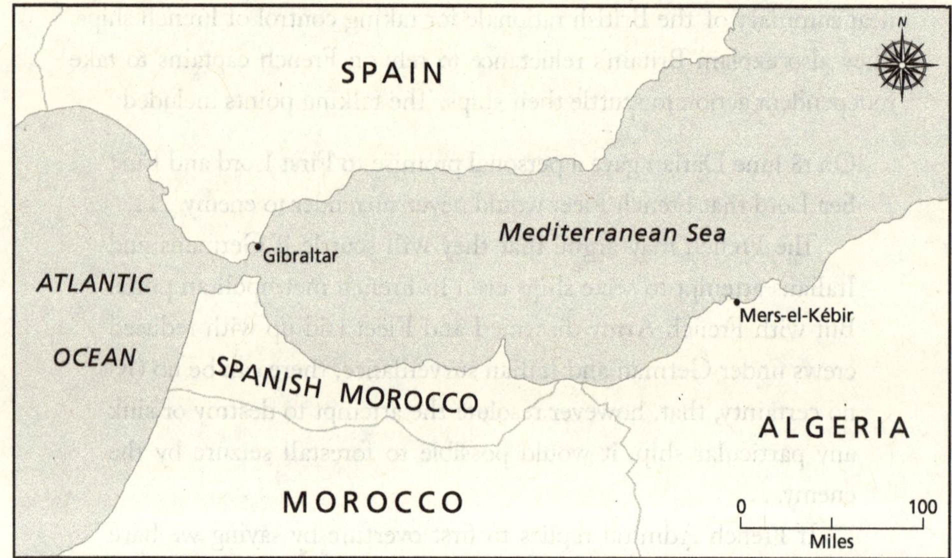

MAP 3. Gibraltar to Mers-el-Kébir

Foresight, *Foxhound*, *Keppel*, *Vidette*, *Vortigern*, and *Wrestler*—had cleared the harbor and were sailing eastward toward Mers-el-Kébir at 17 knots.

Force H had a mysterious encounter with potential disaster along the way. In the dark of night, shortly before 11:00 p.m., a torpedo glanced off the stern of the *Vortigern*, passed beneath the ship, and then exploded far enough off the bow to do no harm. In response, Somerville dispatched two destroyers to hunt for the Italian submarine that launched the torpedo. (There were no German U-boats in the Mediterranean.) After searching for just over an hour in vain, they returned to the body of Force H. It was learned after the war that the Italian submarine *Guglielmo Marconi* fired the torpedo that glanced off the *Vortigern*.[20]

Vice Admiral Somerville deliberated whether or not to lay mines at the entrance to the harbor at Mers-el-Kébir. A minefield would hinder the ability of the French to accept any of Britain's first three alternatives, which called for French ships to sail into a seaborne fighting union with the British or to the sanctuary of a neutral or British port. Somerville also counted on the deterrent effect of the seventeen British warships at the mouth of the harbor. The likelihood of an escape attempt seemed miniscule. Somerville decided to hold the mines in reserve.

After his dinner with Major General Montgomery, Churchill returned by train to London to finalize the details of the next day's action at Mers-el-Kébir. John Colville wrote in his diary that upon Churchill's 10:45 p.m. return to 10 Downing Street, "life became both hot and hectic."[21]

Churchill invited Lord Beaverbrook, a valued confidant, to join A. V. Alexander and Dudley Pound in a meeting to review the next day's forced seizures in British ports, along with the ultimatums and contingencies for the likely assault at Mers-el-Kébir. Beaverbrook, the most unlikely member of Churchill's cabinet, had quickly proven to be its most breathtakingly effective minister despite a background that suggested he was ludicrously ill-suited for his role. Max Aitken was a press baron as well as a baron in the noble sense, having been named First Baron Beaverbrook in 1917. He owned the *Evening Standard* and the *Daily Express*, Britain's most widely read newspaper. Before the war, he supported Neville Chamberlain's policy of appeasement and criticized Churchill for his unrelenting warnings of a coming war. Churchill's column in the *Evening Standard* provided a valued soapbox as well as an important source of income . . . until Beaverbrook cancelled his contract in 1938. In that same year Beaverbrook privately criticized Churchill as "a warmonger," a man who was "turning the thoughts of the peoples of the British Empire to war," and added, "He must be stopped."[22] Edward R. Murrow, a newsman himself, observed, "one of the most interesting things about Mr. Churchill's Cabinet is this: he appears to be putting outstanding critics in positions where they must by their deeds refute their own criticism."[23]

Churchill asked Beaverbrook to build and lead the Ministry of Aircraft Production, an organization that did not yet exist. After reviewing the makeup of Churchill's proposed cabinet, King George VI sent his first letter to his new prime minister: an urgent, handwritten note asking Churchill to reconsider Beaverbrook's appointment.[24] Despite—or perhaps because of—their antagonistic history, Churchill considered Beaverbrook one of his most trusted advisors and turned to him for blunt counsel.

At this late hour on the eve of conflict, with Force H midway in its passage from Gibraltar to Mers-el-Kébir, Churchill's conscience was still troubled by the prospect of an assault on Britain's recent ally, an attack on the forces of a nation that he cherished. Beaverbrook was adamant that ruthless action was justified. If Britain did not decimate the French ships, "The Germans will force the French fleet to join the Italians, thus taking command of the Mediterranean. The Germans will force this by threatening to burn Bordeaux the first day the French refuse, the next day Marseille, and the third day Paris."[25]

Churchill issued the final orders for Vice Admiral Somerville to execute at Mers-el-Kébir. He then grabbed Beaverbrook by the arm and ushered him out to the garden at 10 Downing Street. As Beaverbrook recalled, "There was a high wind blowing. He raced along. I had trouble keeping up with him; and I began to have an attack of asthma. Churchill declared that there was no other decision possible. Then he wept."

At 10:55 p.m. on July 2, six hours after he had sailed from Gibraltar, James Somerville received a brief and pointed cable from the admiralty: "You are charged with one of the most disagreeable and difficult tasks that a British Admiral has ever been faced with, but we have complete confidence in you and rely on you to carry it out relentlessly."[26]

CHAPTER 15

MORE TOUCHY THAN EVER

ALTHOUGH THE BOUNTY from its 1830 invasion of Algeria included the former pirate haven of Mers-el-Kébir, more than one hundred years passed before France developed this small Mediterranean harbor into a base for its navy. In the summer of 1940, with Italy now in the war, the French expected this still-unfinished port to provide the same strategic value in the western Mediterranean that the British base in Alexandria provided to the east. The French and British navies sailed freely into both ports.

The harbor at Mers-el-Kébir sits inside a tight crescent that centuries' worth of tides and storms carved inside a much larger crescent-shaped bay on the northwest coast of Algeria. As ships approached Mers-el-Kébir from the west, their first sight was the beacon of the Cap Falcon lighthouse.

A partially complete twenty-foot-high breakwater, constructed with large stone blocks from a nearby mountain, Djebel Murdjadjo, extended almost one mile from the shore. The breakwater helped define the harbor while it protected anchored vessels from ocean swells and ships' wakes. Not insignificantly, it also offered a degree of protection against potential shellfire from offshore.

In the dark morning hours of July 3, 1940, French ships were moored with no concern for the possibility of combat. The ships were spaced about four hundred feet apart, with their bows and main guns facing the shore.[1] Their sterns, for the most part defenseless, faced the breakwater and the broad Mediterranean Sea where British warships would soon appear with potentially malevolent intent.

Admiral Gensoul later explained to Admiral Darlan that the shallow harbor at Mers-el-Kébir prevented him from mooring his ships with their bows and main guns pointed seaward.[2]

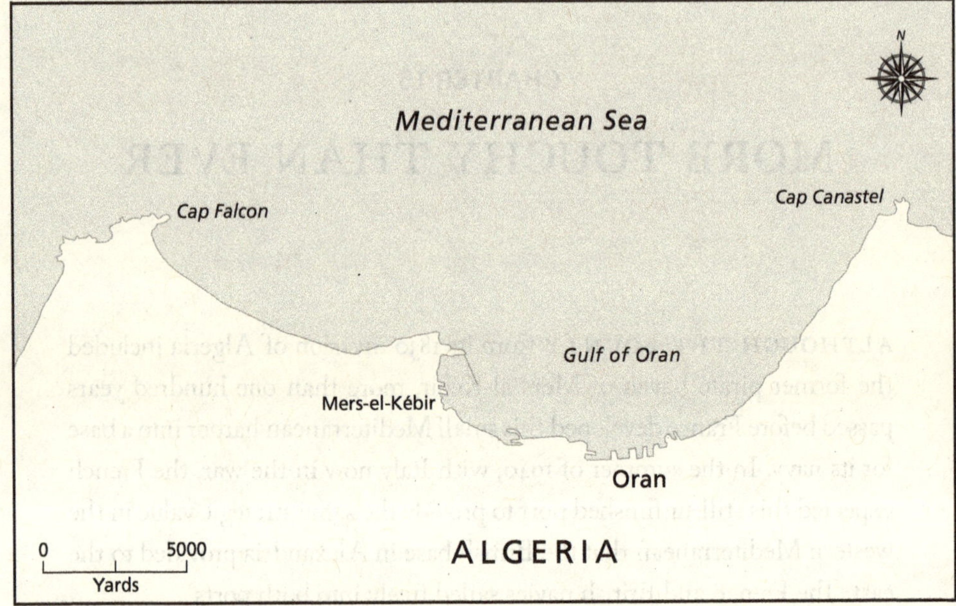

MAP 4. Mers-el-Kébir and Oran

Captain Cedric Holland sailed on board the destroyer HMS *Foxhound* after relinquishing command of the *Ark Royal* for the duration of Operation Catapult. After steaming with Somerville's squadron through most of the night, the *Foxhound* separated and proceeded alone at 4 o'clock on the morning of July 3.

After the admiralty rejected James Somerville's proposal for Holland to sail into the French port twelve hours before the balance of Force H, Somerville elected to surprise the French with Holland's arrival on the *Foxhound* at daybreak on July 3. Somerville and the remainder of Force H would arrive three hours later.

At 5:45 a.m. the *Foxhound* approached Cap Falcon and called the port's war signal station with a request to enter the bay. Permission was granted thirteen minutes later. The men onboard the *Foxhound*, still six miles outside of Mers-el-Kébir, could see the upper works of the French ships above the tall breakwater.

Once inside the bay, the *Foxhound*'s first act was precautionary. The British ship released paravanes—small underwater gliders streamed by

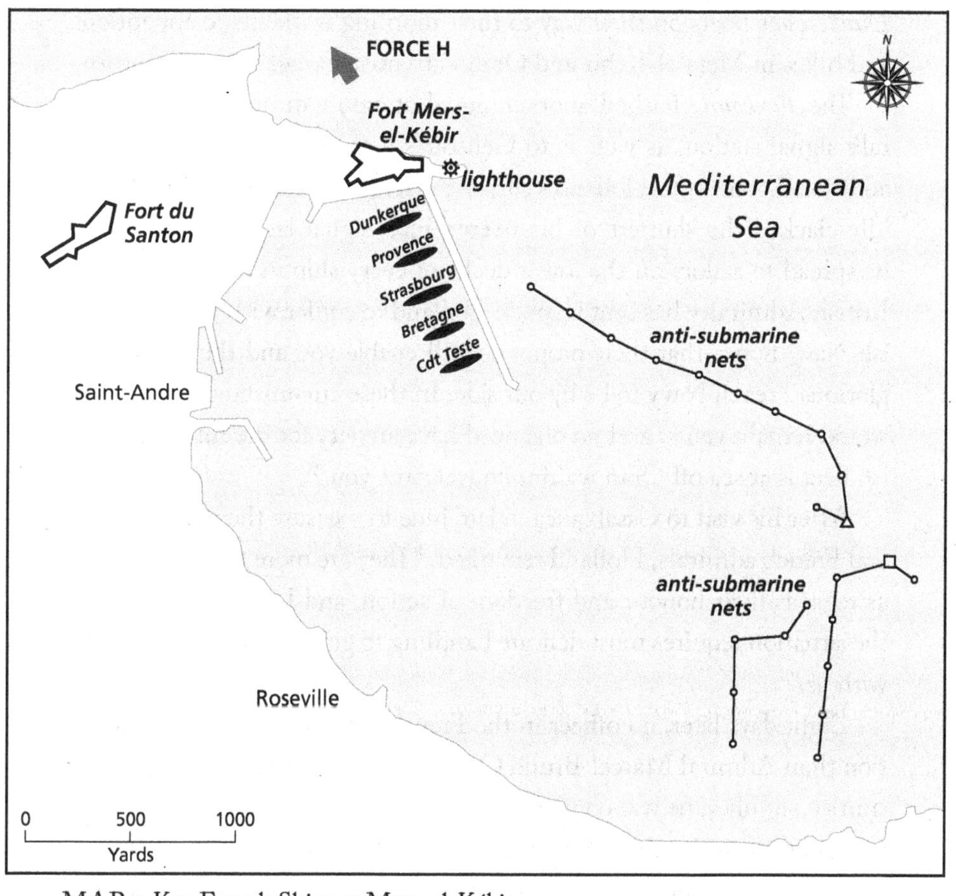

MAP 5. Key French Ships at Mers-el-Kébir

chain from the ship's bow—to cut or snag the moorings of underwater mines that might have protected the harbor entrance.[3]

At 6:30 a.m., with the *Foxhound* inside the bay just outside the port of Mers-el-Kébir, her captain made a request to enter the port to the admiral of the port's station. At the same time, Captain Holland conveyed a signal in French to Admiral Gensoul on board his flagship, the *Dunkerque*:[4] "The British Admiralty has sent Captain Holland to confer with you. Permission to enter."

Receipt of the *Foxhound*'s message was perfunctorily acknowledged, but more than thirty minutes passed without a substantive reply from Admiral Gensoul. At 7:00 a.m., men with shore leave clambered onto the

Dunkerque's boats on their way to their morning workouts, competitions, and hikes in Mers-el-Kébir and Oran with no apparent signs of concern.

The *Foxhound* flashed another signal at 7:09 a.m. to the port admiral's signal station, as well as to Gensoul's flagship. This message added additional context to Holland's surprise arrival. A yeoman of signals rapidly clacked the shutters of his twenty-inch signal lamp to help ensure its spread to sailors on the lower decks of every ship in the harbor: "The British Admiralty has sent Captain Holland to confer with you. The British Navy hopes that their proposals will enable you and the valiant and glorious French Navy to be by our side. In these circumstances your ships would remain yours, and no one need have anxiety for the future. A British fleet is at sea off Oran waiting to welcome you."[5]

After his visit to Casablanca in late June to measure the morale of several French admirals, Holland remarked, "They are more touchy than ever as regards their honour and freedom of action, and I would suggest that the situation requires most delicate handling to get them to fight willingly with us."

Eight days later, no officer in the French Navy faced a touchier situation than Admiral Marcel-Bruno Gensoul. At this moment, shortly after sunrise on July 3, he was confronted without warning by a former ally who was about to insist that he betray his loyalty to his navy's commanding officer and also violate the armistice agreement that his nation had signed with its conqueror. Although there was strategic value in spreading the British message to the crews on the French ships, this blatant undermining of Admiral Gensoul's authority was likely to work against Holland on a day when mutual trust was essential.

Finally, at 7:24 a.m., nearly an hour after her initial request to enter the port, the *Foxhound* received a signal that a pilot was on his way to guide the British destroyer into Mers-el-Kébir. Although the pilot had been instructed to take the *Foxhound* inside the harbor to a berth near the *Dunkerque*, Holland overruled those instructions and insisted on anchoring just off the outer boom—a floating metal-mesh barrier strung across the entrance to the harbor, in place primarily to deter submarines. Two booms helped protect Mers-el-Kébir, one outside the breakwater, one inside. The outer boom was so massive that its six-hundred-foot wide gate was dragged open and closed by tugboats. Holland wished to avoid potential obstructions to an escape if negotiations broke down.

The British captain intended to take the *Foxhound*'s motorboat into the harbor, but that plan was preempted ten minutes later when a small boat from the *Dunkerque* pulled alongside. Holland was pleasantly surprised to see that it carried Bernard Dufay, Gensoul's flag lieutenant, a friend from Holland's time in France who was modestly fluent in English. Before heading toward the *Foxhound*, Dufay had conferred in the admiral's cabin with Gensoul and his chief of staff, Captain Jules Danbé. Gensoul was peeved at the unannounced arrival of Holland, snapping to his aides, "The first time, they sent me a vice admiral [Admiral North, the previous week]. Today it's a captain; tomorrow it will be a midshipman."[6]

Gensoul told Dufay to take the admiral's barge to meet Holland. (An admiral's barge is an admiral's personal boat. Unlike the barges that are towed on American rivers, admiral's barges are motor-driven, they are outfitted with cabins, and some are 60-feet or more in length.) After tying onto the *Foxhound*, Lieutenant Dufay was welcomed on board and led below to meet with Holland. The British captain, carrying a briefcase, thanked Dufay for motoring out to personally take him to the *Dunkerque*. Dufay wasted no time before dashing his friend's enthusiasm, telling him that while Gensoul sent his greetings, no foreign warships were permitted in the port under the terms of the armistice. Dufay offered to deliver any papers that Holland wished to share, and told Holland that Gensoul would send his chief of staff if he required a verbal exchange.

Holland insisted that his orders required him to discuss the documents he carried with no one but Admiral Gensoul. Dufay was unmoved and stated that he also had orders to follow.

Holland had anticipated Gensoul's opening gambit and had prepared a written message that he now handed to Dufay. He asked him to present the message to Gensoul and to let him know that Holland carried proposals "which could only be put to the Admiral himself, personally, and that the matter was of vital importance." After a meeting that lasted just ten minutes, Dufay motored back to the *Dunkerque*.[7]

Among the French seamen who first noticed the presence of the *Foxhound* in the bay, a general train of thought was that she had arrived to invite the French fleet to join Britain in taking the battle to the Italian Navy. On the *Dunkerque*, Officer of the Watch Jean Autric felt an instant wave of exhilaration and liberation: "That's it, the armistice is broken! The English are coming for us." Autric expected an invitation to join Britain in an attack on Mussolini's navy.[8] There was an even more buoyant reaction on the *Strasbourg*, where an officer suggested they invite Captain Holland on board for lunch.[9]

Shortly after Dufay's return to the *Dunkerque*, men on other French ships were astounded by the message conveyed by the flag hoisted on Gensoul's flagship: the signal to "*Prendre les dispositions de combat.*" ["Prepare for combat."][10]

The sudden declaration that this single warship from France's recent ally posed a threat provided an astonishing jolt to seamen throughout the harbor.

The early morning gamesmanship took a severe turn at 8:47 a.m. when Holland received his first direct reply from Admiral Gensoul—a polite but very pointed message, flashed in Morse code: "In reference to your message. Please set sail as soon as possible."[11]

Captain Holland countered Admiral Gensoul's directive to sail from Mers-el-Kébir with a reciprocal stroke of gamesmanship. As a signalman on the *Foxhound* flashed a message that Holland was already en route to Gensoul's flagship in the *Foxhound*'s motorboat, Holland, along with Lieutenant Commanders Spearman and Davies, climbed down to that boat and were on their way toward the *Dunkerque* by 9:05 a.m.

Holland, Spearman, and Davies had no guarantee of safe passage back to the body of Force H when negotiations concluded. Although it was inconceivable that James Somerville would abandon his officers, the *Foxhound*'s commanding officer had received authorization to depart Mers-el-Kébir if he judged his ship was at risk.

Holland intended to motor into the harbor and tie onto the *Dunkerque*. However, the admiral's barge, which once again carried Bernard Dufay, sped toward him. Dufay, in the faster boat, intercepted Holland midway between the restrictive outer boom and the protective breakwater. Holland briefly considered a sudden dash toward the *Dunkerque* but recognized the futility of that idea. At 9:15 a.m. both boats tied to a buoy two hundred yards away from the tugboat that opened and closed the French defense barrier.

Dufay informed Holland that Admiral Gensoul refused to meet with him and added that he had been ordered to prevent—by force, if necessary—Holland from entering the harbor. Dufay added that Gensoul was angry, and his pride had been affronted.

Denied the opportunity to present Britain's demands to the French admiral in person, Holland handed a sealed envelope to Dufay. The envelope, addressed to *Monsieur l'Amiral Gensoul*, contained a printed copy of the British case that Holland had intended to explain in detail and defend in person: "These are the alternatives I hoped to explain to him personally. I'll wait here in *Foxhound*'s motorboat for his answer."

Dufay responded, "I'm afraid there won't be any reply."[12]

After Dufay's boat was untied from the buoy, instead of heading directly back to the *Dunkerque*, it drifted alongside the tug that opened and closed the net defense. Dufay ordered the tug's captain to open fire on the motorboat if Holland attempted a dash toward the inner harbor.[13]

Holland watched Dufay motor back toward the *Dunkerque* and estimated that the British proposals were in Admiral Gensoul's hands no later than 9:35 a.m.

The document that Gensoul read in his cabin had been drafted by Churchill and A. V. Alexander late on July 1. Written in the form of a letter from Vice Admiral Somerville, the text outlined Britain's rationale for this confrontation and ended with Britain's options for compliance.[14]

> To: Monsieur l'Amiral Gensoul from Admiral Somerville.
>
> His Majesty's Government have commanded me to inform you as follows:
>
> They agreed to the French Government approaching the German Government only on conditions that if an armistice was concluded, the French Fleet should be sent to British ports. The

Council of Ministers declared on 18th June that before capitulating on land, the French Fleet would join up with the British Force or sink itself.

Whilst the present French Government may consider that terms of their armistice with Germany and Italy are reconcilable with these undertakings, H.M. Government finds it impossible from their previous experience to believe Germany and Italy will not at any moment which suits them seize French warships and use them against Britain and her Allies. . . .

It is impossible for us, your comrades up till now, to allow your fine ships to fall into power of German or Italian enemy. We are determined to fight on until the end, and if we win, as we think we shall, we shall never forget that France was our ally, that our interests are the same as hers, and that our common enemy is Germany. Should we conquer, we solemnly declare we shall restore the greatness and territory of France. For this purpose we must be sure that the best ships of the French Navy will also not be used against us by the common foe.

In these circumstances H. M. Government have instructed me to demand the French Fleet now at Mers El Kebir and Oran shall act in accordance with one of the following alternatives:

A. Sail with us and continue to fight for victory against the Germans and Italians

B. Sail with reduced crews under our control to a British port. The reduced crew will be repatriated at the earliest moment. If either of these courses is adopted by you we will restore your ships to France at the conclusion of the war, or pay full compensation if they are damaged meanwhile.

C. Alternatively, if you feel bound to stipulate that your ships should not be used against Germans or Italians, since this would break the armistice, then sail them with us with reduced crews to some French port in the West Indies—Martinique for instance—where they can be demilitarised to our satisfaction, or perhaps be entrusted to the United

> States of America, and remain safely until end of war, the crew being repatriated.
>
> If you refuse these fair offers, I must with profound regret require you to sink your ships within six hours. Finally, failing the above, I have the orders of His Majesty's Government to use whatever force may be necessary to prevent your ships from falling into German or Italian hands.

Gensoul, already offended by the arrival of a mere captain to negotiate with him, shared his scornful observation that the "personal" letter from Vice Admiral Somerville had not been signed. A short time after Dufay's launch arrived back at the *Dunkerque*, Admiral Gensoul ordered his ships to light their boilers and begin the six-hour process of raising steam to power their engines.

As the morning sun continued its rise, as Bernard Dufay shuttled back and forth between Holland and Gensoul in the admiral's barge, at ten minutes after 9 a.m., the sixteen ships from Force H that had trailed behind the *Foxhound* through the night slipped into the roads—the calm, sheltered water just outside the harbor at Mers-el-Kébir—with no forewarning. Naval radar, still in its early stages, was not yet deployed on French warships.

The sudden appearance of the imposing British force, including the unmistakable lines of HMS *Hood* and the towering *Ark Royal*, with biplanes already flying off, circling the harbor, and then landing back on her deck in rhythmic circuit, struck an ominous chord. With the exception of the anchored *Foxhound*, the other sixteen ships in Force H steamed back and forth across the bay of Mers-el-Kébir through the morning and afternoon.

The orders and instructions provided to Vice Admiral Somerville included roughly a dozen prewritten, Admiralty-approved messages to share with Admiral Gensoul as circumstances unfolded during the day.

Five ships—the *Hood*, *Valiant*, *Resolution*, *Arethusa*, and *Enterprise*—flashed the message from Envelope "F" to the French ships by signal lamp.

This short greeting, a plea for solidarity, which each British ship flashed three times, read:

> For Admiral Gensoul
>
> From Admiral Somerville
>
> We sincerely hope that the proposals will be acceptable and that we will find you on our side.[15]

CHAPTER 16

DO NOT, REPEAT *NOT*, FAIL

AT SEVEN O'CLOCK on the morning of July 3 in Alexandria—at the same time Cedric Holland approached the lighthouse at Cap Falcon—Vice Admiral René-Émile Godfroy and his chief of staff stepped on board HMS *Warspite* as a Royal Marine band played in their honor.

Admiral Andrew Cunningham, two of his aides, and the two French officers settled into Cunningham's cabin for a formal meeting in a relatively informal setting. The British and French officers sat in comfortable armchairs and conducted the meeting in English. Cunningham noted Vice Admiral Godfroy's "helpful and cordial" demeanor, as well as "the strain under which he was labouring."[1]

After a ritual exchange of pleasantries, Cunningham read a statement that conveyed the British government's hope that Godfroy and his ships would continue the fight against Germany and Italy alongside the Royal Navy. Godfroy absorbed the message in silence "except to say he would have preferred to have this from his own Government."

Cunningham then shared Britain's specific proposals and told the French admiral that he needed to accept "one or other of them that day."

The first proposal read,

> The British Government asks you to put at their disposition the Naval units under your command so that they can continue the struggle against the enemy side by side with the British Navy.
>
> For those who wish to join us the conditions of service and pay will be the same as that of officers, petty officers and men of corresponding rank in the British Navy. Those who do not wish to continue the fight are entirely free to return to France and arrangements will be made soon as practicable for them to do so.

> You are asked to announce these proposals in such a way that they are known to all officers and ships' companies and to make it clear that they are free to make their choice without any constraint.
>
> The British Government guarantees to return to France at the end of the war all ships which have thus taken part with us in the struggle against the enemy.[2]

Godfroy was taken aback by the sudden prospect of sailing his ships under any but a French flag. He stated that "he could not possibly accept it without consulting his Government" (a condition that Cunningham refused to fulfill).

Cunningham then read the second option.

> If you remain convinced that it is not possible to allow your forces to help the British Navy, the British Government asks you to put your ships in a condition in which they cannot go to sea, and leave on board only skeleton crews sufficient to keep the ships in good order.
>
> In this case the British Government guarantees the pay and supplies for the officers and men thus left on board, and that the ships will only be used if the enemy breaks the terms of the armistice concluded between France, Germany and Italy.

This, Godfroy indicated, could very well be an acceptable compromise. He asked for more time to consider the full implications of a commitment of such significance. When Cunningham suggested a 1:00 p.m. deadline, Godfroy replied, "Oh, sooner than that." They agreed to meet again at 11:30 that morning. To ensure that Godfroy knew the full range of alternatives in the British mandate for cooperation, Cunningham also shared the harsh terms of Britain's third and final option: "If these proposals are neither of them acceptable, the British Government asks you as a third alternative to order your forces in Alexandria to sea in order to sink them outside the port in deep waters."

Godfroy avowed that he had no interest in sinking his ships.

Before Godfroy returned to his flagship, Cunningham suggested that he could take solace in the fact that any of the three British options would allow the French to declare *force majeure* and not betray their honor.

After Godfroy departed, Cunningham cabled the admiralty that he expected to know Godfroy's decision by noon and was optimistic about the outcome in his harbor. He believed Godfroy was most likely to accept the second proposal and would reduce crew levels on the French ships to an acceptable minimum.

To Cunningham's shock and dismay, Vice Admiral Godfroy sent a message shortly before noon that he had decided to sink his ships at sea.[3]

Upon reflection, Godfroy's willingness to ignore his orders from Admiral Darlan had reached its limit. He still preferred Britain's second option—to disable his ships and man them with skeleton crews—but since the British would not permit him to seek approval from his admiralty, Godfroy's honor would not permit him to disable his ships in a British-controlled harbor. Godfroy asked Cunningham to delay the sinking of his ships for forty-eight hours to allow time to arrange for the resettlement of his crews.

Cunningham replied with an expression of "profound regret" for Godfroy's decision: "My instructions leave me with no alternative but to accept your choice to take your ships to sea and to sink them in open waters."

Cunningham granted Godfroy's request to delay the sinking for forty-eight hours, adding, "I am therefore under the painful necessity of asking you to proceed to sea to carry out your purpose at 1200 on Friday, 5th July."

Despite agreeing to "the painful necessity" of helping Godfroy sink his ships, Cunningham continued to seek a less drastic resolution in hope of preserving those ships. Although he would take whatever actions were necessary to keep French ships out of German hands, he wished to retain the possibility of them slipping into British control.

Cunningham sent a personal note to Godfroy in which he acknowledged that the French admiral might consider a "reduction of his crews as incompatible with his duty," and asked if he might instead consider emptying his ships' oil tanks and removing the warheads from all torpedoes.[4] To Cunningham's great relief, after a brief period of deliberation, Godfroy agreed to accept this option, and by 5:30 on the evening of July 3, the French ships at Alexandria had already begun to discharge their fuel oil.

Cunningham now hoped that his admiralty would concur that Godfroy had met their demand "to put your ships in a condition in which they cannot go to sea."

As French crews began the work of discharging oil and disarming torpedoes, Vice Admiral Godfroy received a cable commanding him to take an action that current activities rendered impossible: "Weigh immediately and leave Alexandria with all your ships, using force if necessary."

Across the harbor, Andrew Cunningham learned that his admiralty was not satisfied with Godfroy's voluntary move to incapacitate his ships' ability to sail and to fight. Telegram number 1824/3/7/70, which arrived at 8:15 p.m., ordered Cunningham to demand that French ships' companies be "reduced at once by landing or transfer to merchant ships, especially key ratings, before dark tonight."[5]

The telegram ended, "Do not, repeat NOT, fail."

This command was so peculiar in its vehemence that Cunningham later wrote, "It is a perfect example of the type of signal which should never be given," and "It filled me with indignation." In his memoirs, Cunningham added, "At the time I did not believe the signal emanated in the Admiralty and do not believe it now," which inferred that it had emanated from his impatient prime minister.[6] Since darkness had already fallen in Alexandria, and he could not possibly comply with a directive to act "before dark tonight," Cunningham temporarily ignored the order.

Cunningham replied to the admiralty a short time before 1 a.m. on July 4. After noting that he received "Their Lordships" telegram "long after dark," and after providing an update on the status of his negotiations with Godfroy, Cunningham ended, "I fear that in the sense of your 1824/3/7/70 I have failed."[7]

Shortly after receiving and disregarding the "Do not fail" ultimatum, Cunningham received a message from Vice Admiral Godfroy.[8] In one more remarkable display of tolerance and consideration, the French admiral wrote,

> I have just learnt that an ultimatum has been addressed to our Atlantic Fleet by the British Admiralty.

> On the other hand my Admiralty has ordered me to sail, though I have demanded to be assured that the order is authentic.
>
> I have replied that sailing is impossible, but that the situation is definitely changing.
>
> So that I may not incur reproach for having discharged oil-fuel after receiving an order to sail, I have stopped the discharge of oil-fuel pending events.
>
> But that changes nothing. I give you my word as to my intentions which remain unchanged from those I expressed to you in writing this morning.

In a bid to preserve their tactful insubordination and prevent a break in their fragile compromise, Cunningham sent his chief of staff, Rear Admiral Algernon Willis, to persuade the French admiral to continue the discharge of fuel oil from his ships.

By this time, however, Godfroy had learned of the ultimatum that Cedric Holland had delivered at Mers-el-Kébir, and, most ominously, Britain's threat to fire on French ships. As Godfroy wrote in his memoirs, "My views on the situation were instantly transformed."[9]

Godfroy told Willis that any degree of cooperation with the Royal Navy "was no longer possible; that I rejected outright all the proposals of his admiralty and that abandoning the attitude of conciliation that I had had until then, I considered myself, henceforth, as independent of any commitment and free from any action." Whereas Godfroy had earlier been willing to proceed to sea and sink his ships under the cooperative watch of the Royal Navy, he told Willis that if he now saw an opportunity to take his ships to sea, he would attempt to break away, with the full realization that his actions would lead to a battle and bloodshed.

Although Godfroy was irate and his goodwill had dissipated, for all of his bluster, Godfroy knew that he and his ships very likely had no option but to remain in Alexandria. He later wrote, "Indeed, our relatively complicated mooring arrangements, our dispersion, the obligation to carry out, by our own means, long and delicate maneuvers, at close range of the entire British fleet from our first movements, the existence of a strong double boom closing the well-guarded entrance to the port, inevitably condemned any attempt to leave by force to failure and massacre."

To prevent a massacre, if Cunningham threatened force, Godfroy intended to order his captains to scuttle their ships at their berths. In keeping with his previous actions and communications, he remained remarkably deferential. He promised Admiral Willis that if he eventually issued an order to scuttle, "he would do so in a manner as convenient to us as possible."[10]

While Cunningham continued to seek common ground with Godfroy, his admiralty relentlessly pressed him to bring the impasse to a close. Cunningham later acknowledged that "in deference to the wishes of the British Government, and the fact that we could not take our fleet to sea before the French squadron was immobilized, the situation could not be allowed to remain uncertain."[11]

After considering the full range of possible actions, Cunningham settled on a plan to present Godfroy "with a demand to intern or surrender his ships with the result that he would sink them" at sea. Although Cunningham hoped not to have to follow through on his threat, he was not bluffing. If Godfroy refused to comply with the British admiralty's conditions, Cunningham would resolve the stalemate with force. First, however, he would do everything possible to keep the French ships afloat under British control.

Cunningham informed the admiralty that he intended to confront Godfroy on the morning of July 4. In accord with the Admirals' previous agreement, he would order the French ships to be sunk at sea on the morning of July 5, allowing a day to arrange for temporary lodging and swift repatriation of about four thousand French crewmen.

After a long hot day of tense negotiations, Admiral Cunningham "retired to bed, much fatigued and worried" an hour after midnight.[12]

As Cunningham and his men would learn within hours, their worries were justified.

CHAPTER 17

DISCUSS THE MATTER AS OLD FRIENDS

CEDRIC HOLLAND'S MOTORBOAT bobbed gently in the Gulf of Oran, tethered to a buoy midway between the French anchorage and the recently arrived core of Force H. Notwithstanding Bernard Dufay's recent declaration that he was "afraid there won't be any reply," the French lieutenant motored back to Holland's launch at 10:00 a.m. with a message from Admiral Gensoul.

Before Dufay left Gensoul's cabin on the *Dunkerque*, he grabbed a pencil and a signal pad and took down a message dictated by the seething admiral. After tying his boat next to Holland's, Dufay shared Gensoul's exasperation. In his first acknowledgment of the British ultimatum, the French admiral reinforced the assurance he had provided to Admiral North ten days earlier: "The assurances given by Admiral Gensoul to Admiral Sir Dudley North remain unchanged. *En aucun cas* will French warships fall intact into the hands of the Germans or the Italians."[1] Gensoul added that the British should understand that the French ships were prepared to defend themselves by force, if necessary, in the face of Britain's "veritable ultimatum."

Holland had hoped for a more conciliatory response, perhaps even an invitation to motor next to the *Dunkerque* to personally discuss the impasse with Gensoul. Holland crossed from his launch onto the admiral's barge. He asked if he could join Dufay in the barge's cabin so they could sit "and discuss the matter as old friends."[2]

Dufay beseeched Holland to trust the French Navy and added that Gensoul had told him to emphasize "that the term '*en aucun cas*' [which literally translates to "in no case"] means anytime, anywhere, anyway and without further orders from the French Admiralty. These are Admiral Darlan's orders."

After a moment's pause, Holland said, "We had better be frank with each other. I'm trusting you as a comrade and a friend." He then shared the British government's fear that Admiral Darlan had lost his independent control of the French Navy.

In the wake of Dufay's astonished silence, Holland asked when he had last received a signal from Darlan. Dufay, who deciphered every signal that Gensoul received, replied, "About two days ago."[3] When Holland asked if the signal bore Darlan's "Xavier 377" authentication, Dufay expressed surprise that the British were aware of this code. Holland shared his belief, based on Darlan's recent silence, that the French admiral's ability to communicate and command had been constrained by Germany.

Holland now assumed a very personal tack. He described the *aide-memoire* that Dufay had conveyed to Gensoul on his behalf as a clumsy attempt to gain Gensoul's trust. His hope had been to defuse what he knew Gensoul would interpret as a British ultimatum and instead persuade him that it was an expression of hope.[4]

Dufay responded that Gensoul had found the threat of force particularly offensive. In addition, he was once again adamant that the crews of every ship in the French Navy were prepared to sink their ships rather than see them fall into German hands.

Neither officer had more to add. Before he returned to the *Foxhound*'s motorboat, Holland withdrew a small sheaf of papers from his briefcase: a set of notes that he had meticulously typed to guide his planned discussion with Admiral Gensoul. Holland asked Dufay to read the notes written in English on his return passage to the *Dunkerque* before translating them into French for Admiral Gensoul.[5]

Holland had expected to cast his argument to Gensoul as they sat face-to-face in the admiral's cabin. He had carefully orchestrated a line of reasoning and even included two planned pauses near the end, during which he expected to absorb Gensoul's impassioned reaction and then counter his fury. The impact of Holland's argument rendered on paper was significantly diminished.

The case Holland intended to amplify with the force of his personality was now condensed into a two-dimensional set of notes that he handed to Dufay before the two officers went their separate ways:

> The British Government have had suspicions for some days that the Germans and Italians were intending to break the Armistice terms as regards the Navy as soon as a favourable opportunity occurred. The day before yesterday this was confirmed beyond all doubt. Admiral Somerville who is commanding the British Naval Forces at Gibraltar, who had many weeks of close cooperation with your ships during the Spanish Civil War, has therefore been ordered to present certain proposals to you and has sent me for that purpose. This intended action is a dastardly trick which reacts as much against us as it does against you. I have told you here more than I have been ordered to do, but having had the honour of serving with the French Navy and directly under the orders of its Chief who trusted me and gave me his friendship, I feel I wish to help you in every way I can. Because of my close associations with you, I perhaps realise and feel more acutely the circumstances from your point of view. But I must also try and put our point of view to you, if I am permitted to do so.

Holland planned to continue:

> It goes without saying that we trust your Chief and your Admirals in high commands who have spoken for the French Navy. Thus, on the 18th June, Admiral Darlan gave a personal promise to the First Lord and First Sea Lord that the French Fleet would never surrender to the enemy. A few days later, I understand the Admiral of the Fleet sent a telegram to the effect that he hoped personally to maintain the command of the French Navy but should he find himself unable to do so satisfactorily for some unseen reason, he nominated the command successively to Admiral de Laborde, Esteva and yourself. [Holland did not mention Admiral Abrial in his list of Darlan's heirs.] Admiral Esteva's reply to the First Sea

> Lord about that date was in the same sense and he added that if orders were given by the Government as opposed to the Chief to give up the Fleet, he would not obey them. Then you, Admiral, assured Admiral North in the same sense the other day and Admirals Ollive and de Laborde said the same to me. Thus there is the assurance, one might say, of the French Navy, and, Admiral, naturally and very sincerely, we believe you. But in view of what has been found out with regard to the treachery of the Germans and Italians, with the French Army disarmed and the Fleet laid up with reduced crews under German and Italian surveillance, the Government feels that there can be no certainty that however resolute the attempt to destroy or sink the ships, it would not be possible to forestall seizure by the enemy.
>
> Before putting to you the proposals I will, if I may, give you Admiral Somerville's messages. He sends you his sincere wishes adding that he has a most happy recollection of his collaboration with the French Navy and that he will always take with him the souvenirs of the many friendships he has made.[6]

Holland's script repeated the three options contained in the message from Vice Admiral Somerville that he had handed to Bernard Dufay earlier that morning: Sail with the Royal Navy, sail to Britain, or sail to Martinique.

The two planned pauses in Holland's script appeared just before the end. These breaks—if Holland had the opportunity to deliver his words in person—would have added emphasis to Britain's two most ominous demands and would have enabled Holland to immediately parry Gensoul's response. Holland's verbatim script continues:

> (Here I proposed to stop, hoping a discussion on the above would ensue. If nothing came of this, then . . .)
>
> If you do not see your way to accepting one of these fair offers, I must with profound regret require you to sink your ships within six hours.
>
> (Again a stop before putting the final terms.)

> Finally, failing the above, I have orders from H.M. Government to use whatever force may be necessary to prevent your ships from falling into German or Italian hands.

Clearly the last two statements would have carried greater weight, and Holland could have mitigated their noxious impact if he had been able to manage their gradual presentation and discuss them at length with Admiral Gensoul. In printed form, the weight of Britain's argument was diminished, and the sting of the ultimatums was magnified.

Holland watched Lieutenant Dufay motor back to the *Dunkerque* with a copy of the appeal that he had meticulously scripted and planned to deliver to Admiral Gensoul in person. From the distant vantage point of his motorboat, Holland estimated that Dufay tied up to Admiral Gensoul's flagship at 10:50 a.m.

Gensoul digested Holland's case for cooperation much more quickly than he would have if Holland had been sitting across from him with the opportunity to engage the French admiral in a discussion of the British demands—and counter Gensoul's near-certain rejection of those demands. As he read through Holland's document, Gensoul shared a begrudging admission with Dufay: "The British are well informed."[7]

When Gensoul finished reading Holland's script, Lieutenant Dufay made a surprising request. After three round trips across the bay, he asked his commander-in-chief not to send him back for any further discussions with Captain Holland.

The weight of responsibility and his frustration at the standstill had sapped his morale. Dufay later wrote of "the intellectual tension I had been under all morning."[8] Gensoul gestured toward Captain Jules Danbé, his chief of staff, and ordered him to motor out to Holland. To Dufay's chagrin, he ordered him to accompany Danbé.

Before the two officers departed, Gensoul dictated a new message.

When the admiral's barge pulled back alongside Holland's launch at 11:20 a.m., the British captain was surprised but not disappointed to see that Captain Danbé was with Lieutenant Dufay. Holland also knew

Gensoul's chief of staff from his time in France. Danbé handed over a handwritten copy of the message that Gensoul had dictated:

1. Admiral Gensoul can but confirm the reply already sent by Lieutenant de Vaisseau Dufay.
2. Admiral Gensoul had decided to defend himself by every means at his disposal.
3. Admiral Gensoul wishes to draw Admiral Somerville's attention to the fact that the first round fired against us will have the result of putting immediately the whole French Fleet against Great Britain, a result which is diametrically opposite to that which H.M. Government wishes.[9]

With his expectation for a face-to-face meeting dashed for a fourth time, rather than repeat his case to Danbé, and aware of the importance of updating Vice Admiral Somerville on the morning's progress (or lack thereof), Holland decided to return to the *Foxhound*.

Just before heading back to his ship at 11:25 a.m., Holland shook Captain Danbé's hand and made an astonishing admission: "Allow me to tell you, officer to officer, that in your position my reply would have been no different."[10]

For all of his familiarity with French customs, the French language, and the French Navy, Cedric Holland was an imperfect choice for the challenge of negotiating with Marcel-Bruno Gensoul at Mers-el-Kébir. Holland, a respected colleague with a compelling personality, was an unabashed Francophile—a serious flaw for an officer immersed in negotiations with potentially deadly consequences. Holland was perhaps too willing to sympathize with the French position, too trusting in the commitment and ability of French naval officers to resist German takeover attempts, and too confident in his ability to persuade his French counterparts to embrace the British point of view.

Rear Admiral John Godfrey recorded in an unpublished memoir that Holland "had for some time been going through an emotional experience," and in "his estimation of the French, he saw everything French through rose tinted spectacles."[11] In the script that he so meticulously prepared—and was compelled to deliver on paper to Admiral Gensoul—Holland admitted, "Because of my close associations with you, I perhaps realise and feel more acutely the circumstances from your point of view."

Holland and Godfrey had discussed the cause of Holland's "emotional disturbance . . . with great frankness." Although Godfrey was no more specific in his memoir, two reputable historians have written about Holland's involvement with a Frenchwoman during his time in Paris.[12]

Godfrey, Britain's director of naval intelligence in the first three years of the war (and, according to legend, Ian Fleming's model for "M," James Bond's boss), feared that Holland, whom he considered "a great personal friend," appeared to have lost his balance after Britain's breakup with France. In Godfrey's final assessment, "Holland's judgment about French affairs had become gravely impaired and was, in my opinion, useless."

There was also, of course, the matter of relative rank between Holland and Gensoul—an issue that was out of Holland's control, but one of acute sensitivity at Mers-el-Kébir on July 3. Marcel-Bruno Gensoul was keenly offended that James Somerville had sent an emissary of lesser rank to negotiate with him. When Winston Churchill and the British war cabinet attempted to prepare for every conceivable response by Gensoul, they failed to anticipate that the French admiral would be so obstinate and so sensitive to Captain Holland's rank, despite their familiarity.

After the war, Admiral Andrew Cunningham expressed his view that Somerville should have motored in from HMS *Hood* to meet with Gensoul on board the *Dunkerque*, and remarked that "few could resist James's blandishments."[13] Although this would have cut Somerville's contact with the British admiralty through the day, both the Royal Navy and the French Navy would have been better served if Somerville had been untethered from Whitehall and given the opportunity to negotiate directly with his French peer.

The aloof Admiral Marcel-Bruno Gensoul—a man who "was proof against anyone's charms"[14]—would surely have resisted meeting Somerville, just as he brushed off Holland. Somerville, however, would not have been slighted by Gensoul for a disparity in rank, and he would undoubtedly have employed the force of his personality to directly communicate the mortal consequences of a failure to negotiate while there was still time to find a resolution.

But that is hindsight. Like James Somerville and Cedric Holland, Gensoul had orders to follow. But unlike them—and, especially, unlike Admiral Godfroy and Admiral Cunningham at Alexandria—Gensoul was not inclined to compromise or bend his adherence to those orders.

CHAPTER 18

ASKED TO SHOOT HIS BEST FRIEND

REMARKABLY, FRANÇOIS DARLAN did not learn about the simmering crisis at Mers-el-Kébir until the afternoon of July 3, 1940.

Despite the pre-dawn arrival of Captain Holland, followed by Vice Admiral Somerville's ships a short time after 9:00 a.m., Admiral Gensoul waited until 9:45 a.m. to alert his admiralty to the unexpected presence of Somerville's squadron. When Gensoul finally sounded the alarm, his brief message provided an incomplete and misleading picture of the British threat: "English force comprising three battleships, an aircraft carrier, cruisers and destroyers off Oran. Ultimatum sent: Sink your ships in six hours or we shall use force. Reply: French ships will reply to force with force."[1] Gensoul did not mention the option to sail to the West Indies—the least confrontational alternative offered by the British.

To Gensoul's surprise, he did not receive an immediate response from Darlan. As a result of the rickety communications network in France, compounded by the obligations of Darlan's new administrative responsibilities, three hours passed before French officers were able to reach their leader.

Gensoul's cable was received in Nérac, where a radio truck served as the French Navy's temporary communications hub.[2] As if Nérac was not sufficiently remote, Darlan happened to be 175 miles to the north, in Clermont-Ferrand, engaged in meetings with the new French government in his newly added minister of marine role.

A copy of the message was handed to Darlan's chief of staff, Vice Admiral Maurice Le Luc. On his own initiative, Le Luc broadcast an order from Nérac to all French ships in the Mediterranean: "Get under way, ready for action, and report to the admiral in the *Dunkerque* at Oran."

Darlan's assistant chief of staff Jean Negadelle retroactively approved this order on Darlan's behalf after Negadelle finally reached Darlan by telephone shortly before one in the afternoon.

As Captain Holland and Vice Admiral Somerville waited with frustration for an opportunity to parley directly with Admiral Gensoul, they were not yet aware that an attack force had been called upon to reinforce Gensoul's ships, and, perhaps, sink theirs.

Fourteen thousand seamen on British and French ships endured broiling heat on a windless day under a cloudless sky at Mers-el-Kébir.[3] British hands had been at action stations since before nine o'clock that morning, many behind watertight doors that permitted no ventilation. On deck, Ted Briggs, a young signalman on the HMS *Hood*, observed that touching "a handrail was like putting one's fingers on the handle of a poker which had been left in a fire for hours."[4] Men at action stations inside turrets and magazines—many wearing an extra layer of anti-flash gear—toiled in temperatures of 95° Fahrenheit and higher.[5]

After ending his discussion with Jules Danbé, Cedric Holland briefly enjoyed the sweat-cooling relief of a waterborne dash through warm air as he sped back to the *Foxhound* on the ship's motorboat. Back on board the destroyer, Captain Holland read a message that had arrived from Vice Admiral Somerville during his return passage: "Imperative French should know I will not repetition not allow them to leave harbour unless terms accepted."[6]

In the wake of a hectic morning during which he had not been able to converse directly with Somerville, Holland initially intended to ask the *Foxhound*'s captain to take him into the bay for a meeting on the *Hood*. After digesting Somerville's declaration of what the French should know, Holland decided instead to reinforce Britain's position to Admiral Gensoul.

Holland translated Somerville's message into French, tucked his handwritten note into an envelope, and sent Lieutenant Commander Spearman in the *Foxhound*'s motorboat to deliver the note to Captain Danbé.

Vice Admiral Somerville received an update on the status of negotiations in Alexandria and passed it along to Captain Holland. Somerville had been told that the impasse in the Egyptian port was apparently headed toward a resolution in accordance with Britain's objectives. Hopeful that the knowledge of progress at Alexandria would influence Admiral Gensoul to more seriously consider a compromise at Mers-el-Kébir, Holland included a concise update in the message carried by Spearman: "Am informed that Admiral Godfroy is demilitarizing his ships with reduced crews."

Just as Somerville received high-level reports on the progress at Alexandria, Andrew Cunningham received updates on the standoff at Mers-el-Kébir. Cunningham pictured Somerville's "utter repugnance at having to carry out his drastic orders."[7]

During a noon meeting in London, Admiral Dudley Pound brought the war cabinet up to date on the Royal Navy's activities against French ships in home waters. He also shared what he knew about the stalemate at Mers-el-Kébir. To help break that impasse, he argued for fresh consideration of demilitarization—an option that was apparently successful in Alexandria but which the cabinet had previously rejected for Mers-el-Kébir.

To Pound's disappointment, the cabinet rejected this option once again, this time out of concern that Gensoul would interpret its late addition as a sign of weakness.

The cabinet also received an update on President Roosevelt's perspective on the French fleet in a telegram sent by Lord Lothian, Britain's ambassador to the United States. Lothian stated, "I asked him whether that meant that American opinion would support forcible seizure of these ships. He said certainly. They would expect them to be seized rather than that they should fall into German hands and that he would do everything in his power to help this solution. He said that they had offered to buy the Fleet from the French before the Reynaud Government fell but that there was nobody from whom he could buy it today."[8]

Despite Admiral Gensoul's polite admonition to "Please set sail as soon as possible" early that morning, the *Foxhound* had remained in the bay, three miles outside the port of Mers-el-Kébir. Commander Geoffrey Peters, the *Foxhound*'s commanding officer, gradually sensed that his ship would be a ripe target if hostilities escalated, and she had to sail past the shore batteries guarding Mers-el-Kébir. After Spearman delivered Holland's message and motored back, the *Foxhound* sailed outside the outer boom, still within visual signaling distance from the *Dunkerque* but several miles farther away from Admiral Gensoul's flagship.

The additional distance between the ships increased the time Holland would have to travel if an opportunity for a face-to-face discussion eventually arose. Those additional miles and minutes would prove consequential before the day's end.

After Cedric Holland, who was literally in the middle of the standoff between the French and British ships, clarified Britain's intentions with Admiral Gensoul, he sought to verify that Vice Admiral Somerville understood the current French stance as well.

At 11:46 a.m., Holland sent Somerville a signal marked "MOST IMMEDIATE." Holland's message was a paraphrased version of the handwritten note he received from Dufay and Danbé one hour earlier:

(1) Admiral Gensoul confirms former assurances re sinking of ships.
(2) He is determined to fight if force is used.
(3) He draws your attention to fact that first round fired will put whole French navy against us which is opposite of what we want.[9]

Holland added a speculative observation at the end of his note: "From activity in ships apparent intention is to put to sea and fight." And in a separate signal, Holland added, "C.O.S. [Chief of Staff] pointed out preparations to sink ships at any moment and anywhere without further orders from French Admiralty."

Despite this assurance from Gensoul's chief of staff, Somerville would not risk the escape of any of Gensoul's ships. A new message from the first sea lord suggested—but did not order—Somerville to consider laying magnetic mines in the harbor mouth. With his apprehension reinforced, Somerville issued an order to lay the mines. Shortly after one in the afternoon, five Swordfish torpedo bombers lifted off from the flight deck of the *Ark Royal*. Each plane dropped a single mine near the entrance to the harbor.

One pilot reported that the boom, which was open earlier in the day, was now closed. However, contrary to Holland's suggestion that French ships intended to "put to sea and fight," the British pilots detected no apparent signs that French ships were making ready to break out of Mers-el-Kébir. Small boats casually cruised the harbor, travelling between the anchored warships, the quay, and nearby beaches with no signs of being hoisted on board, as they would if a battle was imminent.

The cumulative effect of these conflicting observations would prove calamitous before day's end.

At 12:36 p.m., Somerville sent a disquieting signal to Holland: "Presume there is now no alternative [to] ANVIL."[10]

After a six-minute consideration of Somerville's suggestion that he was prepared to open fire on the French ships, Holland replied with a message that appeared innocuous, but which stimulated Somerville's attention: "Am afraid not. Am awaiting in V/S [Visual Signaling] Touch in case of acceptance before expiration time. Proposals received 0935."[11]

Holland saw no alternative to ANVIL. However, the phrase "expiration time" in his reply raised Somerville's eyebrows. To that point, Somerville had not been sure if Holland had communicated a specific deadline for Gensoul to accept one of the British options. With Holland's confirmation that his signal had been sent at 9:35 a.m., Holland and Somerville were now on the same page. Britain's six-hour window for compliance would close at 3:35 in the afternoon.

The gist of the deadline and the six-hour window were originally conveyed to Admiral Gensoul in the written message Holland begrudgingly handed over to Bernard Dufay during their first meeting in the morning: "If you refuse these fair offers, I must with profound regret require you to sink your ships within six hours. Finally, failing the above, I have the orders of His Majesty's Government to use whatever force may be necessary to prevent your ships from falling into German or Italian hands."

Somerville's exchange with Captain Holland prompted a new consideration. Since Gensoul had been so unresponsive throughout the day, Somerville questioned if Britain was bound by a deadline. With this in mind, he messaged Holland at 1:15 p.m.: "Does anything you have said prevent me from opening fire?"[12]

Holland replied, "Nothing I have said, since terms were not discussed, only handed and reply received. But I would suggest there might be a chance of avoiding ANVIL if Foxhound went in to V/S touch and asked if there was a further message before force employed."[13] Holland believed, and Somerville evidently concurred, that since Gensoul had refused all opportunities to discuss the British terms—which had been handed over and then vaguely dismissed on paper—there was no agreement in force that would delay or prevent the British from opening fire. In fact, Somerville had already decided to act. He informed the admiralty at 1 p.m. that he was prepared to open fire at 1:30 p.m.[14]

In the aftermath of the events at Mers-el-Kébir, Cedric Holland recalled his frame of mind at the moment when Somerville asked him if he had any reason to prevent ANVIL: "My answer to ask for a final reply before the fire was opened was based on my appreciation of the French character, that an initial refusal will often gradually come round to acquiescence."[15]

Holland understood that he had taken on the mantle of the buffer between Marcel-Bruno Gensoul's intransigence and Winston Churchill's desire for action toward a decisive resolution. Holland hoped to prevent the British from firing on the French until every opportunity for compromise had been exhausted: "I had felt most strongly all along that the use of force, even as a last resort, was fatal to the attainment of our object, and I was thus using every endeavor to bring about a peaceful solution."

Holland, who was instrumental in stretching Britain's timetable for compliance by the French, then added, "I therefore take full responsibility for any delay action I may have tried to enforce."

Twelve hours earlier, at 1:35 on the morning of July 3, 1940, during the passage of Force H from Gibraltar to Mers-el-Kébir, the admiralty sent identical cables to Admiral Somerville and Admiral Cunningham: "No time limit for acceptance of demands is contained in your instructions, but it is very important that operations should be completed during daylight hours today Wednesday."[16] In other words, Somerville *had* a time limit, but he still had more than six hours of daylight to work with and leeway to extend the deadline for Gensoul to respond to the British proposals.

After considering Holland's suggestion that "there might be a chance of avoiding ANVIL if Foxhound went into V/S touch," Somerville reasoned that with magnetic mines floating at the entrance to the harbor, and with the seventeen ships of Force H looming on the near horizon—all with their rangefinders tightly focused on targets at anchor behind the breakwater—the French were effectively sealed into their port. As a result, Somerville eased off on his pressure for a prompt decision by Gensoul.

Somerville later reported, "It appeared that the French had no immediate intention of proceeding to sea, and in consequence I decided to give them until 1500 to make a decision."[17] Also, "I was strengthened in this decision by Captain Holland's reply that the use of force might be avoided if FOXHOUND went in to visual sighting touch and asked if there was any further message."

Étienne Sicard, an officer on duty on the French battleship *Bretagne*, which, along with the *Provence* had sailed from Alexandria to Mers-el-Kébir, recorded the general nonchalance of the sailors on French ships. "Still confident that nothing would happen, our men, standing at their fighting stations, were quietly reading magazines, chatting together or exchanging wisecracks."[18]

The *Foxhound* eased slightly back in the direction of Mers-el-Kébir to ensure unbroken visual contact with the *Dunkerque* while each side waited for the other's next step.

While the French and British navies verbally sparred at Mers-el-Kébir and Alexandria, Soviet ambassador Ivan Maisky paid a visit to Winston Churchill at 10 Downing Street. Maisky, who was fluent in English, affable, and well-connected, was a common and welcome presence in London's inner sanctums. He was on amiable terms with Churchill, Lord Halifax, Lord Beaverbrook, and other British luminaries.

In his account of his July 3 conversation with Churchill, Maisky remarked that the prime minister "was full of life and energy, and seemed very cheerful and fresh." He also noted Churchill's "very exhilarated mood."[19]

In their brief meeting, Maisky asked Churchill about two pressing issues: the fate of the French fleet and the future of Britain now that France was out of the war. Before he replied to Maisky's question about the fleet, Churchill took a robust puff of his ever-present cigar. With "a sly flash of his eyes through the bluish smoke," Churchill assured the Soviet Ambassador, "The question is receiving attention."

As to the near-term outlook for Britain, Churchill declared, "My general strategy at present is to last out the next three months."

John Colville's diary entry for July 3 began, "At No. 10 chief interest centres on the Operation CATAPULT. First we hear of the operations at Portsmouth and Plymouth, then the attack on Oran was to take place at 1:30. During the afternoon came news of various postponements in the hope that the French resolve to fight was weakening."[20]

Royal Navy officers had rushed to the quarterdecks of every French ship in Portsmouth and Plymouth between 3:30 and 4:30 that morning after disarming French sentries. French commanding officers were informed of the British takeovers as *faits accomplis* with no warning and no opportunity to negotiate.

In the sole instance of violent resistance, two British officers, one British seaman, and one French warrant officer died during an armed confrontation on the *Surcouf*, the massive French submarine that made a heroic escape from Brest and sailed to Plymouth two weeks before.

The Royal Navy completed the seizures of French ships at Portsmouth, Plymouth, and other British ports by sunrise.

Late on the morning of July 3, with the British and French navies potentially on the verge of battle, General Spears informed Charles de Gaulle of the brewing confrontation at Mers-el-Kébir.[21] Spears noted, "A man of few words, he seldom wasted them to comment on the inevitable, and only moving his head slightly from side to side when forming a sentence of great importance which he might not utter." After a moment's thoughtful silence, de Gaulle expressed his belief that Admiral Gensoul would accept one of the British options, and that bloodshed would be averted.

Spears spent the afternoon in a meeting of a committee that addressed French affairs in Britain. The participants included a representative from the admiralty who received and shared hourly updates on the situation at Mers-el-Kébir. Spears reckoned that Gensoul was "playing for time" in hopes of wasting daylight.

Spears knew Cedric Holland from Holland's time as naval attaché in Paris, and pictured Holland's anguish. "I knew that as the afternoon wore on that Holland must have felt as if he had been put in charge of a firing squad and asked to shoot his best friend."

Admiral Gensoul sent his second message of the day from the *Dunkerque* to his Admiralty's makeshift headquarters in Nérac shortly after 1 p.m.

> Initial English ultimatum was to either join the English Fleet or else destroy ships within six hours to avoid their falling into German [or] Italian hands. Have replied:
>
> First: The latter hypothesis was not for consideration.
>
> Second: Will defend myself with force.
>
> Third: First shot would have practical result of getting whole French Fleet against Great Britain, [the] result diametrically opposed to that sought by British government.
>
> English response: If you get under way without accepting British proposals which are reasonable and favorable, I would regretfully open fire. Captain Holland, who has acted as intermediary, has hinted that disarmament of *Force de Raid* at Mers-el-Kébir could provide the basis for an arrangement. The latter comes under reservations.[22]

Gensoul's two messages would be the subject of debate for decades after the war. Most notably, when he outlined the options offered by the British, Gensoul omitted the possibility of sailing his ships to the French West Indies. Although there is little likelihood that Admiral Darlan or the French government would have risked violating their armistice agreements, awareness of this alternative for independent action might have softened the French reception of the British terms. In 1949, when Gensoul appeared before a French parliamentary inquiry into the events at Mers-el-Kébir, he apologized for his omission.[23]

In addition, Gensoul noted that Captain Holland had "hinted" that disarmament could be acceptable to the British. In his detailed report of the day's action, Holland did not mention a discussion of demilitarization with his French counterparts. In all likelihood, he alluded to the potential for demilitarization to Lieutenant Dufay during one of the discussions on the admiral's barge. Holland's suggestion might have created the impression of a crack in British resolve, as the cabinet had feared.

At 1:30 in the afternoon, seven hours after the *Foxhound* first approached the harbor at Mers-el-Kébir, Vice Admiral Le Luc in Nérac finally reached Admiral Darlan by telephone for a direct conversation. After Le Luc brought him up to date on the slow-boiling impasse between the two navies, Darlan complimented his chief of staff's initiative.

At Darlan's behest, Le Luc sent a signal to Gensoul with orders that threatened to escalate hostilities: "You will make it known to the British intermediary that the Admiral of the Fleet has ordered all French naval forces in the Mediterranean to join you ready for action immediately. You should, then, give your orders to these forces. You will reply to force with force. Summon submarines and aviation if necessary."[24]

One hour later, Darlan shared a summary of the day's events with Marshal Pétain and other members of the new Vichy government, including General Weygand and Paul Baudouin, all of whom absorbed the news in shock and silence.

Vice Admiral Somerville's extension and re-extension of his deadline for Admiral Gensoul to comply with one of the four British options had apparently been for naught, as the French admiral continued to spurn every British attempt to engage in direct dialogue.

As the clock ticked past two in the afternoon with no sign of cooperation, Somerville told Cedric Holland to forward a new message to

Gensoul: "If you accept the terms hoist a large square flag at masthead, otherwise I must open fire at 1500. Your harbour is mined."[25]

Gensoul responded to the threat, not with a large square flag, but by ordering action stations—the command for his men to dash to their combat posts. He also transmitted a plea that was tinged with defiance: "I have no intention of getting under way. I have telegraphed to my government whose reply I am awaiting. Do not create [an] irreparable [situation]."[26]

As Somerville's three o'clock deadline approached, Cedric Holland's emotions careened between the opposite extremes of dread and exhilaration. At ten minutes before three, Somerville sent Holland an updated ultimatum with a thirty-minute reprieve and a lethal promise: "Pass to Gensoul. Accept our terms or abandon your ships, as I mean to destroy them at 1530."[27]

Minutes later, before Holland had a chance to translate and forward Somerville's new message, he was handed a fresh signal from Gensoul. To Holland's great relief, it carried the invitation he had sought throughout the day. The French admiral "was now ready to receive delegates for honourable discussion."[28] Holland conveyed the French admiral's message to Somerville and requested orders to proceed to the *Dunkerque*. Somerville's quick assent to his request was accompanied by a demand to press for an immediate reply to the British terms.

On board the *Hood*, Somerville remained skeptical, suspicious that Gensoul was stalling for time. However, he reasoned "that it was quite possible Admiral Gensoul only now realised it was my intention to use Force if necessary."[29]

Holland elected not to share Somerville's threatened 3:30 bombardment with Gensoul. In hindsight, if Gensoul had been aware of Somerville's intent to destroy his ships, his meeting with Holland would have taken on a very different tone. Holland later logged his impression that Gensoul did not believe the British would fire until the two men met on the *Dunkerque*.

With Holland finally on his way to a meeting in Gensoul's cabin, Somerville shared his tempered optimism in a signal to the admiralty: "Am postponing action and I think they are weakening."[30]

After eight hours of continually mounting frustration, Cedric Holland now had a renewed sense of hope. As he later reflected, "From that moment until I finally went over the DUNKERQUE's side, I thought there was a chance of winning through, and that the French Admiral would accept one or another of the proposals."[31]

The *Foxhound* was still far outside the port, slightly to the north off Cap Falcon, seven and a half miles from the boom and clear of the small minefield the British had laid. That is where Holland and Lt. Cdr. Davies embarked in their motorboat at 3:06 p.m. on their way to the *Dunkerque*.

Holland observed that as they passed the French vessel on watch at the boom, "we were smartly saluted and the crew on deck called to attention."[32] This was the crew that had been instructed to fire upon him earlier in the day if he attempted a headlong dash toward the *Dunkerque*.

The admiral's barge, with Lieutenant Dufay on board, met Holland and Davies just inside the inner net defenses. Once again, Holland's preference was to take his motorboat to the *Dunkerque*, but Dufay had firm instructions from Gensoul to transport the British officers on his barge. Holland left the motorboat secured to a buoy.

Their passage from the *Foxhound* to the *Dunkerque* took slightly more than one hour. At 4:15 p.m., with that priceless hour lost during their transit, Holland and Davies finally arrived on board Admiral Gensoul's flagship.

Vice Admiral Le Luc's early afternoon cable in which he told Gensoul that "the Admiral of the Fleet has given orders for all French forces in the Mediterranean to rally to you immediately" had been sent *en clair*. Not surprisingly, the interception of this unencrypted cable by British monitoring stations stoked anxiety in the admiralty. As Holland and Davies approached Admiral Gensoul's flagship, Dudley Pound informed James Somerville that additional French warships were headed his way.

Somerville replied, "Am awaiting return of delegate whose entry and return delayed by minefield."[33]

At 4:46 p.m. Somerville received an additional message from Admiral Pound that heightened the pressure for a prompt resolution: "Settle matters quickly or you will have reinforcements to deal with."[34]

Somerville immediately signaled all ships of Force H: "Preparative ANVIL at 1730."[35]

Cedric Holland, in the temporary limbo of Gensoul's barge, unaware of the approaching French ships, would now have slightly more than one hour to convince Admiral Gensoul to prevent a deadly battle between the French and British navies.

As the admiral's barge, dwarfed by warships at anchor in Mers-el-Kébir, motored toward the *Dunkerque* at the far end of the breakwater, Cedric Holland was the center of attention. Many of the upper decks were packed with French sailors; some stood at attention.

Holland took note of the posture of the French ships that he passed. "All ships were in an advanced state of readiness for sea. All directors and control positions visible were manned, and all director rangefinders in tops of battleships, with the exception of the 'STRASBOURG' were trained in the direction of our fleet. Tugs were ready by the sterns of each battleship. Guns were trained fore and aft."[36]

Every one of Holland's attempts to persuade Admiral Gensoul with a written plea had been coldly rebuffed. As Gensoul's barge made multiple passes between the *Dunkerque* and the *Foxhound*'s motorboat through the day, both sides aired their arguments and absorbed the other's rebuttals in printed scripts and short notes written by hand on signal pads. The negotiations between Britain and France were now about to enter their final phase: direct, unscripted, and weighted with a full day's worth of emotion.

As Holland climbed on board the *Dunkerque*, as time slipped away, everything rode on this opportunity for the flawed, French-speaking British captain to negotiate face-to-face with the French admiral. From his mastery of the French language to his immersion in the culture of *la Marine nationale* and his proven ability to work amicably with Gensoul and other French officers, Cedric Holland was confident that everything in his career had prepared him for this moment.

CHAPTER 19

THE RED RIBBON OF THE FRENCH LEGION OF HONOR

CEDRIC HOLLAND WROTE this account of the negotiations in Admiral Gensoul's cabin. "I was piped over the side on arrival and received by the Chief of Staff [Captain Danbé]. Although large numbers of the crew were on the upper deck there was a marked lack of officers to be seen, both on our arrival and departure. . . . We were shown into the Admiral's cabin by the Chief of Staff, where we were greeted very formally by Admiral Gensoul."[1]

Holland displayed a subtle but clear sign of his solidarity with the French Navy. The single decoration on his white linen jacket was the red ribbon of the French Legion of Honor, which had been bestowed by Admiral Darlan.[2]

> The Admiral was clearly extremely indignant and angry at the course of events. He commenced by stating that he had only consented to see me at this stage because should we open fire the first shot would not only alienate the whole French Navy, but would be tantamount to a declaration of war between France and Great Britain. That if our aim was to ensure that the French fleet would not be used against Great Britain, the use of force would not achieve our aim. We might sink his ships at Oran but we should find the whole of the rest of the French Navy actively against us.

After completing his preamble, Admiral Gensoul unpacked his grievances:

> He was angry at the sudden presentation of terms which he considered as an ultimatum, and also at the laying of mines at the

entrances to the harbour, which he pointed out prevented him in any case from being able to accept or carry out the three terms (a), (b) or (c), and he rejected out of hand the idea of sinking his ships forthwith, saying it was impossible to abandon the ships at a moment's notice, and he reiterated his former statement given to Admiral North that he would sink his ships to prevent them from falling into German or Italian hands.

The impassioned debate Holland had expected to dive into within hours of his arrival that morning now ensued:

I explained most carefully to him that the British Government were unable to accept this latter statement as a sufficient guarantee that the ships would not fall into enemy hands and be used against us. Although we trusted his word and the similar promises given by Admirals Ollive, de Laborde and Esteva, that they would do everything possible to prevent their ships from falling into enemy hands, we could not trust the Germans or the Italians who would do all they could to achieve this end.

Admiral Gensoul, however, would not listen to this argument, and said he was convinced that the steps taken were adequate to sink his ships whatever happened. I pointed out by sinking his ships, he would be anyway breaking the terms of the Armistice, and by his own action. Should he accept any one of the terms we had offered to him that morning, he would be acting under "Force majeure" and the blame for any action would rest on us.

To this, he replied that, so long as Germany and Italy abided by the Armistice terms and allowed the French fleet to remain with French crews flying the French flag in a French Metropolitan or Colonial port, he would do the same, and not until Germany or Italy had broken their promises would he break the terms laid down, and that these were his orders signed by Admiral Darlan.

Holland responded to Gensoul's commitment to "his orders signed by Darlan" by explaining that both he and Vice Admiral Somerville had stretched the orders they had received from their admiralty, and stressed that unless one of Britain's conditions was "accepted, or immediate preparations made to sink the ships, Admiral Somerville would act under these orders and use force." Holland added, "Admiral Somerville had on his own responsibility, disobeyed those orders by not taking action within the time laid down, thus showing his desire to avoid the use of force if this were possible."

Portholes and air scuttles that would normally have admitted intermittent wisps of relief were screwed shut in response to Gensoul's earlier order to action stations. Drenched in sweat from the oppressive heat in the admiral's cabin, Holland and Gensoul pressed their respective arguments with rising tension.

> It was at this stage, I think that Admiral Gensoul began to think that force might really be used, and he produced a secret and personal copy of the orders received from and signed by Admiral Darlan dated 24th June, timed 1255. It was noted that the opening sentence read that this would be the last cypher message from him that they would receive. This would seem to be a further indication of the argument that I put to Admiral Gensoul through the Flag Lieutenant that morning, that Admiral Darlan was no longer in control.
>
> In giving me these orders, he asked and received my assurances that the contents would not be allowed to be disseminated, as if the Italians or Germans knew of the existence of these orders they would take action immediately. Apart from laying down clearly what steps were to be taken to prevent ships from falling into enemy hands, they mentioned also sailing the French Fleet to the U.S.A. and that ships were not again to operate actively against Germany or Italy.
>
> This appeared to be so close to the term (c) laid down that there seemed to be a chance to persuade the Admiral to accept this latter one. Time was getting very short. It was by then 1700.
>
> Admiral Gensoul however, remained stubborn, and would not give way further except to say that steps had been taken to

commence the reduction of crews that morning by demobilizing a certain number of reservists.

I again pointed out that Admiral Somerville must obey his orders and use force unless the terms were accepted to our satisfaction immediately, to which Admiral Gensoul reiterated that the first shot fired would alienate our two navies and do untold harm to us, and that he would reply to force by force.

Asked if he had received any answer from his Government to the message he had sent that morning, he rather unconvincingly replied that the answer was "resist by force."

An aide entered Gensoul's cabin at 5:15 p.m with a new message from Vice Admiral Somerville. After a quick glance, Gensoul handed the signal pad to Holland without speaking a word: "If one of our propositions is not accepted by 1730, British Summer time I shall have to sink your ships."[3]

In the broad bay outside the harbor, signalmen on HMS *Hood* were ordered to "string together and hoist the series of flags ZHH 1—readiness for instant action."[4]

With just fifteen minutes remaining before Somerville's deadline, Holland realized he had one final chance to prevent catastrophe. He asked for a signal pad and drafted a concise message that he showed Admiral Gensoul before having it flashed by one of the *Dunkerque*'s signalmen to the *Foxhound* and from there to Admiral Somerville on the *Hood*:

To V.A.(H) [Vice-Admiral on the Hood] from Captain Holland via Foxhound.

Admiral Gensoul says crews being reduced and if threatened by enemy would go to Martinique or U.S.A. but this not quite our proposition. Can get no nearer.

Signed Holland[5]

While Holland wrote his message, Gensoul picked up a pencil and drafted a longer statement. Gensoul's note, which outlined "the orders which he intended to obey," was written for posterity and was not flashed to Somerville. Gensoul simply handed it to Holland. It read,

1. The French Fleet cannot do otherwise than apply the clauses of the Armistice—on account of the consequences which would be borne by Metropolitan France.
2. Formal orders have been received, and these orders have been sent to all Commanding Officers, so that if, after the Armistice, there is risk of the ships falling into enemy hands they would be taken to the U.S.A. or scuttled.
3. These orders will be carried out.
4. Since yesterday, 2 July, the ships now at Oran and Mers-el-Kebir have begun their demobilisation (reduction of crews). Men belonging to North Africa have been disembarked.[6]

An officer interrupted the meeting at 5:20 p.m. to hand Gensoul one final cable. Gensoul, at last, read the long-delayed message that Vice Admiral Le Luc had sent three hours earlier at Admiral Darlan's behest, in which he empowered Gensoul to order other French forces to join him. As a result of the crippled French communication system, the message had been read by the British and forwarded to Somerville as a warning before it reached Gensoul.

Holland's urgent message in which he reported the reduction in French crews and the possibility of French ships steaming to Martinique or to America in reaction to a German or Italian threat reached Somerville on the *Hood* at 5:29 p.m., just one minute before his deadline.

Holland and Somerville both knew it fell short of the absolute requirements laid down by Winston Churchill and the admiralty. A promise from Gensoul to immediately steam to Martinique or the United States would have been acceptable. But a flight that was conditioned on indications of a German or Italian takeover could not be countenanced.

Time and the opportunity for compromise were about to run out. With nothing more to accomplish on board the *Dunkerque*, and with Somerville's lethal deadline so near, Captain Holland took his leave. He noted that at this point Gensoul was more amiable than he had been when Holland first arrived on board. But "even at that stage I do not believe that he was certain that fire would be opened."

In his final conversation with Captain Danbé, Holland said that as he headed back to the body of Force H, he would remain alert for signals from the *Dunkerque*. When Holland and Bernard Dufay saluted each other for the final time on that long day, both officers were in tears.[7]

As Holland climbed down to the admiral's barge from the *Dunkerque* at 5:25 that evening, he heard new calls to action stations by French buglers. Holland noted, however, "Very little effort seemed to be made to go to Action Stations." Crew members on several of the ships still stood on their upper decks. On Étienne Sicard's ship, the *Bretagne*, the officer of the watch "saluted smartly as we passed."

The barge made a swift crossing to the net defenses and Holland's waiting motorboat. Holland and Davies transferred back to their sitting boat at 5:35 p.m., untied it from the buoy, and started back at full speed in the direction of Force H.

In the best possible circumstances, Holland and Davies still had at least an hour's passage through seven miles of open water to reach their ship. Holland later noted that they "were clear of the net defences and about one mile to seaward when fire was opened."[8]

PART 4

MORTAL ENEMIES

CHAPTER 20

THE EVIL MINUTE

ELEVEN DAYS AFTER FRANCE signed Germany's armistice agreement in the rail carriage at Compiègne; twelve hours after Cedric Holland approached the lighthouse at Cap Falcon on HMS *Foxhound*; ninety-nine minutes after Holland finally stepped on board the *Dunkerque* for his meeting with Admiral Gensoul; and twenty-nine minutes after Holland left Gensoul's cabin with the two sides still short of an agreement, at 5:54 on the evening of July 3, 1940, a red and white flag—the signal to "Open fire—may be obeyed as soon as seen"—was hoisted on Vice Admiral James Somerville's flagship.[1]

Seconds later the Royal Navy's first shots against their former allies thundered from HMS *Resolution*, followed at twenty-second intervals by HMS *Valiant* and HMS *Hood*.[2] Eight hours of accumulated frustration, along with the simultaneous approach of nightfall and potential reinforcements for Gensoul's ships, had induced Somerville to forego all thoughts of bluffs and warning shots. He informed the admiralty of his action with a terse six-word signal: "Have opened fire on French ships."

In a letter that he wrote to his wife the next day, Somerville lamented, "I did my damndest to make the French Admiral accept our conditions and kept on postponing the evil minute."[3]

On board the *Hood*, seventeen-year-old signalman Ted Briggs, who had helped raise the massive "Open Fire" flag, described blasts so deafening that he felt as if his ears "had been sandwiched between two manhole covers." Briggs later wrote that the "concussions of the *Hood*'s eight fifteen-inch guns, screaming in horrendous harmony, shook the flag deck violently."[4]

The British ships fired from a range of 17,500 yards. The passage of each 2,000-pound round from muzzle to target lasted twenty seconds. Spotter planes from the *Ark Royal* were aloft to provide feedback to Somerville's ships on the accuracy of their broadsides.

Vice Admiral Somerville had eased his ships to the west a short time before they opened fire, which forced French ships to return fire from awkward elevated angles over nearby Fort Santon, standing more than six hundred feet above the shoreline. Although Somerville's maneuver loosened his seal on the harbor at Mers-el-Kébir, he counted on his ad hoc minefield to prevent the escape of any French ships. British gunnery officers used the Mers-el-Kébir lighthouse "as a Laying and Training mark" to perfect their lines of fire, deliberately aiming their first shots short of the lighthouse to confirm their aim, then working their way forward to the sitting French ships with devastating accuracy.

Even the short falls had deadly consequences, blasting the breakwater and raining shards of stone on the *Bretagne*, *Strasbourg*, *Provence*, and *Dunkerque*.[5] A French historian wrote of "dozens of sailors" who were "reduced to bloody rags" by those fragments.[6]

At 5:57 p.m., three minutes after opening fire from his vantage point ten miles offshore, Vice Admiral Somerville saw and heard an enormous explosion from the midst of the French warships. This blast was soon followed by "an immense column of smoke several hundred feet high." Another, smaller explosion followed about a minute later.[7]

A massive bloom of smoke—punctuated by sharp bursts of amber flame—enveloped the harbor. British fire control officers had close to zero visibility of the now moving targets they had sighted with meticulous care in the previous hours. Pilots and spotters in their circling biplanes also struggled to make out the details of the chaos in the crescent at Mers-el-Kébir. The shelling continued, nonetheless.

The give-and-take barrage agitated every bodily sense of the French seamen. Concussive blasts that knocked men off their feet accompanied ear-bursting explosions. Billowing smoke and a thick haze of oil mist was so dense that men could taste the vapor that also stung their eyes. A bouquet of noxious odors, including the stench of burnt cordite and the reek of fuel oil—some of it floating on the surface, some of it burning—saturated the air.

Somerville assumed that the initial large explosion "was caused by the blowing up of a battleship in the *Bretagne* class." "*Bretagne* class" was the name assigned to three super-dreadnaught battleships constructed by France during World War I—the *Bretagne* and the *Provence*, both of which were at Mers-el-Kébir, and the *Lorraine*, which sailed under Vice Admiral Godfroy at Alexandria. He suspected that the second, smaller explosion was from a French destroyer.

Vice Admiral Somerville's assumption about the large blast, which could be heard forty miles away, was correct.[8] The *Bretagne* was hit by a barrage of fifteen-inch shells, each of which delivered nearly a half ton of high explosive. Although she had slipped her mooring within seconds of the first shell-splash, the *Bretagne* had been slow to make her way from the jetty, and her stern was devastated by the initial salvoes. As a column of flame rose several hundred feet into the air, she began to settle into the harbor.

Water poured in through the gaping hole in the aft section of the *Bretagne*, crippling her ability to maneuver. On board the wounded ship, Étienne Sicard saw flame and smoke from the *Bretagne*'s stern and from multiple gun turrets. When spotters in her crow's nest attempted to abandon their stations, they found their ladders searing hot. Several who attempted to descend by rope crashed to the deck when their lines caught fire.

When the *Bretagne*'s commanding officer issued the order to abandon ship, his men ran to the fore part of the burning vessel and dove into the harbor.[9] Before Sicard reached the bow, he saw, heard, and felt another large explosion after a British shell hit a powder hold. After listing severely to starboard, the *Bretagne* capsized in less than one minute. Sicard later recalled, "everything cracked and moaned as the bridge was hurled into the water. . . . I sank down . . . about 40 feet under the water but was able to . . . keep my breath. . . . By the time I reached the surface the *Bretagne* had already almost disappeared."[10]

A thick layer of fuel topped the water and blackened every man afloat. Random wisps of fire taunted the swimmers with the potential of horrific death. Although the fuel did not burst into flames, the slick coating complicated the work of rescuers in gruesome ways, making it next to impossible to pull exhausted and wounded men from the harbor, even when clutched by their hair in desperation.

French journalist Pierre Varillon shared stories of "innocent victims" and "obscure heroes" in the immediate wake of the assault in his 1949 book about Mers-el-Kébir.[11] A seaman from the *Dunkerque* dove into the oil-saturated water a dozen times, bringing a comrade to the surface each time before he finally collapsed, exhausted. A quartermaster who suffered a broken collarbone and swam with one arm made three rescue dives.

Étienne Sicard swam for roughly thirty minutes before one of the small French launches searching for survivors rescued him. Sicard was one of the fortunate few from the *Bretagne*, which lost 1,079 men and sustained the most casualties by far of the ships under Admiral Gensoul's command.[12]

In the summer of 1941, salvage divers found the remains of dozens of men who were presumed to have survived for hours—perhaps even days—on board the *Bretagne* after the attack, trapped in the ship's mangled hulk, only to die lingering deaths.[13]

French ships, which had raised steam throughout the afternoon, were in motion within minutes of the first British shell-falls and maneuvered through the suddenly cluttered harbor with random degrees of fortune. The *Strasbourg* vacated her berth just before the multiple splashes of a salvo and was the most fortunate by far. Multiple misses followed in her wake. The wake of the *Strasbourg* proved to be a perilous location.

The *Mogador*, a destroyer steaming a slight distance behind the *Strasbourg*, was struck by a fifteen-inch shell near her stern. The force of this explosion set off the depth charges carried on her deck, which further obliterated one hundred feet of the destroyer's stern.[14] Although thirty-seven men were killed, the *Mogador* was more fortunate than the *Bretagne* in that she remained sufficiently seaworthy to be towed and beached on the shoreline.[15]

After escorting Cedric Holland and Lieutenant Commander Davies back to their waiting motorboat in Admiral Gensoul's barge, Bernard

Dufay made it back on board the *Dunkerque* five minutes before the British opened fire on his ship.[16] Although she immediately returned fire, the *Dunkerque* was neither as nimble nor as fortunate as the *Strasbourg*. While other vessels cast off their lines within seconds of the first shell splashes, the *Dunkerque* remained secured to the jetty for a mystifying few minutes. An inquiry revealed later that "the deck parties fore and aft responsible for casting off had either gone to action stations within the ship or had fled for cover once the ships guns had opened up and the first British shells began to fall."[17]

Once she was finally underway, Gensoul's flagship was struck in her stern. (The propensity for French ships to attract shellfire to their sterns was not coincidental; it was a consequence of their stern-out mooring at Mers-el-Kébir.) That fifteen-inch shell did minimal harm, but an ensuing broadside of three additional armor piercing shells severely damaged the *Dunkerque*, with catastrophic effect to her crew.

The least destructive of the three shells ricocheted off the turret of one of the *Dunkerque*'s upper thirteen-inch guns. A fragment punched into a different turret, set fire to a stack of ammunition, and asphyxiated the gun crew.[18] The second shell pierced into a boiler room, causing the sudden release of high-pressure steam. Pierre Varillon described mechanics whose faces were erased by the sudden rush of scalding vapor.[19] That second shell also sliced the electrical cabling to the rudder. As a result, the 26,500-ton battleship, finally underway from the jetty, "had to be steered manually using an emergency four horsepower Renault motor."[20]

The most damaging blast tore a hole at the waterline amidships. A sudden flood of salt water fouled the ship's fuel oil and damaged the ship's electrical system. Dozens of men were mangled, ripped, crushed, and charred beyond recognition.[21]

In a cruel stroke of irony, the *Dunkerque* had been specifically targeted throughout the barrage by HMS *Hood*, her sailing partner from early in the war. This was not deliberate malice. Rather, the *Hood* was ordered to target "the northernmost vessel in the line of warships lying at the mole," which happened to be the *Dunkerque*.[22]

Captain M. J. M. Seguin, the commander of Admiral Gensoul's flagship, ordered the beaching of the *Dunkerque* on the shore of St. André on the far side of the harbor. Despite the damage she had suffered, the *Dunkerque* fired at least forty shells back in the direction of the *Hood* as she made her way to the shore.[23]

The disposition of the French ships relative to Force H resulted in especially awkward firing angles over Fort Santon. The battleship *Provence* had been the first French ship to return fire, unleashing a salvo as her crew cut the lines that secured her to the breakwater.

The *Provence* had to fire "over and across the *Dunkerque*," adding to the cacophony on Gensoul's flagship. The *Provence* performed this acrobatic feat with remarkable precision, with one deadly exception. A fire control officer on the *Dunkerque* bled to death after the base of a shell fired from the *Provence* clipped him and severed his femoral artery.[24]

As *Provence* steamed from her berth, she too was hit in the stern by a fifteen-inch shell, which ignited a large fire. The impact of the blast also knocked a section of armor plate awry, which resulted in severe flooding. *Provence* temporarily dropped anchor in the harbor and was later beached.

Father R. P. de Gueuser, a Jesuit chaplain, tended to the divine concerns of sailors on the *Provence*. After offering a general absolution to the men on his ship—"Recite an act of contrition, then do your duty. . . . Long live France!"—Father de Gueuser knelt to provide direct comfort to the men most in need of a priest's ministrations, "reciting the prayers of the dying . . . consoling, absolving, closing the eyes" of the dead; an angel of consolation in the midst of hellfire.[25]

As French gunners returned fire, their initial shots fell wide, but their accuracy improved with every salvo, helped by bursts of color that were specific to each French ship. The shells of each vessel carried a dye with a unique pigment—red, green, blue, and magenta for the *Dunkerque*, *Strasbourg*, *Provence*, and *Bretagne*, respectively—splattering a palette in the bay that enabled gunnery officers to track their aim as they straddled British ships, splashing closer with every salvo.[26]

With French shells falling close, the captain of HMS *Enterprise* ordered the six depth charges on her quarterdeck to be jettisoned to avoid potential catastrophe.[27] HMS *Wrestler*, which had been positioned to guard the harbor's entrance, was an especially vulnerable target for gunners from the forts above Mers-el-Kébir. In his report to Vice Admiral Somerville, *Wrestler*'s commanding officer recorded his desperation: "Smoke was made and drastic alterations of course enabled punishment to be avoided although at the time it did not seem possible that the ship could avoid being hit and probably sunk." Before Somerville ordered her to withdraw out of range, the *Wrestler*'s commander estimated that "at least one hundred shells of 4-inch to 6-inch caliber" had splashed near her, with some shell fragments falling on her deck.[28]

At 6:04 p.m., ten minutes after the first shots were fired, a "yellow and blue vertically halved flag" was hoisted on the *Hood*'s masthead, signaling the ships in Force H to cease fire.[29] The three British capital ships—the *Hood*, *Resolution*, and *Valiant*—had each fired twelve salvoes, a total of 144 fifteen-inch (or 380mm) rounds.[30] The British had fired with remarkable accuracy. Only five shots landed outside the harbor, one of which decapitated the lighthouse that overlooked Mers-el-Kébir.

The French ships had fallen silent, and Somerville reasoned "that by ceasing fire I should give them an opportunity to abandon their ships and thus avoid further loss of life." He ordered his ships to make smoke, providing a defensive screen of man-made fog against French gunners. Stokers in the engine room of each vessel adjusted their valves, "admitting just too much oil and shutting off just too much air" into their furnaces, causing extraordinary clouds to billow from their funnels.[31]

Force H, now wrapped in a protective veil, eased to the west, out of range of the guns firing from the fort at Mers-el-Kébir, but still close enough to resume their shelling of the French ships if necessary. When Somerville received a report that French planes in Oran were scrambling for a possible attack, he ordered his ships farther out to sea. Even after Force H halted its barrage, signalmen on the *Dunkerque* sent repeated messages by wireless and signal lamp, imploring the British to cease fire. To help ensure an end to the carnage, Gensoul complied with a demand that Captain Holland had passed along earlier in the afternoon: "If you accept the terms hoist a large square flag at the masthead."

Gensoul ordered Bernard Dufay to find a square of fabric that was large enough and bright enough to be visible to Force H. It could not be a white flag due to the indelible implications of that signal. And so, at 6:13 p.m., a signalman raised a bedspread—colored beige, with light blue stripes—atop the beached *Dunkerque*. As Gensoul later wrote, "the English proposals were temporarily satisfied and I therefore did not hesitate to use this signal for a few minutes."[32]

Although the gunfire had paused and the French were standing down, Somerville was concerned that his mission to incapacitate Admiral Gensoul's *Force de Raid* had not yet been fulfilled. At 6:35 p.m., Somerville signaled, "Unless I see your ships sinking, I shall open fire again."[33]

CHAPTER 21

THE WORST POSSIBLE OUTCOME

BRITISH NAVAL HISTORIAN David Brown, author of the most detailed account of the run-up to the attack at Mers-el-Kébir, believed: "The worst possible outcome of Operation 'Catapult' was an escape by French capital ships."[1]

The worst happened.

Within minutes of the first British shots, their spotting aircraft reported French ships in motion, with several steaming in the direction of the mined entrance to the port. The British barely missed a knockout blow on one of their coveted targets. A salvo splashed into the *Strasbourg*'s vacated mooring at 5:59 p.m.

The *Strasbourg* departed in such haste that she left her anchors in the grasp of the mud at the bottom of the harbor. Their chains slipped through their hawseholes as she cast off her stern lines.[2] Although the *Strasbourg* escaped a direct hit, she endured scars, scrapes, and charred teak planks on her decks from raining debris in the aftermath of the explosions that surrounded her—mostly from the obliterated *Bretagne*. Less visible but more significant, a small chunk of concrete from the smashed jetty impeded an air intake valve, which resulted in an immense cascade of dark smoke from the *Strasbourg*'s funnel.[3]

With five magnetic mines planted at the mouth of the harbor, James Somerville believed that Admiral Gensoul would accept that his ships were trapped. He was equally confident that no French captain would attempt to break free on his own.

When a pilot from one of the *Ark Royal*'s aircraft reported at 6:20 p.m. that "a *Dunkerque*-class destroyer" had made its way out of the harbor and was heading east, Somerville discounted the information. (The

Dunkerque and the *Strasbourg* were the only two ships in the *Dunkerque* class.[4]) The escape of a French ship was barely conceivable, and there had been multiple false reports through the day from airborne observers. As Somerville later wrote, "In view of other reports of movements which had subsequently been cancelled, the difficulty of observation due to smoke and the certainty I entertained that the French would abandon their ships, I did not attach sufficient weight to this report."

The *Strasbourg* used the heavy pall of smoke that enveloped the French ships to her advantage. In addition, although British magnetic mines still imperiled her path, her escape route had been widened within the past hour when machine gunners on a French destroyer demolished several buoys that supported a portion of the antisubmarine boom that blocked the harbor.[5] Captain Louis Collinet deftly and fortuitously maneuvered the *Strasbourg* away from Mers-el-Kébir, out of reach of Somerville's ships. Collinet's boldness paid off as the *Strasbourg* slipped the harbor at 6:13 p.m., accompanied by five destroyers (the *Kersaint*, *Lynx*, *Le Terrible*, *Tigre*, and *Volta*).[6] Once she reached open water, the *Strasbourg* sped to the northeast with her small convoy in the direction of the naval base at Toulon on the French Mediterranean coast.

While Vice Admiral Somerville struggled to trust reports of a breakaway battleship, the *Strasbourg* sped to the northeast at twenty-eight knots. At the same time, Somerville ordered Force H to ease in an opposite direction, northwest, at eighteen knots to evade fire from the batteries of the fort overlooking Mers-el-Kébir.

Finally, at 6:30 p.m., almost half an hour after the *Strasbourg*'s break for freedom, a report from yet another British reconnaissance pilot convinced Somerville that a ship had escaped . . . although no one knew which French ship had made its way out of the harbor. By this point, the *Strasbourg* had opened a gap of twenty-five miles between itself and Force H.

The methodical choreography of takeoffs and landings on the deck of the *Ark Royal* skipped a beat at the worst possible time for James Somerville. He had ordered a wave of six Swordfish torpedo, spotting, and reconnaissance (TSR) planes—open cockpit, three-seat biplanes that could carry either bombs or torpedoes—to follow up on the initial shellfire and

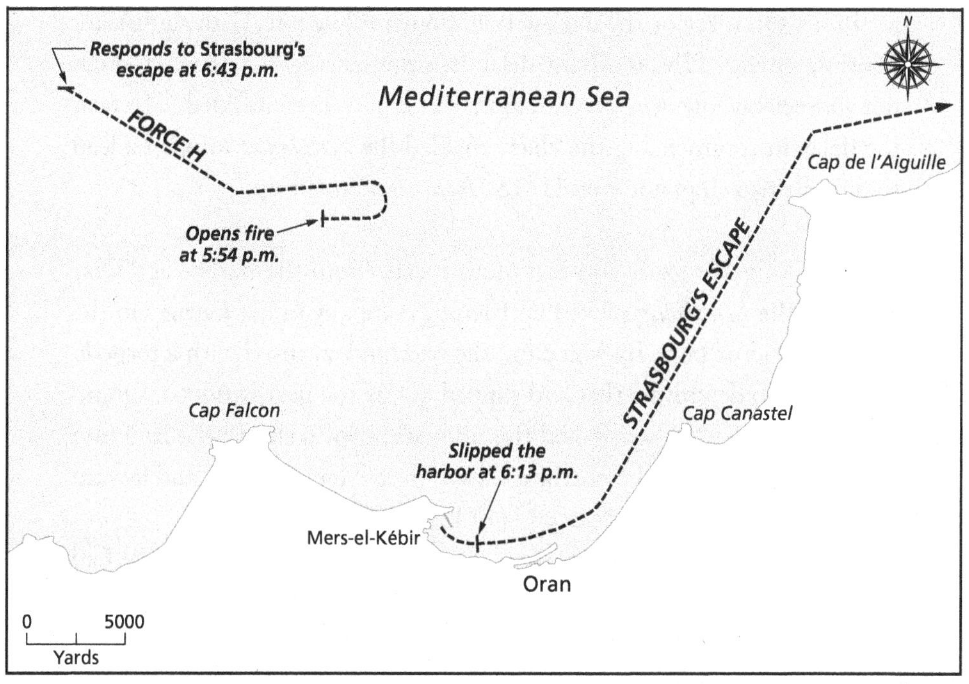

MAP 6. *Strasbourg*'s Escape

administer a coup de grace on any surviving French ships with an airborne torpedo attack.[7] However British spotter planes over the harbor were now running low on fuel and needed to land. The torpedo bombers' departures were held back until 6:25 p.m. as the deck remained clear for the return of the reconnaissance aircraft.

As a result of the delay, and in response to multiple confirmations of the movement of French vessels, Somerville ordered the Swordfish to divert from their planned attack on the wounded ships in the harbor. Instead, they would fly in pursuit of the French battleship that was steaming to the east.

At 6:43 p.m., Somerville finally ordered his fastest cruisers and destroyers—with the *Hood* in the van—to pursue the fleeing French ships. He now accepted that either the *Dunkerque* or the *Strasbourg* had escaped. The British did not know, and remained unsure for more than twenty-four hours, which ship had gotten away.

In his summary of the day's action, Somerville wrote, with significant understatement, "The resultant delay in commencing the chase, though not appreciably affecting the situation, could have been avoided."[8] In fact, the delay in commencing the chase enabled the *Strasbourg* to open a lead that no British ship, not even HMS *Hood*, could make up.

After making her swift and fortuitous escape from the harbor at Mers-el-Kébir, the *Strasbourg* picked up friendly company in her journey to the safety of a home port. By 7:30 p.m., she had rendezvoused with a torpedo boat and two destroyers that had slipped out of the nearby port of Oran.[9] Six cruisers from Algiers joined this ad hoc convoy a short time later and continued to speed to the northeast, away from Mers-el-Kébir and toward Toulon on the Mediterranean coast of France.[10]

The French reinforcements that Churchill, Pound, and Somerville had feared never materialized in the proximity of Force H. Only a handful of ships heeded Vice Admiral Le Luc's message to "Get under way, ready for action, and report to the admiral in the *Dunkerque* at Oran." By the time they finally approached Mers-el-Kébir, they joined the *Strasbourg*'s convoy instead of engaging Force H.

The fragment of Force H led by HMS *Hood*, still in hopeless pursuit of the *Strasbourg*, never made-up significant ground. Unlike the British ships, however, the Swordfish torpedo bombers from the *Ark Royal* were able to catch up to the fleeing French ships. The massive plume of dark smoke that streamed from *Strasbourg*'s choked funnel made her an easy target to follow. Captain Collinet was told that a resolution to his ship's heavy tail of smoke would require the temporary shutdown of one of her boilers. Since this would have reduced her speed from twenty-eight knots to twenty knots, Collinet elected to delay the repair.[11]

Captain Collinet reported that one British bomb fell less than one hundred feet off the port side of the *Strasbourg*.[12] Aside from that near miss, and despite reports from the *Ark Royal* pilots of shots fired, torpedoes launched, and contact flashes against the darkening sky, the *Strasbourg* and her entourage suffered no damage in their passage away from Mers-el-Kébir.

The *Strasbourg* and her shielding destroyers had continued to widen the gap and were now several dozen miles ahead of the *Hood*. Somerville called off the chase by the British ships at 8:20 p.m.[13] HMS *Hood* and company altered course to the west, back toward the body of Force H.

Somerville summarized his rationale for abandoning the futile chase in the dark evening seas: "The prospects of locating and engaging the French battlecruiser at night were small," and "I did not consider that the possible loss of British ships were justified as against the possibility of French ships being allowed to fall into German or Italian hands."[14]

After a French reconnaissance pilot reported that the British pursuers had reversed course, Captain Collinet ordered a reduction in speed to allow repairs that would reduce the *Strasbourg*'s billowing smoke. To the horror of the officers who opened the armored hatch to the boiler room, twenty-five men were unconscious and five were dead, victims of toxic fumes and excessive heat. Despite that grim discovery, after the incapacitated men were tended to and ventilation repairs were completed, the *Strasbourg* resumed her journey at full speed with a less prominent tail of smoke after a one-hour delay.[15]

The *Strasbourg* completed her voyage home, free from additional harassment. With her jubilant crew lining her decks, the ship eased into the French naval base at Toulon shortly after nine o'clock on the evening of July 4. Her welcome included boisterous cheers from the crews of anchored ships and overlapping renditions of *La Marseillaise*, the national anthem of France, played by multiple ships' bands. Having escaped Force H, the *Strasbourg* was now "safely" nestled in a harbor where she was potentially vulnerable to the whims of Adolf Hitler and his naval commanders.

At 10 Downing Street, John Colville noted that by 7:00 on the evening of July 3, "signals began to come through that we were heavily engaged with the French." Chief of the Imperial General Staff (CIGS), General Sir John Dill, told Colville that he had observed Churchill pacing the room, muttering, "Terrible, terrible."[16] Colville also recorded Dill's observation that "he had never seen anything comparable, that two nations who were fighting for civilization had to turn and rent each other while the barbarians sat back and laughed. It was indeed the most tragic irony in history, and an event that could not have been entertained as possible a fortnight ago."

Additional details streamed in from Mers-el-Kébir while Churchill met with the chiefs of staff at 11:30 p.m. According to Colville, Churchill remarked to A. V. Alexander "that the French are fighting with all their vigour for the first time since the war broke out." Churchill added that he expected Britain and France to be at war the following day.

French warplanes sporadically pestered the now dispersed ships of Force H during the last ninety minutes of sunlight on the evening of July 3. Four bombs fell within fifty yards of the *Wrestler* but did no damage.[17]

After the *Strasbourg* made her stunning escape, pilots in Somerville's spotter planes reported that although several French ships were beached, others remained afloat in the harbor at Mers-el-Kébir. Somerville planned to employ Swordfish aircraft from the *Ark Royal* in a follow-up attack on the morning of July 4. Naval airmen would launch torpedoes at any French ships that were still afloat. With the likely menace of enemy submarines growing by the hour, Somerville wanted a quick, efficient, and lethal operation. There would be no forewarning to Admiral Gensoul.

Somerville's intended follow-up was thwarted by awful weather. Force H encountered heavy fog during the night of July 3 into July 4. By 4:00 a.m., fog in the Gulf of Oran had completely enveloped Somerville's ships. The weather remained so poor through the early morning hours that Admiral Lionel Wells, the vice admiral commanding aircraft carriers on board the *Ark Royal*, reported that he saw no alternative other than to abandon the planned operation.[18]

Somerville had received multiple messages from Gensoul "stating that his ships were hors-de-combat and that he was ordering personnel to evacuate their ships." With his ships potentially vulnerable targets of revenge, and with misgivings that another attack would be inhumane, Somerville returned to Gibraltar instead of resuming the attack on Mers-el-Kébir.

British ships suffered no direct hits during the exchange of shellfire at Mers-el-Kébir. HMS *Hood* and HMS *Wrestler* incurred "superficial damage." Two men on the *Hood* suffered minor wounds. Five British planes were downed. With the exception of two men from one of the Swordfish aircraft who were killed, all the crews were rescued.[19]

The foul weather in the western Mediterranean provided Admiral Gensoul, his ships, and his men with a temporary—if short-lived—respite from hostilities. Six ships, the *Strasbourg* and the five destroyers that joined her dash for freedom, were now gone. The harbor at Mers-el-Kébir, though less crowded, was a panorama of ruin.

The *Dunkerque* was aground on the beach of Saint André. The *Provence* was beached on the nearby shore of Roseville. The remains of the *Mogador*, now without a stern, were beached at Bains la Reine. The hulk of the *Bretagne* was beneath the harbor that was fouled with oil and littered with debris.

Work crews remained on the beached *Dunkerque*, fighting small fires, working to restore power, and searching for survivors. Every section of the ship revealed fresh horrors to the men tasked with rescue and repair, with bodies of fellow seamen crushed, shredded, steamed, or charred—often beyond recognition. Gensoul and his staff moved ashore to quarters in nearby Oran late on July 4.

Even before the returning British ships were secured in Gibraltar at 7:00 on the night of July 4, the British admiralty conceived a new assignment for Force H. As James Somerville scribbled in his pocket diary, "Now have orders to take on *Richelieu* at Dakar. How I loathe it all."[20]

CHAPTER 22

THIS IS NO TIME FOR DOUBT OR WEAKNESS

AS MEMBERS OF PARLIAMENT SETTLED into the Palace of Westminster on the afternoon of July 4, 1940, most, if not all, were aware of a violent engagement between the French and British navies the previous day, but few knew the details. Shortly before four o'clock, Winston Churchill stood to describe the events at Mers-el-Kébir to a hushed and packed Commons:

> It is with sincere sorrow that I must now announce to the House the measures which we have felt bound to take in order to prevent the French Fleet from falling into German hands.
>
> When two nations are fighting together under long and solemn alliance against a common foe, one of them may be stricken down and overwhelmed, and may be forced to ask its Ally to release it from its obligations.
>
> But the least that could be expected was that the French Government, in abandoning the conflict and leaving its whole weight to fall upon Great Britain and the British Empire, would have been careful not to inflict needless injury upon their faithful comrade, in whose final victory the sole chance of French freedom lay, and lies.[1]

Churchill summarized the takeover of French ships in British ports. He provided an overview of the still active events in Alexandria. After saluting the "very gallant" Vice Admiral Godfroy, Churchill proclaimed, "But the most serious part of the story remains," and moved on to a more somber passage.

Churchill specifically mentioned, and complimented, James Somerville as "an officer who distinguished himself lately in the 'bringing-off' of over 100,000 Frenchmen during the evacuation from Dunkirk." He also noted the role of Cedric Holland, "a carefully chosen British officer . . . lately Naval attaché in Paris."

Churchill stood before the members of the house twenty-four hours after Holland climbed on board the *Dunkerque*. Somerville and Holland had not yet filed their detailed reports of the previous day's proceedings. In that vacuum, Churchill spoke of naturally assumed meetings between the British and French:

> All day the parleys continued, and we hoped until the afternoon that our terms would be accepted without bloodshed. However, no doubt in obedience to the orders dictated by the Germans from Wiesbaden, where the Franco-German Armistice Commission is in session, Admiral Gensoul refused to comply and announced his intention of fighting.
>
> Admiral Somerville was therefore ordered to complete his mission before darkness fell, and at 5.53 p.m. he opened fire upon this powerful French Fleet, which was also protected by its shore batteries. At 6 p.m. he reported that he was heavily engaged. The action lasted for some 10 minutes and was followed by heavy attacks from our naval aircraft, carried in the "Ark Royal." At 7.20 p.m. Admiral Somerville forwarded a further report, which stated that a battle cruiser of the "Strasbourg" class was damaged and ashore; that a battleship of the "Bretagne" class had been sunk.

The British were still unsure of the identity of the ship that had escaped: "While this melancholy action was being fought, either the battle cruiser 'Strasbourg' or the 'Dunkerque,' one or the other, managed to slip out of harbour in a gallant effort to reach Toulon or a North African port and place herself under German control."

Churchill turned his attention to the carnage at Mers-el-Kébir, and to the French ships now under British control:

> I fear the loss of life among the French and in the harbour must have been heavy, as we were compelled to use a severe measure of force and several immense explosions were heard. None of the

British ships taking part in the action was in any way affected in gun-power or mobility by the heavy fire directed upon them. I have not yet received any reports of our casualties, but Admiral Somerville's Fleet is, in all military respects, intact and ready for further action.

A large proportion of the French Fleet has, therefore, passed into our hands or has been put out of action or otherwise withheld from Germany by yesterday's events. The House will not expect me to say anything about other French ships which are at large except that it is our inflexible resolve to do everything that is possible in order to prevent them falling into the German grip.

Churchill offered no apologies and faced the future with his trademark resolve. As he neared the climax of his address, the prime minister turned in a slow circle, his arms spread wide, taking in the grave expressions of the men and women assembled in all four sides of the historic hall.[2]

I leave the judgment of our action, with confidence, to Parliament. I leave it to the nation, and I leave it to the United States. I leave it to the world and to history.

Now I turn to the immediate future. We must, of course, expect to be attacked, or even invaded, if that proves to be possible—it has not been proved yet—in our own island before very long. We are making every preparation in our power to repel the assaults of the enemy.

In the fullest harmony with our Dominions, we are moving through a period of extreme danger and of splendid hope, when every virtue of our race will be tested, and all that we have and are will be freely staked. This is no time for doubt or weakness. It is the supreme hour to which we have been called.

John Colville wrote that members of the Commons "listened enthralled and amazed. Gasps of surprise were audible" during Churchill's somber address as they absorbed barely conceivable details of a violent clash with Britain's recent ally.[3] American military attaché Colonel Raymond E. Lee, who witnessed Churchill's address from the Distinguished Strangers gallery, observed that Churchill "reveled in this great moment and his complete competence in dealing with it."[4]

To this time, Churchill's acceptance as prime minister from the opposition Labour and Liberal parties had been tepid at best. As Churchill ended his speech and took his seat on the treasury bench, members of Parliament unexpectedly began to rise and cheer as one without respect to party. As the cheering continued its cascade, Churchill lowered his chin into his chest as tears flowed down his cheeks. He was, for the first time—fifty-five days after assuming the mantle of prime minister—heartily embraced by all members of Parliament.

In the wake of the speech, as Churchill left the house, Colville heard him murmur to member of Parliament and former secretary of state for war Leslie Hore-Belisha, "This is heartbreaking for me."[5]

While the prime minister addressed the House of Commons, Lord Halifax, Britain's foreign secretary, shared the government's description of the previous day's events in the House of Lords. Halifax, of course, supported Churchill's decision to attack the French fleet; but on a personal level, he considered the British action "perfectly hateful" and a "beastly business."[6]

The two leaders' speeches were similar; in fact, they matched word-for-word in several sections, as if Churchill's speech served as the template for Halifax's address. However, much of what Halifax had to say was unique, and he made the speech his own. But the most striking statement that appears only in Lord Halifax's address rang with a pronounced Churchillian tone: "As regards the Government of Marshal Pétain, I am bound to observe that they placed the redemption of a promise to the enemy before the fulfilment of a solemn pledge to an Ally."[7]

CHAPTER 23

IT IS CRAZY TO FIGHT AMONG OURSELVES

AN AIDE AWAKENED Andrew Cunningham before sunrise on the morning of Thursday, July 4, 1940, with an urgent message from his French counterpart. Vice-Admiral Godfroy's letter, which preempted the ultimatum Cunningham planned to send that morning, began, "I have the honor to inform you that the situation no longer allows me and the forces that I command to even consider the solution which we spoke about last evening as acceptable."[1]

Godfroy's ire had ignited when he learned the details of Britain's assault on the French ships at Mers-el-Kébir. Cunningham later wrote about Godfroy's uncharacteristically fiery letter, in which the French admiral "repudiated every undertaking he had given, reserved to himself complete liberty of action, and left me no doubt that he proposed to try and get to sea, if necessary by fighting his way out of harbour."[2]

When Cunningham walked onto the deck of the *Warspite*, he saw French ships raising steam, and French turrets turned toward British ships. Godfroy later explained his turnabout: "Enlightened by what had happened at Mers-el-Kébir, I had, by daybreak on July 4, made all arrangements for an immediate fight."[3]

At first light, the harbor at Alexandria already stirred with the taut energy of naval crews preparing to sail their warships into battle. The unique circumstance of two warring fleets preparing to battle in the same harbor amplified the tension.

Cunningham wrote in his memoirs, "We, of course, were not behindhand in our preparations. Where necessary our battleships were kedged round to bring their broadsides to bear. Our destroyers and submarines were warned off to torpedo the French ships at once if they moved from their berths or opened fire."[4]

If July 3 at Mers-el-Kébir ended in the worst possible way for Britain, a battle in the confines of the harbor at Alexandria on July 4 would be an even greater disaster. A deadly battle that was specifically triggered by the British attack at Mers-el-Kébir would be a tragedy. Godfroy wrote that although he watched British vessels snaking through the harbor, "ready to launch their torpedoes at us," he was determined not to fire the first shot. If Cunningham's ships opened fire, Godfroy believed his men would have time to respond with torpedoes at close range.[5]

Despite this surprise turn of events, Cunningham had multiple advantages on his side, including that of time. "I knew it would take the French ships six to eight hours to raise steam and be ready to move." That might provide enough of a cushion to convince Godfroy and his men "to see reason" and refuse to fight or sail.[6]

As if the anxiety that filled the air was not sufficiently dense, a small squad of Italian bombers flew overhead at 8 a.m. Although the French and British crews were on the brink of combat, Cunningham was heartened to see crewmen from at least one French ship engage and fire at the Italian aircraft whose attack was ineffective and caused no casualties.[7]

To this point Cunningham had resisted any impulse to appeal directly to Godfroy's men. Now, with their compromise about to fracture and perhaps degrade into a bloodbath, Cunningham sought to convince French officers and ratings to challenge Godfroy's inclination to fight. Cunningham cabled his admiralty: "Am attempting to sow dissension among his ships' companies."[8]

A British officer translated a message into French to convey "the helplessness of their situation." The message was flashed by signal lamp multiple times to all French ships. As an extra measure, the message was also chalked onto large blackboards set on launches that slowly skimmed through the harbor. The message read,

> The British admiral does not want to sink your ships. What is the point of needlessly sacrificing lives while fighting against superior

> force? Our regrets for what happened are as deep as yours. We must do no more. We only ask that your ships be put in a condition where they cannot sail because if they leave they could fall into enemy hands. Liners which can take you to France are arriving soon. Great Britain continues the fight to destroy the Boches and the Italians and to re-establish France. It is crazy to fight among ourselves.[9]

Godfroy recorded his reaction to Cunningham's message:

> "The admiral does not want to sink your ships." If it was a frank and sincere affirmation—as I had no doubt—if he was really determined not to do it, then everything would probably work out.
>
> "My regrets for what happened are as deep as yours. We must do no more." It was really not possible to remain insensitive to this honest testimony of disapproval of the outrage of Mers-el-Kebir.
>
> "It's crazy to fight among ourselves." How can we not agree with this implicit disavowal of the actions which had led to this risk of fratricidal struggle?[10]

British officers, men who had worked with their French counterparts in port and at sea for the better part of two months, returned to the French ships to which they had been assigned and reasoned directly with their opposite numbers.

Cunningham's approach, which combined empathic dialog with an overt willingness to take deadly action, had the intended effect. Cunningham noted that "it was interesting to see the leaven gradually working among the French sailors."[11] French officers received their British counterparts "with cordiality and nowhere with hostility."

Commander Philippe Auboyneau of the French Navy, who had previously been quartered on the *Warspite*, had moved back to Godfroy's flagship after France signed the German armistice agreement. On the morning of July 4, he shuttled between the two admirals and played an integral role in helping their navies find common ground.

Godfroy was astonished when, at 2 p.m., his ships' commanders arrived at his flagship and requested a meeting. Godfroy later learned that Auboyneau had organized this meeting after visiting Cunningham's flagship.[12] After speaking with his officers for close to an hour, Vice Admiral Godfroy asked to meet with Admiral Cunningham on the *Warspite*. With input from his men—Philippe Auboyneau, in particular—René-Émile Godfroy finessed a solution that he could live with, an outcome that was also palatable to Andrew Cunningham and those who had hectored Cunningham from Whitehall and Downing Street. Godfroy refused to accept any of the three specific proposals presented by Cunningham. Instead, he offered to allow his force to remain "immobilized."[13] Godfroy added, "Auboyneau . . . told me that he had the impression that if I agreed to 'demilitarize' our ships, Admiral Cunningham would consider himself satisfied and would accept that this was done under my sole control, and not under British material constraints."

Godfroy, in his nuanced proposal, offered to "unload the majority of the fuel oil," to reserve a reduction in manpower "for later discussion," and to dismantle the obtorators (which prevented the calamitous escape of propellant gas from his big guns during firing) and deposit them at the quarters of the French consulate general in the city of Alexandria. The vague accommodation on the reduction of French crews removed the final obstacle that had prevented British approval of an agreement between the two admirals. Cunningham immediately accepted Godfroy's proposal and complimented his counterpart's "great dignity" in the matter.[14] This thoughtful compromise was a testament to the two bold and reasonable men who maintained direct, frequent, and candid communications, two experienced leaders who presumed they had earned the leeway to selectively disregard orders from their remote superiors who demanded more belligerent measures.

The French ships—drained of their fuel, disarmed, more lightly manned, and no longer a threat to flee or to fight—were now indisputably under British control.

Cunningham noted a short time afterward, "Never in my life have I experienced such a whole-hearted feeling of thankful relief."[15] Cunningham extended "a large share of the credit" to the British captains who "prevailed upon their opposite numbers."

Cunningham also praised Auboyneau for his tireless work toward a peaceful resolution. Auboyneau would join Charles de Gaulle's Free French forces before month's end, after first sending Admiral Darlan a respectful letter of apology for switching sides.[16] Darlan, on his part, stated on multiple occasions during the next two years that he now respected only one British officer: Andrew Cunningham.

Cunningham sent a brief message to the admiralty about the settlement at 3:30 on the afternoon of July 4, then followed with additional details in a signal that ended: "With the completion of the . . . de-fueling and de-arming measures I shall feel quite free to take the Fleet to sea to continue operations against the enemy."[17]

Cunningham had consistently deflected and sometimes turned a virtual blind eye to the unsubtle and sometimes "almost inept in its unwisdom" orders from his superiors. As Cunningham and Godfroy responded to events and orders during the first week of July, they did so with the impact on their opposite number in mind. They resolved the impasse in Alexandria without bloodshed or the destruction of a single ship. Cunningham ultimately did not, repeat, NOT fail in his mission to prevent the French ships from falling into German hands.

Early on the evening of July 4, several hours after he sent his summary of the events and their resolution in Alexandria to the British admiralty, Cunningham received a joint message from the first lord of the admiralty and the first sea lord: "After what must have been a most trying and anxious time your negotiations have achieved complete success. We offer you our most sincere congratulations. The Prime Minister also wishes his congratulations to be sent to you."[18]

It took the French just three days to reduce their crews in Alexandria by 70 percent. The men who disembarked were repatriated to France.

To Admiral Cunningham's great relief, with the French ships demilitarized in their berths, he now had freedom of action to sail at will against the Italian Navy. Malta was especially vulnerable and was in dire need of British support and resupply. Dozens of British subjects, including Cunningham's wife and two nieces, were rescued by the end of July 1940.[19]

Vice Admiral Godfroy wrote a letter to Cunningham in late July, in part to explain his "present reserve," and also to assure Cunningham that he looked upon him "with the same respect and sympathy as before." However, "I feel obliged to take into account for some time the grief of officers and petty officers of my squadron who have lost sons or brothers at Oran and would perhaps be hurt if we behaved as if nothing had happened."[20]

Admiral Godfroy and Force X remained in the purgatory of Alexandria for almost three years—despite pleas from Cunningham, and even Admiral Darlan, to ally with the Royal Navy. Godfroy joined the Free French Navy and sailed with British ships once again in May 1943 after the Allies routed Axis forces from North Africa.

Cunningham wrote that despite any residual bitterness carried by Godfroy over Mers-el-Kébir, "no success of the British fleet passed without his letter of cordial congratulation, no loss without his letter of sympathy."

Godfroy returned to the south of France after the war. He died in January 1981 at the age of ninety-six.

In October 1943, as Admiral Dudley Pound lay dying from the effects of a brain tumor, Winston Churchill asked Andrew Cunningham to succeed Pound as first sea lord.

After the war's end, the New Year's Honours' list of 1946 included Cunningham's elevation to Viscount Cunningham of Hyndhope.[21] The bonnie fechter was now a peer in the House of Lords. When the French government awarded Cunningham their Médaille militaire, he joined Winston Churchill as one of the only two living recipients of this most special honor.

Cunningham retired from the navy in June 1946. One of his most cherished possessions—a bell from his former flagship HMS *Warspite*—hung outside his house at Bishop's Waltham in Hampshire. The *Warspite*'s bell now rang only to summon Lord Cunningham from his garden.[22]

Andrew Cunningham's autobiography carries this passage near the end: "I have no profound philosophy of life to propound. As perhaps I have shown, I have always been inclined to rebel and to speak out against decisions that I felt to be wrong. Otherwise, I think I have usually taken things as I found them, and tried to make the best of them."[23]

Cunningham died in 1963 at the age of eighty and was buried at sea—not in his beloved Mediterranean but in the waters off the coast of Portsmouth.

CHAPTER 24

THAT FILTHY JOB IS OVER AT LAST

THE SMOKE AND THE FOG and the haze of uncertainty had cleared by July 5, 1940, and the British now knew the locations of all their primary targets. The *Strasbourg* was the ship that escaped, and the *Dunkerque* sat damaged on the harbor shore at Mers-el-Kébir. Was the *Dunkerque* still a threat? Was she sufficiently impaired to remove her from battle for at least a year? One careless comment by one of Admiral Darlan's heirs provided the answers the British were seeking. In a bid to boost morale in the suddenly reeling French Navy, Vice Admiral Jean-Pierre Esteva issued a press communiqué with uplifting news: "The damage to *Dunkerque* is minimal and the ship will soon be repaired!"[1]

The British wasted little time in formulating Operation Lever to further her disrepair. Instead of sailing to Dakar to take out the *Richelieu*, James Somerville and Force H were directed back to Mers-el-Kébir to complete the demolition of the *Dunkerque*.

Somerville shared his ongoing qualms about taking additional lives of his former allies in a July 6 letter to his wife Mary:

> Just before we sailed last night I made a final appeal to the Admiralty pointing out that this second bombardment of Dunkerque at Oran would inevitably mean not only a lot more French officers and men but also civilians [would be killed?—garbled handwriting] as the ships were quite close to the town of St Andre. I said that the Wednesday action must have caused very heavy casualties and asked if some means couldn't be found to induce the French to demilitarise the ships to avoid further bloodshed.

The admiralty accepted Somerville's recommendation for demilitarization, but he was taken aback by the specific line of action they formulated. Somerville had evidently hoped for admiralty-to-admiralty negotiations. Instead, to Somerville's astonishment, he was initially told to forewarn the French and provide them with an opportunity to stave off an attack by fully demilitarizing the *Dunkerque*. Somerville noted:

> Admiralty suggested my sending in a delegate to propose to the French they should do this and if they didn't agree I must bombard. I replied that the French would never receive a delegate after what has happened and that any warning to them would result in their attacking me with every submarine and aircraft available.
>
> Eventually at 3 a.m. this morning [while Somerville was en route] they said I could attack with torpedo aircraft only. Before they had turned down my suggestion to do so, they said it wouldn't be sufficiently effective.[2]

To perpetuate his July 3 claim that his ships had been abandoned, Admiral Gensoul had ordered the *Dunkerque*'s antiaircraft guns to remain unmanned. Although a small number of crewmen remained on Gensoul's flagship, they were in salvage mode, working at a relaxed pace and even sleeping on the ship's open deck at night.[3]

As one precaution against a follow-up attack, three patrol boats stood by alongside, available to evacuate the remaining crew if necessary. The patrol craft, which had previously been engaged in antisubmarine duties, remained armed with depth charges.

The repeat engagement with the French fleet at Mers-el-Kébir on July 6 conformed to the British script every bit as well as Operation Catapult had on July 3. Once again, very little went according to plan. On this day, however, the Royal Navy's broken plans worked out for the best. With the *Dunkerque* beached on the shoreline of the town of Saint André, Somerville planned to skim torpedoes from low-flying Swordfish torpedo bombers flown from the *Ark Royal*. The torpedoes were set to stream and explode in shallow water. As the *Ark Royal* steamed ninety miles offshore, a wave of six Swordfish took off from her deck at 5:20 in the morning. They sighted their target and flew in low, just above the smashed and debris-strewn breakwater.

The first British torpedo run had slight apparent impact: The *Dunkerque* was unscathed. The only casualty was the *Terre-Neuve*, one of three patrol boats sitting at her side.[4] The torpedo that hit the *Terre-Neuve* failed to explode but speared a large hole in her hull, which caused *Terre-Neuve* to recede into the shallow water. A torpedo from the second wave of Swordfish scored a direct hit—not on the *Dunkerque* but on the helpless *Terre-Neuve*. When that torpedo exploded, fourteen of the depth charges on board the sunken patrol boat also exploded—"the equivalent of eight air-launched torpedo warheads."[5] Most of the damage from that secondary explosion was to the *Dunkerque*'s starboard bow, which now settled more deeply into the water. One hundred and eighty officers and men died on the *Dunkerque* on July 3. Thirty additional victims lost their lives on July 6, burned, shattered, and buried under twisted steel.[6]

James Somerville, still laden with guilt, finally had cause for modest relief. "I was thankful to find that we had lost no-one in this operation, as it was my fault it had to be carried out."[7] Somerville underscored the finality of the July 6 operation in a letter to his wife: "The ships must be completely knocked out so that filthy job is over at last." With a tone of exasperation, he concluded, "I don't know what other butcher's work awaits me, but as things are it looks as if the French will actually declare war on us by now so then at least they will be legitimate enemies."[8]

The British did not learn until months later that the follow-up attack and the detonation of the depth charges did not completely destroy the *Dunkerque*. The attack, however, accomplished the British objective of immobilizing the *Dunkerque* for a lengthy period. After sitting out of action at Mers-el-Kébir for more than a year, she sailed to the French naval base in Toulon in February 1942, still only partially repaired. There she joined the *Strasbourg* and the core of the French fleet.

Admiral Gensoul, still nominally in command of the remnants of his *Force de Raid*, flew to Toulon on the evening of July 7. With his squadron at Mers-el-Kébir in tatters and the *Dunkerque* barely salvageable, Gensoul hoisted his flag on the *Strasbourg*.[9]

With the *Dunkerque* out of commission, and the *Strasbourg* out of reach, two coveted French vessels remained in play.

When the *Jean Bart* slipped the shallow channel at Saint-Nazaire and made her slow way to Casablanca, she was an unfinished vessel. The dockyard repair facilities in that Moroccan port were inadequate for a ship of the *Jean Bart*'s size and complexity. The French could not feasibly complete her construction and arm her for battle as long as she remained in Casablanca. Britain's leaders were comfortable that she had minimal fighting value. The admiralty decided, and even informed the French, that they would not attack her.[10]

Somewhat to the surprise of the Allies, the *Jean Bart* fired on two American warships from her static berth when the Naval Battle of Casablanca came to her in November 1942. Although she suffered more damage than she inflicted, the *Jean Bart* traded salvoes with the battleship USS *Massachusetts* and the heavy cruiser USS *Augusta*.[11] The *Jean Bart* played no further active role in the war.

That left the *Richelieu*, anchored once again at Dakar.

A British naval squadron, led by Captain Richard Onslow on the aircraft carrier *Hermes*, approached the African harbor early in the morning of July 7. Onslow, who had been promoted to the temporary rank of Acting Rear-Admiral for the duration of the operation, presented local French authorities with a short list of terms for cooperation or submission akin to those rejected by Admiral Gensoul at Mers-el-Kébir.[12]

The local governor general dismissed the British demands as "shameful." Later in the day, the British intercepted a French order to all ships at Dakar telling them to "meet attacks from the English enemy with the utmost ferocity."[13]

When the British threatened to destroy Admiral Gensoul's *Force de Raid* at Mers-el-Kébir, some French officers believed their recent allies were bluffing. Four days later, in the wake of the British attack, the French had context that had been lacking on July 3.

No one in Dakar suspected a bluff.

Unlike Admiral Gensoul, who took few measures to protect his ships, the *Richelieu*'s commanding officer, Captain Paul Marzin, sought to ensure that his battleship was not vulnerable to a surprise attack. The *Richelieu* was anchored just outside the port, facing south, positioned with her uncommonly lethal battery of eight 15-inch guns aimed in the most likely direction of any ships that dared approach. To forestall torpedo raids, the French cushioned the *Richelieu* with rows of cargo ships on her port and starboard sides.[14]

Marzin was not about to wait for the Royal Navy to open fire. Unbeknownst to the British, he planned to sortie on the morning of July 8, and use the *Richelieu*'s massive firepower to sink the *Hermes*.[15] Unbeknownst to Marzin and the French, the *Hermes* had orders to "fly off her Swordfish to destroy the Richelieu" that same morning.[16]

Before either attack was launched, Royal Navy Lieutenant Commander Robert Bristowe conceived a plan on his own initiative to attack the *Richelieu* at minimal risk to the *Hermes* and her crew. Bristowe, who had retired from the Navy in 1933 and pursued a successful career as a stockbroker in London's "City," had been mobilized back into the navy and assigned to the *Hermes* six days before Britain's September 1939 declaration of war on Germany. Admiral Onslow approved Bristowe's mission and supported his recruitment of a small group of volunteers.

A short time after darkness fell on the night of July 7, Bristowe and nine Royal Marines climbed down into a small wooden motor-launch, their faces and hands blackened with burnt cork, and their launch painted matte black.[17] Bristowe and his crew motored toward the *Richelieu* in the dark at the slow pace of three knots. Even at that speed, on a night fraught with risk and worry, Bristowe feared the launch's small phosphorescent wake would attract attention. Fortunately, no one spotted them. Concerned that the boom supporting the harbor's submarine nets might be mined, Bristowe cut his motor, held his breath, and let the wooden boat glide safely over the metal barrier.

Bristowe sighted the protective rows of merchant ships and used them to guide his way toward the *Richelieu*. By 2:10 a.m., Bristowe was within thirty yards of the *Richelieu*'s stern. The men muscled four depth charges—each the size of a forty-gallon drum—over the side in the hope of "wrecking propellers and flooding stern compartments."[18] Bristowe and his confederates knew that of the multiple threats to their lives that night, the most serious would be when the depth charges exploded.

But the *Richelieu* was anchored in surprisingly shallow water, and the charges failed to explode. To Bristowe's chagrin, the massive French battleship "was not lifted out of the water as we had all expected."[19] His daring mission was apparently for naught. Bristowe and his disappointed crew completed a safe return to the *Hermes.*

In the hour before sunrise, six Swordfish aircraft took flight from the *Hermes* for a follow-up attack on the *Richelieu.* The planes made the best of the small gaps between the merchant ships that surrounded the French battleship and dropped shallow-water torpedoes—much in the way the British attacked the wounded *Dunkerque* at Mers-el-Kébir.

A popular version of this story claims that Bristowe's sitting depth charges were set off by one of the British torpedoes. The most credible version holds that one of torpedoes launched from a Swordfish shredded the *Richelieu*'s stern. The French suffered no casualties, but the explosion ripped an eight-hundred-square-foot hole in the French battleship.[20] The wounded *Richelieu* was maneuvered into the port at Dakar and was surrounded with torpedo nets to forestall future attacks.[21] Water continued to flood into the *Richelieu*, and she gradually settled stern-first into the mud.[22] With limited repair facilities in Dakar, the damage from the British torpedo kept the *Richelieu* out of the war for more than a year.

In a radio address on July 14, 1940—Bastille Day, or "*La Fête Nationale*" in France—Winston Churchill declared,

> Our painful task is now complete. Although the unfinished battleship, the *Jean Bart*, still rests in a Moroccan harbor and there are a number of French warships at Toulon and in various French ports all over the world, these are not in a condition or of a character to derange our preponderance of naval power. As long, therefore, as they make no attempt to return to ports controlled by Germany or Italy, we shall not molest them in any way. That melancholy phase

in our relations with France has, so far as we are concerned, come to an end.[23]

Although Churchill and his top admirals believed Hitler's navy could potentially grab the *Strasbourg* from her berth at Toulon at any time, they were confident that the threat to Britain from France's four most dangerous ships had been eliminated for one year at the very least. The British campaign against these French ships had concluded, but the French ships' stories had not yet reached their end.

CHAPTER 25

YOU'RE NOT ALLOWED TO HAVE A HEART IN WARTIME

THE BITTER EMOTIONS THAT smoldered inside François Darlan on July 3, 1940 erupted in full fury the following morning. Darlan's voice trembled as he declared his intention to exact revenge on the British.

Darlan believed he had been betrayed by his former brothers-in-arms and argued for the bombing of the British naval base at Gibraltar, home to the squadron that attacked his ships. When Marshal Pétain added his support, former president Pierre Laval cautioned, "We have just lost one war. Are we about to start and lose another?"[1]

A small flight of French aircraft approached Gibraltar on July 5. Whether by accident or intent, their bombing run was a feeble act of symbolic revenge. No ships were harmed as all the bombs fell outside the harbor, into the bay.

Darlan advocated a joint operation with the Italian Navy to liberate Admiral Godfroy's Force X at Alexandria. After Marshal Pétain initially spoke in favor of this attack, Paul Baudouin and General Weygand were instrumental in its cancellation.[2]

In a July 5 statement, Darlan saluted his fallen sailors and condemned the British: "I respectfully salute those of our comrades who died courageously for their country. They would probably have preferred to die in a fair fight instead of being murdered."[3] The Vichy government formally broke diplomatic relations with Great Britain on July 8.

Darlan's ire was undiminished by the passage of time. During a December 1940 conversation with American envoy Robert Murphy, Darlan claimed that his family had been ruined five times by the British, but never by the Germans. Britain's high command, in his estimation, was "utterly imbecile." As for Winston Churchill—"the drunken Churchill"—he "had no word strong enough" to denounce the man "who had crawled to him on his knees" in the month preceding their breach, "only to turn on him at Mers-el-Kébir."[4]

British newspapers tempered their applause with empathy.

The editors of London's *Daily Herald* expressed their pride in Britain's leaders for their "fearless and terrible decision."[5] *The Observer* described the episode as one of "human reluctance and relentless necessity."[6] *The Times* stated, "There can be little pleasure in contemplating the defeat of enemies whom we believe to be at heart our friends, and who were fighting, not for their country, but for a point of honour, which was rooted in the dishonour of their political chiefs."[7] *The Times* also suggested, "That HITLER feels deprived of an expected fighting contingent for his own fleet, . . . is shown by the incoherent fury with which the seizure has been denounced in the Nazi Press. Great Britain is accused of stabbing a mortally wounded ally in the back, and the British people are exhorted to punish the crime by hanging MR. CHURCHILL in Trafalgar Square."[8]

Some American papers printed an eloquent, two-paragraph summary from the *Associated Press*:

> The British Navy has fallen with reluctant ferocity upon the fleet of its old French Ally, and in battle and by threat of battle has wrested the great bulk of it from the reaching grasp of Germany.
>
> This, the strangest of all naval actions in the world's history, was announced yesterday in the House of Commons by Prime Minister Winston Churchill in a speech that was like no other ever heard in its ancient halls.[9]

To no one's surprise, Churchill and Britain were condemned in French newspapers. "On the night of the armistice," wrote François Mauriac in *Le Figaro*, "we did not think that anything worse could have happened to us. And then, suddenly . . . this ambush at Mers-el-Kébir and all these sacrificed sailors. . . . Monsieur Winston Churchill has arrayed against England—for how many years—a united France."[10]

The arrival in Paris of London newspapers that were perceived to celebrate Mers-el-Kébir as a great British naval victory helped sustain French indignation.[11]

James Somerville shared his raw misery and lingering dread in a July 4 letter to his wife. Reflecting on the officers and men under his command in the hastily assembled Force H, he wrote, "We all feel thoroughly dirty and ashamed that the first time we should have been in action was an affair like this."[12]

In the same letter, Somerville added, "I shouldn't be surprised if I was relieved forthwith. I don't mind because it was an absolutely bloody business to shoot up those Frenchmen. The truth is my heart isn't in it and you're not allowed to have a heart in wartime."

Somerville also confessed, "I hate the idea of being regarded as the 'unskilled butcher of Oran.'"

Before Somerville completed his mission with the follow-up attack on the *Dunkerque*, a telegram from the admiralty arrived, with begrudging appreciation from the first lord and first sea lord: "While we are sorry that you did not put DUNKERQUE in the bag, we congratulate you on measure of success so far achieved. Request all under your command may be informed that their Lordships appreciate efficiency with which the bombardment was carried out. The Prime Minister wishes to be associated with the above."[13]

A brutally harsh note of condemnation, signed by a dozen French officers whom Somerville considered akin to brothers, followed one week later:

> The Commander and the Officers of the DUNKERQUE inform you of the deaths, for the honor of their flag, on July 3 and 6, 1940, of nine officers and 200 men from their battleship.
>
> They return to you the attached mementoes, which they had of their comrades in arms of the British Royal Navy, in whom they had placed all their trust.
>
> And they express to you on this occasion all their bitter sadness and their disgust at seeing that these comrades did not hesitate to

> soil the glorious flag of St. George with an ineffaceable stain, that of an assassination.[14]

A small collection of badges, ribbons, and other mementos from the men slain on the *Dunkerque* accompanied the note.

One of Somerville's first conversations in the wake of the carnage at Mers-el-Kébir was with Walter Knight-Adkin, the dean of Gibraltar and former chaplain of the fleet, who joined him for dinner on board HMS *Hood*. Somerville later described their conversation:

> Had a long talk with him afterwards about Oran and my feelings on the matter. He was very sympathetic and understanding. His view was that we had got back to the Old Testament days and that in order good should survive and evil be crushed it was necessary for the innocent to suffer. He may be right, but I find it difficult to accept—at least, when I'm the instrument chosen to inflict the suffering.[15]

Three months after firing on Admiral Gensoul's ships, Somerville wrote to his wife, "Just as we were thinking of going back [to Gibraltar—after an operation in the Atlantic] yesterday I got a charming message to say it was rumoured the whole of the Toulon fleet was coming out to have a scrap with us. Not wishing to have an Oran done on me I decided to stay out [at sea]."[16]

Somerville's sense of duty was his bedrock. "If I didn't feel that in war one can only have one loyalty and that is to the King and Government I shouldn't hesitate to ask to be relieved at once. But I feel it would be wrong and a stab at the country if I did."[17]

After James Somerville and Andrew Cunningham expressed their initial objections to the admiralty's plans, they followed their orders (however imperfectly) and moved on. Admiral Dudley North, on the other hand, made the career-wrecking decision to share his objections in a letter to First Lord A. V. Alexander in the *aftermath* of the Mers-el-Kébir and Alexandria operations.[18]

The admiralty delivered the first in a series of reprimands in a terse message: "the opinions of Senior Officers are always of value before an operation is carried out; but once the operation has taken place, Their Lordships strongly deprecate comments on a policy which had been decided by the Admiralty." In addition, "Their Lordships fully realized how repugnant the operation would be to all officers concerned, but they cannot allow such considerations to influence decisions in war and are surprised that comment of the kind received should be made."[19]

Winston Churchill expressed his disdain for North in a letter to Alexander: "It is evident that Admiral Dudley North has not got the root of the matter in him, and I should be very glad to see you replace him with a more resolute and clear-sighted officer."[20]

First Lord of the Admiralty A. V. Alexander delivered a withering rebuke in a meeting with Admiral North in January 1941. As North wrote years later, "Mr. Alexander said that I never ought to have written such a letter, that it was not my business to decide who were the King's enemies."[21]

In his report on the events at Mers-el-Kébir, Marcel-Bruno Gensoul wrote that he had avoided meeting with Captain Holland out of concern that doing so might breach France's armistice with Germany.[22]

Gensoul offered additional reasons for his actions and inactions in testimony to a postwar French commission that investigated the doings of the Vichy government. He stated that he was "haunted" by the prospect of sinking his ships or seeing them "sunk by the British," and he "did not consider for a single moment the possibility" of sailing to Martinique "under the escort and menace of English ships" or sailing to America "with English guns trained upon my ships."[23]

As for why he did not convey the full list of British options to his admiralty on July 3, 1940, Gensoul effectively sold out his two principal aides: "I can no longer explain why I did not do that nor why my staff officers [including Danbé and Dufay] did not call my attention to this omission. The telegrams were prepared very hastily and this must be attributed to the circumstances of the moment."[24] Gensoul betrayed his aides again in separate testimony: "I blamed myself for it afterwards. But, how is it that, in my entourage, it was not pointed out to me that there would be interest in making a somewhat more complete report?"[25] When Danbé's name appeared on a list of recommended awards and decorations, Gensoul crossed it off, only to be overridden by Admiral Darlan.[26]

It did not take long for Admiral Darlan to usher Gensoul into obscurity. After meekly enduring multiple attacks from the Royal Navy and overseeing the burial of more than one thousand of his sailors, Gensoul did not speak with Darlan until July 19, 1940, when Darlan visited Toulon. Darlan was brusque and refused to discuss Mers-el-Kébir.

Gensoul debarked from the *Strasbourg* on August 10, 1940 and was assigned to organize the navy's social works. This officer, once described by Cedric Holland as "a small man in a big position," acquired an unofficial title befitting his new small position: "first social worker of the sea."[27] He was placed on the retired list two years later.

American naval historian Arthur J. Marder wrote to Gensoul in 1972 and queried his perspective on the events at Mers-el-Kébir after the passage of more than thirty years. In a handwritten letter, the ninety-two-year-old Gensoul replied in French to Marder's question: "If you could relive your experiences of that unhappy day, is there anything you would do differently?" The retired admiral replied,

> First, considering everything, my course of action would be the same, the fundamental reason being not to break the Armistice which had just been concluded, with all the dramatic consequences that would result for France and the French, and not having in my possession, moreover, the elements necessary to arrive at a different judgement.
>
> Second, until the very last moment, I hoped for a peaceful solution, and it is for that reason that I avoided making any movement to sail, or even opening fire on British aircraft which were coming in to drop mines in the channel: thus putting myself in a position of inferiority in regard to the British force, allowing it to choose its own moment and its own formation for opening fire.[28]

Gensoul died in 1973 at the age of ninety-three. He kept no diary and destroyed the notebook in which he recorded the events of July 1940.[29] A British naval liaison paid his respects at Gensoul's funeral, wearing civilian clothes at the request of Gensoul's family.[30] A British officer who knew

Gensoul well, but asked not to be quoted by name, shared with Marder, "I am afraid that, since Oran, Admiral Gensoul's life must have been a very shallow and miserable one."[31]

When Major General Edward Louis Spears met with Charles de Gaulle on the evening of July 3, 1940 and shared what he knew about the attack at Mers-el-Kébir, he was surprised by the French general's subdued reaction. "His calmness was very striking, the objectivity of his views astonishing. He had evidently done a lot of thinking."[32]

De Gaulle acknowledged that the Royal Navy's actions were inevitable from the British vantage point. Nonetheless, he was uncomfortable with the prospect of a formal collaboration with an ally who had attacked and killed his countrymen. De Gaulle was demoralized to the degree that he considered moving to Canada, to Montreal specifically, where he would withdraw from public life.

Spears reinforced the importance of de Gaulle's leadership to those Frenchmen who wished to carry on the fight. After a single night's reflection, de Gaulle told Spears on July 4 that he would continue to fight on the side of the British. De Gaulle returned to the BBC's studios for an address aimed at France as well as at Frenchmen in England. In an uncensored and unsparing speech on July 8, de Gaulle both reproached Britain and acknowledged the logic of its actions. He also rejected any perception that the British had enjoyed a military victory worthy of celebration.

> There is not a Frenchman who has not heard with pain and anger that ships of the French fleet have been sunk by our Allies. This grief and anger come from the innermost depths of our being.
>
> I . . . ask the British to spare us, as well as themselves, any portrayal of this hateful tragedy as a direct naval success. To consider it such would be both unjust and out of place.[33]

De Gaulle acknowledged that the French fleet had been "at the mercy of the enemy," and he understood that inaction could be fatal to both France and Britain: "There cannot be the slightest doubt that, on principal and of necessity, the enemy would have used them against Britain or against our own Empire. I therefore have no hesitation in saying they are better destroyed." He added, "I prefer to know that even the *Dunkerque*—our dear, magnificent, powerful *Dunkerque*—is stranded off Mers-el-Kébir, rather than learn one day that she has been manned by Germans and used to shell British ports. . . . Our two peoples—our two great peoples—are still linked together. Either they will both succumb, or they will triumph side by side."

After the Allies won the war, Charles de Gaulle was named chairman of the Provisional Government of the French Republic and later served as his nation's president for ten years. De Gaulle's provisional government tried Philippe Pétain and sentenced him to death for treason. After offers of asylum for the marshal from Britain, Switzerland, Brazil, America, and other countries were rejected, de Gaulle commuted Pétain's sentence to life in prison and exiled him to the tiny Île d'Yeu off the western coast of France for the remainder of his life. Muddled with severe dementia, the disgraced hero of World War I died in 1951 at the age of ninety-five. De Gaulle died in 1970 at the age of seventy-nine.

Winston Churchill aspired to impress President Roosevelt with Britain's ruthless action, just as he wished to convince all of the United States that Britain was in the war for the long run. According to Roosevelt biographer, Robert Sherwood, Britain's aggression against the French fleet at Mers-el-Kébir "served forcibly to underscore Churchill's defiant assurance that 'we will fight them in the streets' and 'never surrender.'"[34]

When President Roosevelt met with Count René de Saint-Quentin, the Vichy French government's ambassador to the United States, on July 19, 1940, the ambassador urged FDR to protest the British seizure of French ships and stressed that Vichy France was "a free and sovereign state."

Roosevelt scolded de Saint-Quentin, "Even if there was only an extremely remote possibility that your fleet would pass into German hands, the British government had good reason to act as it did. I would not have acted otherwise. I am a realist."[35]

Nevada's Key Pittman chaired the United States Senate Committee on Foreign Relations. This influential and outspoken legislator had been unsparing in his gloomy outlook for Britain. Several days before the action at Mers-el-Kébir, Pittman called upon Churchill to abandon the British

Isles, based on his belief that the British would not be able to defend their home. Pittman added that "nothing the United States has to give can do more than delay the results."

In the wake of events at Mers-el-Kébir, Senator Pittman revealed a stunning change of heart: "Every member of the United States' Senate approves Churchill's course and applauds his courage in preventing the use of the French navy by Hitler. It was the fear that this step would not be taken that shook the confidence of some of us to the power of British defense."[36]

Churchill later boasted that his decisions "produced a profound impression in every country. Here was this Britain which so many had counted down and out, which strangers had supposed to be quivering on the brink of surrender to the mighty power arrayed against her, striking ruthlessly at her dearest friends of yesterday. . . . It was made plain that the British War Cabinet feared nothing and would stop at nothing."[37]

Galeazzo Ciano, Italy's foreign minister and Benito Mussolini's son-in-law, shared sentiments similar to Churchill's in a July 4, 1940, diary entry: "It is too early to judge the consequences of the British action. For the moment it proves the fighting spirit of His British Majesty's fleet is quite alive and still has the aggressive ruthlessness of the captains and pirates of the seventeenth century."[38]

At 7:14 on the evening of July 3, 1940, a lookout on a British destroyer spotted a small boat speeding across the open bay outside Mers-el-Kébir flying a white flag and a white ensign.

The motorboat carried Cedric Holland and Lieutenant Commander Davies, now safe, more than ninety minutes after they climbed down to the admiral's barge from the now stricken *Dunkerque*. The British officers had completed their passage between the French and British squadrons, reflexively ducking their heads, literally under fire as shells crossed overhead, each salvo passing with the shuddering thunder of an express train at full throttle.[39]

HMS *Forester* detached to pick up Holland and his colleagues, who were now fifteen miles offshore.[40] With their fuel running low, and the sun descending toward the horizon, Holland and company, exhausted from the long, tense day, unleashed spontaneous cheers of the saved and thankful as the destroyer swung around for them to climb on board. The *Foxhound*'s motorboat was abandoned, left floating in the bay just outside Mers-el-Kébir.

Cedric Holland's assessment of the events on July 3 was quite similar to James Somerville's. Holland's frustration mirrored Somerville's with the shared sense that if Gensoul would have met with him earlier in the day, and if Holland had been afforded more time to press his arguments in person and directly counter Gensoul's resentment, he and Gensoul would have reached a peaceful resolution. The fact that Admiral Gensoul initially "received the terms by letter through the hands of an intermediary . . . [eliminated] all possibility of a friendly interview and amicable discussion."

"Holland continued, As it was, he took the proposals in the form of an ultimatum, and for this reason, together with the national dislike of the French for being rushed into negotiation, he became stubborn and would not listen to argument, though, as the day wore on, he did gradually take up a less uncompromising attitude. When I boarded 'DUNKERQUE,' I still had a faint hope that it was not too late for a peaceful settlement."[41]

Holland's impression was that "up to the very last" Gensoul did not believe that the British would open fire.

Somerville offered unequivocal support for Holland in his report on Operation Catapult. He complimented his personally chosen negotiator, noting that Holland "carried out his most difficult task with the greatest tact, courage and persistence. That he failed in his mission was not his fault. That he so nearly succeeded is greatly to his credit."[42]

Holland's morale was shattered in the aftermath of July 3. His anguish was more intense, and its expression was more tangible than Somerville's, as evidenced in his letter to the vice admiral, aircraft carriers sent two days after his failed negotiations:

> I have the honour to submit that, owing to the altered circumstances which have now arisen, I may be relieved of my command at sea.
>
> The use of force at Oran on 3rd July, 1940, was to me not only repugnant, but in my opinion useless to attain the end sought by His Majesty's Government.

> I was glad to have been ordered to carry out the unpleasant task of informing the Senior Officer at Oran of the British terms, as I consider (rightly or wrongly) that I had a better chance of making Admiral Gensoul submit to them than anyone else had.
>
> But after my long, close and trusted association with Admiral Darlan and so many of the officers and men of the French Navy, I am unable wholeheartedly or with energy to carry out active warfare at sea against the French Navy, who have had hostilities thrust upon them by us.
>
> I very much regret asking that this request may be favourably considered, since my one desire is actively to pursue this war on sea against the Germans and Italians with all my energy and capability.[43]

James Somerville shared with his wife that he had persuaded "Poor Hooky" to withdraw his letter of resignation. Holland's letter never reached the attention of the admiralty, and he remained captain of the *Ark Royal* for another nine months until April 1941. That service was followed by a seven-month stint as chief of staff to Lord Gort at Gibraltar, and then two years as director of naval communications at the admiralty.

Holland was promoted to rear admiral in November 1943 and served in southeast Asia through the end of the war. When General Seishirō Itagaki surrendered local Japanese forces at Singapore in September 1945, he did so across the table from Rear Admiral Cedric Holland on board his flagship HMS *Sussex*.

Decades after Holland's death at the age of sixty in 1950, Vice Admiral Brian Schofield (who, while still a captain, was Holland's assistant in Paris and remained in touch with Barbara Holland) recalled that, unlike James Somerville, who helped resolve his torment by pouring it out in letters to his wife, "Holland talked very little about Oran with his wife other than to say that he felt he could have won the day if he could have had another two hours with Gensoul, whom he described as 'an obstinate old codger.'"[44] Schofield believed, "Oran took years off his life."[45]

The Vichy government did not hesitate to employ "the martyrs of Mers-el-Kébir" for propaganda purposes. The victims of British shells and torpedoes were buried in a cemetery near the harbor where they died. Standing before rows of hastily constructed coffins, Admiral Gensoul intoned to the unhearing victims, "You had promised to obey your superiors in whatever they might command you to do for the honor of the Flag and the greatness of the arms of France. If there is a stain on a flag today, it is certainly not on yours."[46]

Sweeping images of Gensoul, immaculate in his tropical white uniform and parade gloves, surrounded by rows of coffins, were shown in every French cinema. The somber memorials perpetuated an emotional response well after the ships settled into the muck of the harbor and the bodies of the slain men were interred for eternal rest.

When considering the emotional impact of what, from the French perspective, was undeniably a tragedy, it is fair to measure the British attack at Mers-el-Kébir against Japan's attack on the U.S. Navy at Pearl Harbor seventeen months later.

For perspective: 1,257 French seamen died at Mers-el-Kébir, including 1,012 on a single ship, the *Bretagne*.[47] At Pearl Harbor, 2,335 American military personnel were killed, including 1,177 on the USS *Arizona*. The population of the United States at the time (132 million) was more than three times the population of France (40 million).

Japan, of course, had not been a recent ally of America.

A statue of Winston Churchill stands in the heart of Paris. This ten-foot-tall depiction of Sir Winston watches over Avenue Winston Churchill, close to both the Champs-Élysées and the River Seine. The £250,000 cost of the statue was generously funded by contributions from the French public.

Queen Elizabeth II joined French president Jacques Chirac at the statue's unveiling on November 11, 1998, the eightieth anniversary of the first armistice that was signed in Marshal Foch's rail car at Compiégne. The queen delighted the assembled crowd when she addressed them in both French and English.

This bronze likeness of France's most resolute ally leans forward in confident stride, walking stick in hand, lips pursed, a hint of triumph in his narrowed eyes. This was Winston Churchill as he marched down

France's most sacred boulevard at the side of General Charles de Gaulle on a different November 11—in 1944, five months after the Allies landed at Normandy, and three months after they liberated Paris from its German occupiers.

The statue was modeled on a photograph of that triumphant walk down the Champs-Élysées. Winston Churchill, who spoke of his affection for France throughout his life, had fulfilled the vow he made in July 1940 to "restore the greatness and territory of France."

For some in France, bitter memories of the action at Mers-el-Kébir have festered from generation to generation. Fifty-nine years after Churchill's decision to attack the French fleet, a fresh reminder of those harsh sentiments unexpectedly appeared in Paris.

Just under a year after its unveiling—on November 1, 1999—one or more vandals desecrated the statue, smeared Churchill's hands with blood-red paint, and scrawled the charge "Mers el Kébir, 1300 killed" at its base.[48]

PART 5

EPILOGUE

CHAPTER 26

YE ARE FORGERS OF LIES

ON SEPTEMBER 3, 1939, *Grossadmiral* Erich Raeder, the commander-in-chief of Adolf Hitler's navy, confided his bitter reaction to the day's consequential events in a war journal entry: "Today the war against France and England broke out, the war which, according to the Führer's 's previous assertions, we had no need to expect before 1944."[1]

Just forty-one days earlier, Hitler had assured an assembly of naval officers that under no circumstances would Germany enter into a war with Great Britain. Hitler acknowledged that such a war "would mean *Finis Germaniae*."[2]

Despite an aggressive shipbuilding campaign during the preceding decade in belligerent disregard of a series of naval treaties, Admiral Raeder's U-boat-centric navy still lacked sufficient numbers of battleships, destroyers, aircraft carriers, and cruisers to challenge the navies of Britain and France.

A comparison of key elements of the British, German, and French navies at the beginning of the war illustrates Germany's disadvantage. The British totals below include its dominions' navies.[3]

	BRITISH	GERMAN	FRENCH
Battleships and battle cruisers	15	2	5
Cruisers	58	10	19
Destroyers	178	32	70
Submarines	71	57	79
Aircraft carriers	7	0	1

In January 1939, eight months before the Allies' declaration of war, Hitler had approved Raeder's Z plan, which provided for the construction of six new battleships, four aircraft carriers, and an additional complement of smaller warships. The two men clashed on the timetable for the ships' completion, however. Raeder argued that 1948 was a realistic expectation. Hitler declared that the six battleships, in particular, could be built in less time: "If I can build the Third Reich in six years, then the navy can surely build these six ships in six years."[4]

War was a sudden reality in the fall of 1939, and Raeder could not have been more disconsolate about the fleet he was about to order into war. "The surface forces are so inferior in number and strength, that they can no more than show that they know how to die gallantly and are thus willing to create the foundations for later reconstruction."[5]

One exception—a German surface ship that was superior in strength—was the *Bismarck*. Launched on Valentine's day 1939, the battleship *Bismarck* was the most massive ship in the German fleet on the day it first sailed. Adolf Hitler beamed from the dockside as a granddaughter of Otto von Bismarck smashed a bottle of champagne against the ship's bow and declared, "On the order of the Führer, I baptize you with the name '*Bismarck*.'"

Admiral Raeder vowed to the Führer that the 2,200 officers and men on board the *Bismarck* would honor the memory of its namesake "to their last breath."[6]

One month before Hitler's armies attacked Belgium, Holland, and Luxembourg, Germany launched unprovoked invasions of Denmark and Norway. The German Navy played an instrumental role in the invasions, but their success was short-lived. The British and Norwegian navies got the best of their foe in several deadly confrontations during the brief campaign. Although they inflicted grievous damage on the Royal Navy, including the loss of nine destroyers and an aircraft carrier,[7] the heavy toll the Germans paid relative to the size of their fleet underscored Admiral Raeder's earlier warning that Germany's surface fleet "can no more than show that they know how to die gallantly."

In the week that followed their invasion, ten German destroyers—almost half of the destroyers in the *Kriegsmarine*—were sunk.[8] The German Navy, its surface fleet in particular, which had begun the war at a numeric disadvantage, was now virtually obliterated.

After Germany overran France, with the German destroyer fleet now ravaged, logic suggested that Germany would seize France's newest and largest warships.

However, to the dismay of his admirals and generals, to the disappointment of his ally Benito Mussolini, and contrary to Winston Churchill's fears and expectations, Hitler had no desire to seize the French fleet. He had a different priority. After the war, the Allies discovered a memorandum of a June 1940 meeting between Hitler and Mussolini in which Hitler's rationale was revealed:

> The Fuehrer explained in detail what a great increase in strength the French fleet would represent for England, if it were to put itself at Britain's disposal. . . .
>
> It would therefore be best to try to reach agreement with a French government to neutralize the fleet. . . .
>
> Above all the French fleet must be prevented from reaching England. . . . It would also be a favorable solution if the French fleet scuttled itself.[9]

Galeazzo Ciano detested Hitler. In his estimation, however, Hitler drafted the French naval clause with a deft hand. "I cannot be accused of excessive tenderness toward him, but today I truly admire him." Ciano understood that Hitler's absolute priority was to quickly remove France from the war.[10]

> Hitler, on the other hand [in contrast to Mussolini] wants to avoid an uprising of the French Navy in favor of the English. From all that he says it is clear that he wants to act quickly to end it all. Hitler is now the gambler who has made a big scoop and would like to get up from the table, risking nothing more. Today he speaks with a reserve and a perspicacity which, after such a victory, are really astonishing.

After conquering France, Hitler anticipated a near-term resolution of his differences with Britain—either in battle or by treaty. He did not expect to need the French ships to achieve his goal, but he perceived that British possession of those ships would prolong Britain's ability to resist. Thus, he was every bit as anxious to keep the French ships out of British hands as Churchill was to prevent those ships from falling into German hands.

As they awaited the details of Germany's armistice terms in June 1940, most French leaders expected Germany to claim their fleet. No one outside of Germany or Italy—not Winston Churchill, not François Darlan, not Franklin Roosevelt—knew Hitler's intentions. In the end, his objective was the complete opposite of his enemies' expectations.

François Darlan's name was permanently scarified in the minds of many in Britain when he refused to order the French fleet to sail to British, American, or French colonial harbors in the summer of 1940. By Christmas Eve of 1942, the day on which he was assassinated, Darlan had earned the scorn of additional detractors in Germany, America, Algeria, and even France.

During the course of 1941, Darlan's résumé ballooned with titles, including vice president of the council, minister of national defense, minister of foreign affairs, minister of the interior, minister of war, and commander of the army. For all intents and purposes, he was the operational head of Marshal Pétain's Vichy government. He was officially designated the successor—some referred to him as the dauphin—to the octogenarian Pétain.

With France's former ties to Britain now in tatters, and with an opportunity to exact revenge against Winston Churchill and the former brothers-in-arms who had doubted his honor, Darlan demonstrated his willingness to collaborate with Germany. His most notorious achievement was the negotiation of the Paris Protocols in May 1941. Darlan provided Germany with access to certain military facilities in France's African colonies, including a port in Tunisia through which supplies flowed to General Rommel's Afrika Corps.[11] In fairness, Darlan reaped a relative windfall in return. Germany reduced the "occupation costs" that France paid from 400 million to 300 million French francs per day and also agreed to free 83,000 prisoners of war, primarily aged veterans who had served in both world wars.[12]

Half a year later, Darlan played a more treacherous hand when he suggested that he still had a "very well informed intelligence service" and access to "valuable information on British ships' movements and intentions" that he was willing to share with Admiral Raeder.[13] Darlan also declared his aspiration for a "European Fleet" in which the *Strasbourg* and other French warships would sail "on Germany's side."[14]

Despite the French admiral's conspicuous inclination to collaborate with Germany against Britain, Adolf Hitler disliked Darlan. In April 1942, German authorities pressured Darlan to resign from all of his posts with the exception of commander of the armed forces. Pierre Laval, a former prime minister of France and a favorite of the Führer, replaced Darlan in the Vichy government.

François Darlan flew to Algiers on November 5, 1942 to visit his twenty-eight-year-old son Alain, a lieutenant in the French naval reserve, who had been stricken by poliomyelitis, and was feared to be near death.[15] By unlucky coincidence, the United States, Britain, and Free French launched Operation Torch—an attack by land, sea, and air—on Algeria three days later. American troops briefly held the elder Darlan under house arrest, hoping they could persuade him to use his still considerable influence to convince local French forces to forsake resistance against the Allies. After that hope was fulfilled, Andrew Cunningham wrote, "Darlan was the only man in North Africa who could have . . . brought the authorities and people of North Africa in to help us in the struggle against the Axis."[16]

Nonetheless, "the Darlan deal," which was brokered by U.S. General Mark Clark, met with hostility in Britain, America, and France. Marshal Pétain stripped Darlan of his remaining responsibilities in the Vichy government, as well as, by month's end, his French citizenship.[17] Although President Roosevelt termed the deal "a temporary expedient,"[18] and General Dwight Eisenhower referred to Darlan as a "deep-eyed villain,"[19] both men defended the decision to work with the French admiral. Winston Churchill reluctantly accepted the deal as well and offered this explanation during a secret session of the House of Commons: "I am sorry to have to mention a point like that, but it makes a lot of difference to a soldier whether a man fires his gun at him or at his enemy."[20] Darlan was not blind to the controversy. In a letter to Mark Clark, Darlan noted, "I am but a lemon which the Americans will drop after it is crushed."[21]

Fernand Bonnier de La Chapelle brought the Darlan deal to a sudden end. The twenty-four-year-old was waiting in an anteroom as Darlan walked into his office after lunch on December 24, 1942. At the sound of a pistol being cocked, Darlan spun in Bonnier's direction. Bonnier fired two shots at point-blank range, hitting Darlan in the mouth and in the ribs, perforating a lung.[22] Darlan died on the way to the hospital. A naval aide grabbed Bonnier at the scene.

To this day, divergent strains of rumor hold that British, American, or French plotters were behind the still-unsolved assassination. Bonnier was a disposable asset for whomever he served. His coffin was reportedly ordered even before his trial opened on Christmas day. He was shot by a firing squad the following day.

After a Roman Catholic funeral mass, attended by Dwight Eisenhower, Mark Clark, Andrew Cunningham, and other Allied officers, the French Navy claimed Darlan's body and buried the fallen admiral in the fortress wall in Algiers. Darlan was reinterred in April 1964—in the naval cemetery at Mers-el-Kébir—in the company of almost 1,300 men who had not expected to die for him in July 1940.[23]

The German partitioning of France into free and occupied zones came to an end on November 11, 1942. The Allies' invasion of north Africa and the capitulation of French forces by order of Admiral Darlan provoked Adolf Hitler to call for the military occupation of the entire country—with one small exception. The naval base at Toulon was the lone remaining oasis of independence in metropolitan France. The *Strasbourg* and most French warships still afloat sat at anchor in this port on France's southern Mediterranean coast. The partially repaired *Dunkerque* was also at Toulon, isolated in a dry dock.

Twenty-eight months after the attack at Mers-el-Kébir, Britain still coveted the French capital ships. In a meeting with General Eisenhower in early November, at a time when François Darlan was still alive, Winston Churchill commented, "If I could meet Darlan, much as I hate him, I would cheerfully crawl on my hands and knees for a mile if by doing so I could get him to bring that fleet of his into the circle of Allied forces."[24]

Adolf Hitler still feared, and soon acted to prevent, that outcome. At four o'clock on the morning of November 27, 1942, when Admiral Jean de Laborde—who succeeded Darlan as head of the French Navy—learned that German tanks had breached the gates at Toulon, he broadcast an urgent order: "*Sabordez la flotte*!" The command to scuttle the fleet was broadcast by radio and flashed by signal lamp. Small motorboats raced throughout the harbor to extend de Laborde's *Sabordez* message. To spread the alert as widely and quickly as possible, the siren on the *Strasbourg*, de Laborde's flagship, wailed.[25]

The *Strasbourg*, the battleship that had escaped Vice Admiral Somerville at Mers-el-Kébir, was the first ship to sink at her berth. Her sister ship, the *Dunkerque*, a floating wreck, had limped to Toulon from Mers-el-Kébir in February 1942 to complete her repairs. It was now time for the French to sink her for good. Engineers flooded the dry dock in which she rested and ripped away the patches that had sealed the holes left by shells from HMS *Hood* and depth charges from the unfortunate *Terre-Neuve*. As the *Dunkerque* settled into the waters of Toulon, explosive charges ripped through her turrets and bridge.

The self-destruction of the French ships was thorough. Weaponry, communications equipment, and navigational tools were mangled beyond use. De Laborde's Navy scuttled three-quarters of their warships at Toulon.[26] The harbor at Toulon was shallow, thirty-nine-feet-deep on average.[27] Some vessels capsized, others sat with their hulls submerged and their superstructures visible above the water. The Italian Navy would later salvage several French ships.

Twenty days before his assassination, François Darlan looked back in a December 4, 1942 letter to Winston Churchill:

> On June 12, 1940, at Briare, at the Headquarters of General Weygand, you took me aside and said to me: "Darlan, I hope that you will never surrender the Fleet." I answered you: "There is no question of doing so; it would be contrary to our naval traditions and honour." . . . If I did not consent to authorize the French Fleet to proceed to British ports, it was because I knew that such a decision

would bring about the total occupation of Metropolitan France as well as North Africa.

I admit having been overcome by a great bitterness and a great resentment against England as a result of the painful events which touched me as a sailor; furthermore it seemed to me that you did not believe my word. One day Lord Halifax sent me word . . . that in England my word was not doubted, but that it was believed that I should not be able to keep it. The voluntary destruction of the Fleet at Toulon has just proved that I was right, because even though I no longer commanded, the Fleet executed the orders which I had given and maintained, contrary to the wishes of the Laval Government.[28]

Winston Churchill's belief that Adolf Hitler would eventually renege on his promise not to grab the French fleet was borne out. And yet, just as Admiral Darlan had sworn to Churchill and Admiral Dudley Pound, and just as Admiral Gensoul had promised Cedric Holland, James Somerville, and Dudley North, French captains purposely scuttled their ships in the face of an attempted German takeover.

Churchill, the members of his war cabinet, and the senior men in his admiralty had misjudged François Darlan and his senior officers. After years of French promises and British doubts, after Dudley Pound's declaration that "we have no use for words," the men of the French Navy proved their honor with their deeds at Toulon.

Admiral Erich Raeder's solemn vow that the crew of the *Bismarck* would honor the memory of their ship's namesake "to their last breath" was fulfilled in May 1941 with assistance from James Somerville and the Royal Navy.

When the *Bismarck* finally entered the war after two years of sea trials, modifications, and combat-readiness training, she encountered HMS *Hood*, which was no longer Somerville's flagship, in her first battle. On the morning of May 24, 1941, in a clash that lasted just seventeen minutes, a sudden fireball erupted as the *Hood* was split in two, almost amidships. She sank in just three minutes, one of the most stunning losses in Royal Navy history. Only three members of her 1,419-man crew were rescued.

One of the three was eighteen-year-old Ted Briggs, the signalman who had helped hoist the red and white "Open fire—may be obeyed as soon as seen" flag on the *Hood* at Mers-el-Kébir.

A reconstituted Force H, still under the command of Vice Admiral Somerville and still with the carrier *Ark Royal* at its core, set off from Gibraltar, part of the Royal Navy's wide-ranging mission to avenge the *Hood*. Force H closed on the *Bismarck* on May 26, 1941 and shadowed the German battleship from a safe distance while awaiting reinforcements. In that interim, a torpedo from one of the *Ark Royal*'s Swordfish biplanes permanently jammed the *Bismarck*'s rudder during a late-night attack. Although the *Bismarck* retained her lethal firepower, Somerville reported that the massive battleship was now a vulnerable target, unsteerable and adrift in the heavy seas.

As the sun rose the following morning, observers on multiple British ships witnessed a relentless barrage on the wounded pride of the German Navy. A short time later, Winston Churchill stood before the House of Commons to brief members of Parliament on what he termed "an episode of arresting character." After noting that the *Bismarck*'s fate had not yet been sealed, the prime minister took his seat and responded to questions from Members of Parliament.

At 10:35 a.m., the heavy cruiser HMS *Dorsetshire* closed on the hulk of the *Bismarck* and helped usher her to the bottom of the Atlantic with torpedoes fired at close range. It is widely believed that the *Bismarck*'s crew helped complete her demise by detonating scuttling charges in her final hour. A short time after the *Bismarck* sank, John Colville rushed to Churchill's side and handed him a slip of paper.[29] The prime minister rose from his seat and announced, "I do not know whether I might venture, with great respect, to intervene for one moment. I have just received news that the *Bismarck* is sunk."[30] The House erupted in jubilation.

In February 1942 James Somerville was assigned to take on a new foe in a different theater. As commander of the Eastern Fleet, he risked peril in combat against the much larger and more lethal Imperial Japanese Navy.

After two heavy cruisers in the Eastern Fleet, HMS *Cornwall* and HMS *Dorsetshire* (the ship that launched the fatal torpedoes into the

Bismarck), were sunk by Japanese dive bombers, Somerville dispatched a cruiser and two destroyers to search for survivors. Eleven-hundred men were rescued after spending thirty hours in the sea. The dividend of so many lives saved proved to be worth that risk. A member of Somerville's staff noted that the rescue was "one of the best reasons why sailors in the fleet worshipped him."[31]

The composition of the Eastern Fleet changed on a routine basis as a result of losses and revised priorities in seas around the world. Somerville wrote in a letter to Dudley North, "My chief preoccupation of late has been to try and keep my small ration of butter evenly spread over the very large hunk of bread which is my portion."[32]

In March 1944, Somerville's Eastern Fleet received a most unlikely reinforcement, the French battleship *Richelieu*. After the British attacked her in July 1940, the *Richelieu* remained under slow repair in Dakar. When Germany completed its occupation of France and the majority of the French fleet self-scuttled at Toulon at the end of 1942, the crew of the *Richelieu*, along with the commanders and crews of other French ships in Africa, defected to the Allies. The *Richelieu* sailed to America for repairs and modernization. After six months of work in the Brooklyn, New York, naval yard and one month of firing exercises in the Chesapeake Bay, the *Richelieu* sailed back toward the war and joined Somerville's Eastern fleet.[33] The battleship that Somerville had once been ordered to destroy now sailed with his fastest ships against Japanese battleships, cruisers, destroyers, and carriers, and remained an active and effective component of the Eastern Fleet through the end of the war.

Somerville, who had taken an early interest in naval aviation and the use of carrier aircraft in particular, now had multiple modern aircraft carriers under his command, most notably the USS *Saratoga*, which sailed with the Eastern Fleet for a brief time early in 1944. Somerville's brush with the *Saratoga* inspired a poignant observation about the changed world order and the flipped balance between the American and British navies.

When Somerville "went afloat with my flag flying" to call on Captain John Cassady, the *Saratoga*'s commander, he was greeted with naval honors. "I felt it a bit incongruous, however, with the bands playing 'Rule

Britannia' when America has by far and away the largest fleet of any nation in the world."[34]

In the spring of 1944, Andrew Cunningham, now first sea lord, asked Somerville to accept a post that horrified his friend: a shore appointment as head of the British Admiralty Delegation in Washington, DC. The battle for support and supplies from America was almost as important to Britain as her fight against Germany and Japan. Somerville's persistence and personality would help ensure that Britain's navy received an adequate share.

Somerville's command of the Eastern Fleet had been so effective that Winston Churchill objected to his posting to Washington. The Eastern Fleet had enjoyed a series of successful attacks against Japanese bases due in no small part to Somerville's initiative, training, and tactical execution. Churchill implored First Lord of the Admiralty A. V. Alexander,

> Admiral Somerville has added new claims to our confidence by his brilliant attack at Sabang while the main Japanese Fleet was at Singapore. Why do we want to make a change here at all?
>
> It seems to me he knows the theatre, has right ideas about it and is capable of daring action. Does he want to go to Washington and give up his fighting command?[35]

In subsequent letters, Churchill added that Somerville was "keen and sprightly in the last degree,"[36] and that to "send this officer on this great command to Washington would be a squandering of our war power."[37] On this occasion, contrary to previous aspersions cast by Somerville and others on his independence, A. V. Alexander remained steadfast in the face of Churchill's arguments. In alliance with Andrew Cunningham, Alexander eventually won his argument with Churchill over Somerville's redeployment. James Somerville's last day at sea was August 23, 1944.

With Britannia no longer ruling the waves, Somerville's primary responsibility was to negotiate for the resources required to sustain Britain's navy as a viable sea-fighting force. He pressed for fuel, ammunition, and the use of dockyards in the Pacific. Somerville was a member of the British delegation at the Yalta Conference in February 1945, where he participated in meetings of the combined chiefs of staff.

Despite his initial misgivings—along with a distaste for the social obligations and the internaval politics that he never got over—Somerville thrived once again in this new position. The scratching up of a small boat that he rowed on the Potomac River helped him feel more at home. "I had a grand pull on Sunday afternoon," he mentioned in a letter to a friend.[38]

On May 8, 1945, the day the war in Europe came to an end, James Somerville was promoted to admiral of the fleet, the ultimate rank for an officer in the Royal Navy. Accolades poured in from all points of the compass. For Somerville, who had been dismissed from the navy in the year before the start of the war and then spent the next six years proving his extraordinary fitness for duty, the most thoughtful of the many kind sentiments that came his way was bestowed by Admiral Bob Burnett, who included a reference to the Bible verse Job 13:4—a scornful nod to the doctors who had declared Somerville a medical invalid, unsafe and unfit for duty in 1939. "But ye are forgers of lies, ye are all physicians of no value."[39]

Admiral of the Fleet Sir James Somerville retired in peace to the small Somerset town of Dinder, where Somervilles had lived since 1457.[40] He died on March 19, 1949 at the age of sixty-seven.

CODA

THE UNNECESSARY WAR

AT A TIME WHEN World War I was generally called "The Great War," Franklin D. Roosevelt asked Winston Churchill what he thought the new war would be named. Churchill suggested, "The Unnecessary War."[1]

Churchill's response begs the question, Was the British attack on the French ships at Mers-el-Kébir necessary?

Despite his apprehension before the fact, Churchill had no public regrets about his decision to secure or destroy the French ships and no misgivings about the consequences of Britain's actions. As he later wrote about the Royal Navy's attack on Admiral Gensoul's *Force de Raid*, "No act was ever more necessary for the life of Britain."[2]

The life of Britain in July 1940 depended on her ability to control the seas, specifically the ability to resist the expected cross-channel invasion by Hitler's Wehrmacht and the ability to preempt a blockade and sustain the daily lives of British citizens with the free flow of essential materials. If Germany had combined the core of the French fleet—the *Dunkerque, Strasbourg, Richelieu,* and *Jean Bart,* in particular—with the U-boats and destroyers of the *Kriegsmarine*, the combined forces could have compromised Britain's ability to defend and supply her shores. Winston Churchill would not allow the German Navy to surround his island.

Despite Hitler's declaration in the Franco-German armistice agreement that he did not intend to use the French fleet, Churchill was not about to trust a promise from the German chancellor. Any suggestion that Hitler would never add French ships to Admiral Raeder's navy would have seemed preposterous in 1940.

Churchill had multiple assurances in hand—from François Darlan, Paul Reynaud, and Philippe Pétain, as well as from Darlan's loyal fraternity of admirals in Atlantic and Mediterranean ports—that French naval officers had plans in place to scuttle their ships in the face of German takeover attempts. The promises of French politicians and admirals paled in comparison with what Churchill termed "the real facts of the situation." Despite their best intentions, Churchill did not believe the French would have the opportunity to honor their vows to scuttle. He expected mortal threats and lightning attacks to overwhelm French seamen before they could act to defend or sink their ships. As the Royal Navy proved in Plymouth and Portsmouth, French ships under foreign control were indeed vulnerable to abrupt seizure.

To their vast credit, French naval officers deliberately scuttled their surviving fleet in the harbor at Toulon to prevent its seizure by Germany. The mettle and the integrity of French admirals and captains was greater than Churchill was willing to ascribe to them in 1940. The men of the French Navy proved their honor and earned admiration for posterity with this defiant act.

The French ships in Alexandria were peacefully demilitarized. This same action would have prevented bloodshed at Mers-el-Kébir. However, in contrast with Admiral René-Émile Godfroy, who joined candid negotiations with Admiral Andrew Cunningham at Alexandria, Admiral Marcel-Bruno Gensoul refused to parley directly with Captain Cedric Holland until late on July 3, 1940. We now know that Holland hinted (at the very least) that Britain might find demilitarization an acceptable measure. We also know that Admiral Gensoul expressed no interest in that option.

On the surface, James Somerville's selection of Cedric Holland to negotiate with Admiral Gensoul was ideal. In terms of language skills and personal relations with officers in the French Navy, there was no better candidate. Holland, however, lacked the stonehearted temperament necessary to overcome Gensoul's intransigence. Andrew Cunningham believed it would have been more productive for Somerville to deal with Gensoul directly, with Cedric Holland at his side to translate.[3]

From a hardware standpoint, the British campaign to destroy or secure the most dangerous ships in François Darlan's navy was a mixed success. The *Bretagne*, which had been commissioned in 1916, was demolished. The *Dunkerque*, one of Britain's four primary targets, was damaged to the extent that she was not put back into battle against Britain. At Dakar, repairs to the *Richelieu* would take more than a year, and her guns would never fire upon Royal Navy ships. The *Jean Bart* remained unfinished, effectively marooned in Casablanca. Apart from the inspirational value of the story of her escape, the *Strasbourg* spent most of the war at anchor in Toulon and made no consequential impact on the further course of the war. Additional French ships were secured in Alexandria, Plymouth, Portsmouth, and other ports.

The deaths of 1,257 French seamen were more significant than the loss of any French vessels. Their martyrdom turned the opinion of most Frenchmen against Churchill and Britain, nowhere more so than in the French Navy. In demanding the seizure of French ships and authorizing attacks on those that would not yield, Churchill risked war with France. Was the potential outcome worth the risk?

The French response to Britain's attacks was meek in every aspect. Her navy, though not eliminated, ended up diminished as a threat to Britain. The leaders of France recognized that their only hope to escape from German control was for Britain to win the war. American Ambassador William Bullitt echoed that sentiment after meeting with Marshal Pétain on July 4, 1940 in the aftermath of the attack at Mers-el-Kébir: "Pétain recognized that only a defeat of Hitler by some other power can restore independence to France. He is therefore, sincerely desirous of a British victory. Pétain was inclined to minimize the "breach" by attributing it to Churchill's personal lack of balance."[14]

Speaking for himself and for all of Britain, Churchill stated that they had "but one thought, to win the war and destroy Hitlerism." And, with indispensable help from Britain's allies, they did.

Churchill knew that his action would not alienate the only prospective ally that truly mattered. Britain's attack at Mers-el-Kébir assured America of Churchill's resolve. It fortified Franklin Roosevelt's inclination to do everything within his admittedly constrained power to supply and support Britain during the time when Britain and its dominions fought Germany and Italy on their own.

Six months after the events at Mers-el-Kébir, in the course of a midnight-till-2 a.m. discussion, the prime minister summarized the progress of the war for the benefit of Harry Hopkins, whom Roosevelt sent to assess Churchill's character and fortitude. As recounted by John Colville, Churchill told Hopkins, "He believed that Oran had been the turning point in our fortunes: it made the world realise that we were in earnest in our intentions to carry it on."[5]

Colville perfectly captured the stark significance of Churchill's action in his introduction to Warren Tute's book about the events at Mers-el-Kébir: "Throughout the entire world it became clear that the British had burned not merely the French boats but their own."[6]

Churchill's former private secretary added that "the vision of a total and immediate victory for Nazi Germany, so vivid in June 1940, already began to seem a trifle blurred in July." The ruthless attack on Britain's recent ally demonstrated that Churchill was unlike any other leader Adolf Hitler had encountered.

When Churchill determined that Britain's best course was to eliminate the French fleet as a risk in July 1940, he based his decision on what he knew at the time. He would not trust Adolf Hitler's vow that he would not seize France's largest ships. He lacked confidence in François Darlan and his admirals' ability to defend the independence of their fleet. A German invasion of Britain was assumed to be the natural next step after the capitulation of France. Hitler's confidence that he would either crush Britain or force the harsh terms of a treaty was never higher than in the immediate aftermath of the fall of France. During the afternoon of July 3, 1940, the French Navy added a dire dimension to the dispute at Mers-el-Kébir when they broadcast an appeal for warships in other ports to reinforce Admiral Gensoul's *Force de Raid*. Those reinforcements materialized too late to help Gensoul, but their threat could not be ignored, and that threat was a significant factor late on that July day.

As the leader of a nation at war, Winston Churchill was responsible for the whole machine—military and civilian. He inspired the masses with his eloquence, but he understood the finite impact of even the most inspirational words and phrases. As Churchill knew, "It is events that move the world."[7]

Admiral Marcel-Bruno Gensoul faced a brutal predicament on July 3, 1940. He had the ability to prevent his recent friends and former allies from firing on his ships. But if he surrendered his ships—or, in his mind, worse, joined forces with the Royal Navy—he would have betrayed Admiral Darlan and violated the German armistice agreement. Gensoul had two practical alternatives available to avoid destruction and bloodshed: to demilitarize his ships or steam them to Martinique or America under the cover of British duress. In all likelihood, if he had parleyed with Cedric Holland early in the day, the two men would have devised a compromise that worked for both sides. When he spurned every opportunity for a peaceful solution as Force H waited in the bay off Mers-el-Kébir, vulnerable to the approach of French reinforcements, Admiral Gensoul assumed responsibility for the outcome of his decision.

If Britain had not attacked the French ships and killed 1,257 French seamen at Mers-el-Kébir, the Allies would still have won the war. However, given the evidence at Churchill's disposal in June and July 1940, the assault at Mers-el-Kébir was a necessary attack. Britain's prime minister could not risk the loss of the *Dunkerque*, *Strasbourg*, *Richelieu*, or *Jean Bart* to German or Italian control.

Winston Churchill was fighting a war.

NOTES

CHAPTER 1. WINSTON IS BACK

1. Kenneth Poolman, *The Kelly* (W. W. Norton, 1954), 64.
2. William Manchester, *Winston Spencer Churchill: Alone, 1932–1940* (Little, Brown and Company, 1988), 556. The lee is the side away from which the wind is blowing.
3. Winston Churchill, *The Second World War: The Gathering Storm* (Houghton Mifflin Company, 1948), 410.
4. Admiral Sir Guy Grantham to Arthur J. Marder, August 21, 1968, UCI, Arthur J. Marder papers, MS-F002, BA05-A-1. Box 1.
5. "Things That Happen in War Time," *The Clarion*, November 23, 1914.
6. Rear Admiral Paul Auphan and Jacques Mordal, *The French Navy in World War II* (Naval Institute Press, 1959), 221.
7. Colin Smith, *England's Last War Against France* (Phoenix, 2010), 37.
8. Lord Mountbatten to Cedric Holland, September 15, 1949, NMM, Holland family papers, HND/5/2, Letters received by Holland, 1921–1949.
9. Cedric Swinton Holland Service Records, TNA, Royal Navy Service Records, ADM 196/52/257.
10. Arthur R. Hinks to Cedric Holland, December 15, 1921, NMM, Holland family papers, Letters received by Holland, 1921–1949, HND/5/2.
11. Kenneth Poolman, *Ark Royal* (William Kimber, 1956), 130.
12. David Brown, *The Road to Oran* (Frank Cass, 2004), 8.
13. Auphan and Mordal, *French Navy in World War II*, 25.
14. Churchill, *The Gathering Storm*, 500.
15. John Jordan and Robert Dumas, *French Battleships: 1922–1956* (Seaforth Publishing, 2009), 122.
16. Smith, *England's Last War Against France*, 38.
17. Churchill, *The Gathering Storm*, 164.
18. Churchill, *The Gathering Storm*, 501.
19. HC Deb. (8 Nov. 1939) (353) col 258.
20. William L. Shirer, *The Collapse of the Third Republic* (Simon and Schuster, 1969), 537.
21. Glyn Prysor, *Citizen Sailors* (Penguin Books, 2012), 26.

CHAPTER 2. UNTIL THEY WIN OR GO DOWN WITH THEIR FLAG FLYING

1. Friedrich Ruge, *Der Seekrieg—The German Navy's Story: 1939–1945* (United States Naval Press, 1957), 15, 34.
2. Ruge, *Der Seekrieg*, 49.
3. "British Sea Might Centering on *Spee*," *New York Times*, December 15, 1939.
4. Colin Smith, *England's Last War Against France* (Phoenix, 2010), 38.
5. Dudley Pope, Graf Spee*: The Life and Death of a Raider* (J. P. Lippincott, 1957), 237.

6. *Fuehrer Conferences on Naval Affairs, 1939–1945* (Naval Institute Press, 1990), 69.
7. David J. Bercuson and Holger H. Herwig, *The Destruction of the Bismarck* (The Overlook Press, 2001), 24.
8. Keith Bird, *Erich Raeder: Admiral of the Third Reich* (Naval Institute Press, 2013), 143.
9. Richard Collier, *1940: The Avalanche* (The Dial Press, 1979), 24.
10. Ruge, *Der Seekrieg*, 82.
11. Winston Churchill, *The Second World War: The Gathering Storm* (Houghton Mifflin, 1948), 562.
12. Willi Frischauer and Robert Jackson, *The Altmark Affair* (Macmillan, 1955), 237.
13. Norman Longmate, *How We Lived Then* (Pimlico, 2002), 89.
14. Churchill, *The Gathering Storm*, 563.
15. Smith, *England's Last War Against France*, 39.
16. Philippe Lasterle, "Marcel Gensoul (1880–1973), un amiral dans la tourmente," *Revue historique des armées* 219 (2000): 80.
17. Fifteen-inch guns fired shells that were fifteen inches in diameter, five-feet long, and packed with close to a half-ton of explosives.
18. David Brown, *The Road to Oran* (Frank Cass, 2004), 9.

CHAPTER 3. FACTS ARE BETTER THAN DREAMS

1. André Maurois, *Why France Fell* (John Lane, 1940), 63.
2. Reynaud's formal title was President of the Council of Ministers. "Premier" and "Prime Minister" are acceptable—and interchangeable—references. "Prime Minister" is used throughout this book, except when "Premier" appears in quoted passages.
3. Galeazzo Ciano, *The Ciano Diaries* (Howard Fertig, 1973), 238.
4. Julian Jackson, *The Fall of France* (Oxford University Press, 2003), 127.
5. Winston Churchill, *The Second World War: The Gathering Storm* (Houghton Mifflin Company, 1948), 575.
6. John Harvey, ed., *The Diplomatic Diaries of Oliver Harvey* (Collins, 1970), 219.
7. HC Deb. (5 Oct. 1938) (339) col. 364.
8. Jackson, *Fall of France*, 125.
9. Pierre Lazareff, *Deadline: The Behind-the-Scenes Story of the Last Decade in France* (Random House, 1942), 312.
10. Clare Boothe, *Europe in the Spring* (Alfred A. Knopf, 1941), 156.
11. Sanche de Gramont, *The French: Portrait of a People* (G. P. Putnam's Sons, 1969), 148.
12. Churchill, *The Gathering Storm*, 549.
13. Winston Churchill, "Dwelling in the Cage of the Tiger," Radio Broadcast from London, March 31, 1940.
14. William L. Shirer, *The Collapse of the Third Republic* (Simon and Schuster, 1969), 603.
15. Angus Calder, *The People's War* (Pantheon Books, 1969), 77.
16. Colin Coote, *Editorial: The Memoirs of Colin R. Coote* (Eyre & Spottiswoode, 1965), 184.
17. HC Deb. (7 May 1940) (360) col. 1150.
18. A. J. P Taylor, *From the Boer War to the Cold War* (Penguin Press, 1994), 305.
19. John Barnes and David Nicholson, *The Empire at Bay—The Leo Amery Diaries: 1929–1945* (Hutchinson, 1988), 292.
20. Leo Amery, *My Political Life*, vol. 3: *The Unforgiving Years: 1929–1940* (Hutchinson, 1953), 360.

21. Harold Macmillan, *The Blast of War: 1939–1945* (Harper & Row, 1967), 57.
22. HC Deb. (8 May 1940) (360) cols. 1283–1362.
23. Macmillan, *Blast of War*, 62.
24. Andrew Roberts, *Walking with Destiny* (Viking, 2018), 509.
25. Churchill, *The Gathering Storm*, 410.

CHAPTER 4. NOT ILLUMINATED BY THE MERCY OF CHRIST

1. William L. Shirer, *The Collapse of the Third Republic* (Simon and Schuster, 1969), 605.
2. Richard Collier, *1940: The Avalanche* (The Dial Press, 1979), 67.
3. Winston Churchill, *The Second World War: Their Finest Hour* (Houghton Mifflin Company, 1949), 42.
4. Admiral Sir William James to Marder, February 22, 1975, UCI, Arthur J. Marder papers, MS-F002, BA05-A-1. Box 1.
5. Major L. F. Ellis, *The War in France and Flanders: 1939–1940* (Her Majesty's Stationery Office, 1953), 309.
6. In addition to Churchill, the war cabinet included Lord President of the Council Neville Chamberlain, Lord Privy Seal Clement Atlee, Foreign Secretary Lord Halifax, and Minister without Portfolio Arthur Greenwood.
7. Shirer, *Collapse of the Third Republic*, 699.
8. Colin Smith, *England's Last War Against France* (Phoenix, 2010), 16.
9. Lieutenant Commander P. K. Kemp, *Key to Victory: The Triumph of British Sea Power in World War II* (Little, Brown and Company, 1957,) 17.
10. Charles de Gaulle, *The Complete War Memoirs of Charles de Gaulle* (Simon and Schuster, 1959), 64.
11. Richard M. Watt, *Dare Call It Treason* (Simon and Schuster, 1963), 214.
12. General Pierre Héring, *La Vie Exemplaire de Philippe Pétain* (Paris-Livres, 1956), 77.
13. Anthony Eden, Earl of Avon, *Eden Memoirs: The Reckoning* (Houghton Mifflin Company, 1965), 117.
14. Major General Sir Edward Spears, *Assignment to Catastrophe*, vol. 2: *The Fall of France: June 1940* (William Heinemann Ltd, 1954), 101.
15. Robert and Isabelle Tombs, *The Sweet Enemy* (William Heinemann, 2006), 555.
16. HC Deb. (4 June 1940) (361) col. 791.
17. "Germans Applaud Candid Churchill," *New York Times*, June 6, 1940.
18. Ian Ousby, *Occupation: The Ordeal of France—1940–1944* (St. Martin's Press, 1997), 38.
19. Robert Wright, *Dowding and the Battle of Britain* (MacDonald, 1969), 104.
20. Churchill, *Their Finest Hour*, 154.
21. Ronald C. Rosbottom, *When Paris Went Dark, The City of Light Under German Occupation* (Little, Brown and Company, 2014), 41.
22. Alexander Werth, *The Twilight of France, 1933–1940: A Journalist's Chronicle* (Harper & Brothers Publishers, 1940), 166.
23. Churchill, *Their Finest Hour*, 153
24. Samuel Rosenman, ed., *The Public Papers and Addresses of Franklin D. Roosevelt—1940 Volume* (MacMillan & Co., 1941), 265.
25. Churchill, Their *Finest Hour*, 153.
26. Spears, *Fall of France*, 219.
27. Spears, *Fall of France*, 148.
28. Spears, *Fall of France*, 202.

29. Spears, *Fall of France*, 203.
30. Spears, *Fall of France*, 207.
31. Spears, *Fall of France*, 209.
32. The Deputy Ambassador in France (Biddle) to the Secretary of State, (Paris) Tours, June 14, 1940, *Foreign Relations of the United States Diplomatic Papers, 1940, General, Volume I*, Office of the Historian, https://history.state.gov/historicaldocuments/frus1940v01/d215.
33. Churchill, *Their Finest Hour*, 182.
34. General Carl von Clausewitz, *On War*, vol. 3 (Kegan Paul, Trench & Trubner & Co. LTD, 1908), 210.
35. Lord Ismay, *Memoirs of General The Lord Ismay* (Heinemann, 1960), 128.
36. John Colville, *The Fringes of Power* (The Lyons Press, 1985), 157.
37. Spears, *Fall of France*, 265.
38. Spears, *Fall of France*, 194.
39. Spears, *Fall of France*, 266.
40. Spears, *Fall of France*, 279.
41. Spears, *Fall of France*, 282.
42. Spears, *Fall of France*, 284.
43. Spears, *Fall of France*, 286.
44. Spears, *Fall of France*, 289.
45. Spears, *Fall of France*, 290.

CHAPTER 5. AND THUS WE SHALL CONQUER

1. Major General Sir Edward Spears, *Assignment to Catastrophe*, vol. 2: *The Fall of France: June 1940* (William Heinemann Ltd, 1954), 291.
2. HC Deb. (16 Oct. 1940) (365) cols. 701–702.
3. John Colville, *The Fringes of Power* (The Lyons Press, 1985), 160.
4. Walter Thompson, *Assignment Churchill* (Farrar, Straus and Young, 1955), 194.
5. Winston Churchill, *The Second World War: Their Finest Hour* (Houghton Mifflin Company, 1949), 215.
6. Thompson, *Assignment Churchill*, 194.
7. Spears, *Fall of France*, 273.
8. Churchill, *Their Finest Hour*, 211.
9. Churchill, *Their Finest Hour*, 212.
10. Jean Lacouture, *De Gaulle, The Rebel: 1890–1944* (W. W. Norton and Company, 1990), 207.
11. Spears, *Fall of France*, 298.
12. Noel Barber, *The Week France* Fell (Stein and Day, 1976), 262.
13. Spears, *Fall of France*, 300.
14. Spears, *Fall of France*, 298.
15. Spears, *Fall of France*, 307.
16. Spears, *Fall of France*, 293.
17. Churchill, *Their Finest Hour*, 210.
18. Churchill, *Their Finest Hour*, 230.
19. Churchill, *Their Finest Hour*, 182.
20. Spears, *Fall of France*, 305.
21. General Sir Edward Louis Spears to Winston Churchill, November 24, 1948, CAC, Spears: Assignment to Catastrophe, Source Material, SPRS 8/20.

22. Lacouture, *De Gaulle, The Rebel*, 244.
23. James Leasor, *War at the Top—Based on the Experiences of General Sir Leslie Hollis* (House of Stratus, 1959), 92.
24. Anthony Heckstall-Smith, *The Fleet That Faced Both Ways* (Anthony Blond, 1963), 70.
25. David Brown, *The Road to Oran* (Frank Cass, 2004), 41.
26. René Pierre Eugène Caroff, *Les Forces Maritimes de l'Ouest* (Service historique de la Marine, 1954), 326.
27. Charles Williams, *Pétain: How the Hero of France Became a Convicted Traitor and Changed the Course of History* (Palgrave Macmillan, 2005), 166.
28. I. C. B. Dear, *The Oxford Companion to World War II* (Oxford University Press, 1995), 414.
29. Churchill, *Their Finest Hour*, 216.
30. Churchill, *Their Finest Hour*, 217.
31. Spears, *Fall of France*, 294.
32. Spears, *Fall of France*, 294.
33. Spears, *Fall of France*, 312.

CHAPTER 6. YOU DO NOT NEGOTIATE AN ARMISTICE

1. Nicolaus von Below, *At Hitler's Side: The Memoirs of Hitler's Luftwaffe Adjutant, 1937–45* (Greenhill Books, 1980), 62.
2. William L. Shirer, "*This is Berlin*" (The Overlook Press, 1999), 288.
3. William L. Shirer, *Berlin Diary: The Journal of a Foreign Correspondent* (Alfred A. Knopf, 1941), 422.
4. *Documents on German Foreign Policy, Series D (1937–1945)*, vol. 9: *The War Years: March 18–June 22, 1940* (United States Government Printing Office, 1956), 644. Hereafter: *DGFP*.
5. General Maxime Weygand, *Recalled to Service: The Memoirs of General Weygand* (Doubleday & Company, 1952), 202.
6. Richard Collier, *1940: The Avalanche* (The Dial Press, 1979), 140.
7. *DGFP*, 646.
8. Dr. Paul Schmidt, *Hitler's Interpreter* (William Heinemann Ltd., 1951), 183.
9. *DGFP*, 653.
10. *DGFP*, 654.
11. Albert Kammerer, *La Verité Sur l'Armistice* (Editions Médicis, 1944), 653.
12. William L. Shirer, *The Collapse of the Third Republic* (Simon and Schuster, 1969), 882.
13. 400 million is from Jean-Pierre Patat and Michael Lutfalla, *A Monetary History of France in the Twentieth Century* (St. Martin's Press, 1986), 97. This levy was reduced to 320 million in 1941, and raised to 500 million in late 1942 when the free zone was eliminated. One French franc was equal to 0.0223 U.S. dollars in 1940; from David Challis, Archival Currency Converter 1916–1940, https://canvasresources-prod.le.unimelb.edu.au/projects/CURRENCY_CALC/. In 1940, 400 million FF would have equaled $8,920,000. A U.S. dollar in 1940 would be worth $21.91 in 2024; from CPI Inflation Calculator: https://www.in2013dollars.com/us/inflation/1940?amount=1. What would have been $8,920,000 in 1940 is $200,570,003 in 2025.
14. Shirer, *Collapse of the Third Republic*, 880.
15. The full text of the Franco-German armistice agreement appears in *DGFP* on page 671. It can also be found online at Yale Law School's online Avalon Project, Documents in Law, History and Diplomacy, https://avalon.law.yale.edu/wwii/frgearm.asp.

16. Eleanor M. Gates, *End of the Affair* (University of California Press, 1981), 284.
17. Pertinax, *The Gravediggers of France* (Doubleday, Doran & Company, 1944), 441.
18. Shirer, *Collapse of the Third Republic*, 883.
19. Shirer, *Collapse of the Third Republic*, 883.
20. Henry H. Adams, *Years of Deadly Peril* (David McKay Company, 1974), 189.
21. The Ambassador in the United Kingdom Kennedy to the Secretary of State Hull, June 22, 1940, *Foreign Relations of the United States Diplomatic Papers, 1940, General and Europe*, vol. 2, Office of the Historian, https://history.state.gov/historicaldocuments/frus1940v02/d532.
22. Albert Kammerer, *La Passion de la Flotte Française* (Librairie Arthéme Fayard, 1951), 15.
23. George Melton, *From Versailles to Mers el-Kébir: The Promise of Anglo-French Naval Cooperation, 1919–1940* (Naval Institute Press, 2015), 5.
24. Herve Coutau-Bégarie and Claude Huan, *Lettres et notes de l'amiral Darlan* (Economica, 1992), 186.
25. Jules Moch, *Rencontres Avec . . . Darlan et Eisenhower* (Plon, 1968), 138.
26. Pierre Varillon, *Mers-el-Kébir* (Amiot-Dumont, 1949), 65.
27. Charles de Gaulle, *The Complete War Memoirs of Charles de Gaulle* (Simon and Schuster, 1959), 76.
28. Rear Admiral Paul Auphan and Jacques Mordal, *The French Navy in World War II* (Naval Institute Press, 1959), 17.
29. David Dilks, ed., *The Diaries of Sir Alexander Cadogan: 1938–1945* (G. P. Putnam's Sons, 1972), 248.
30. Kammerer, *La Passion de la Flotte Française*, 135.
31. Gerald Pawle, *The War and Colonel Warden* (Alfred A. Knopf, 1963), 12.
32. Hervé Coutau-Bégarie and Claude Huan, *Darlan* (Librairie Arthème Fayard, 1989), 151.
33. Moch, *Rencontres Avec . . . Darlan*, 67.
34. Alain Darlan, *L'Amiral Darlan Parle* (Amiot-Dumont, 1952), 36.
35. Alexander Werth, *France: 1940–1955* (Henry Holt and Company, 1956), 81.
36. Vice Admiral Jules-Théophile Docteur, *La Grande Énigme de la Guerre: Darlan—Amiral de la Flotte* (Le Grand Livre du Mois, 1948), 60.
37. Winston Churchill, *The Second World War: Their Finest Hour* (Houghton Mifflin Company, 1949), 229.
38. Coutau-Bégarie and Huan, *Darlan*, 26.
39. *DGFP*, 646.
40. Weygand, *Recalled to Service*, 197.
41. Shirer, *Collapse of the Third Republic*, 886.
42. *DGFP*, 668.
43. Shirer, *Collapse of the Third Republic*, 899.
44. Philip Ziegler, *London at War, 1939–1945* (Pimlico, 2002), 83.
45. HC Deb. (18 June 1940) (362) cols 59–61.

CHAPTER 7. TWO ESCAPES

1. Minutes of Meeting Held in First Sea Lord's Room at the Admiralty, June 7, 1940, PRO, First Sea Lord's Personal War Records, ADM 205/4.
2. Winston Churchill, *The Second World War: Their Finest Hour* (Houghton Mifflin Company, 1949), 239.
3. Cordell Hull, *The Memoirs of Cordell Hull*, vol. 1 (Macmillan & Co., 1948), 792.

4. Sir Llewellyn Woodward, *History of the Second World War: British Foreign Policy in the Second World War*, vol. 1 (Her Majesty's Stationery Office, 1970), 298.
5. William L. Shirer, *The Collapse of the Third Republic* (Simon and Schuster, 1969), 858.
6. George Melton, *From Versailles to Mers el-Kébir: The Promise of Anglo-French Naval Cooperation, 1919–1940* (Naval Institute Press, 2015), 171.
7. John Jordan and Robert Dumas, *French Battleships: 1922–1956* (Seaforth Publishing, 2009), 171.
8. Record of Conversation held at Bordeaux on June 18, 1940 between first lord, first sea lord, and Admiral Darlan, PRO, ADM 205/4. Jordan and Dumas added that the *Clemenceau* was not bombed until 1944 and was not commandeered by Germany.
9. Alec de Montmorency, *The Enigma of Admiral Darlan* (E. P. Dutton, 1943), 92.
10. Hervé Coutau-Bégarie and Claude Huan, *Lettres et notes de l'amiral Darlan* (Economica, 1992), 208.
11. Rear Admiral Paul Auphan and Jacques Mordal, *The French Navy in World War II* (Naval Institute Press, 1959), 87.
12. David Brown, *The Road to Oran* (Frank Cass, 2004), 31.
13. Auphan and Mordal, *French Navy in World War II*, 89.
14. Colin Smith, *England's Last War Against France* (Phoenix, 2010), 1.
15. Jordan and Dumas, *French Battleships*, 124–25.
16. Stephen Roskill, *The War at Sea: 1939–1945*, vol. 1 (Her Majesty's Stationery Office, 1954), 236.
17. Auphan and Mordal, *French Navy in World War II*, 92.
18. René Pierre Eugène Caroff, *Le Théâtre Atlantique*, Tome 2: *aprés le 25 juin 1940* (Marine nationale E. M. général, Service historique, 1959), 156.

CHAPTER 8. ANY ENEMY OR EX-ALLY

1. Sir Llewellyn Woodward, *History of the Second World War: British Foreign Policy in the Second World War*, vol. 1 (Her Majesty's Stationery Office, 1970), 312.
2. Gilbert Martin, *The Churchill War Papers*, vol. 2: *Never Surrender, May 1940–December 1940* (W. W. Norton & Company, 1995), 393.
3. Woodward, *History of the Second World War*, 298.
4. Woodward, *History of the Second World War*, 308.
5. Jacques Benoist-Méchin, *Sixty Days That Shook the West—The Fall of France: 1940* (G. P. Putnam's Sons, 1963), 454.
6. David Brown, *The Road to Oran* (Frank Cass, 2004), 145.
7. First Sea Lord's signal, 0124, June 23, 1940.
8. Albert Kammerer, *La Passion de la Flotte Française* (Librairie Arthéme Fayard, 1951), 101.
9. Brown, *Road to Oran*, 88.
10. Esteva's reply is mentioned in the script that Cedric Holland handed to Bernard Dufay in the bay at Mers-el-Kébir on July 3, 1940.
11. Vice Admiral Jules-Théophile Docteur, *La Grande Énigme de la Guerre: Darlan—Amiral de la Flotte* (Le Grand Livre du Mois, 1948), 45.
12. Woodward, *History of the Second World War*, 313.
13. William L. Shirer, *The Collapse of the Third Republic* (Simon and Schuster, 1969), 888.
14. Paul Reynaud, *In the Thick of the Fight: 1930–1945* (Simon and Schuster, 1951), 563.
15. Major General Sir Edward Spears, *Assignment to Catastrophe*, vol. 2: *The Fall of France: June 1940* (William Heinemann Ltd, 1954), 209.

16. Noel Barber, *The Week France Fell* (Stein and Day, 1976), 297.
17. Pertinax, *The Gravediggers of France* (Doubleday, Doran & Company, 1944), 311.
18. Kammerer, *La Passion de la Flotte Francaise*, 118.
19. HC Deb. (25 June 1940) (362) col 304.
20. HC Deb. (25 June 1940) (362) col 305.
21. John Colville, *The Fringes of Power* (The Lyons Press, 1985), 126.
22. Shirer, *Collapse of the Third Republic*, 892.
23. Henry H. Adams, *Years of Deadly Peril* (David McKay Company, 1974), 194.
24. Jean Lacouture, *De Gaulle, The Rebel: 1890–1944* (W. W. Norton and Company, 1990), 231.
25. Winston Churchill, *The Second World War: Their Finest Hour* (Houghton Mifflin Company, 1949), 230.
26. Jules Moch, *Rencontres Avec . . . Darlan et Eisenhower* (Plon, 1968), 146.
27. Hervé Coutau-Bégarie and Claude Huan, *Lettres et notes de l'amiral Darlan* (Economica, 1992),188.
28. Henri Ballande, *De l'Amiraute a Bikini, Souvenirs des jours sans joie* (Presses de la Cite, 1957), 97.
29. Simon Berton, *Allies at War* (Carroll & Graff Publishers, 2001), 29.

CHAPTER 9. A STATE OF STUPEFIED MISERY

1. Denis Baldensberger, *Mers-el-Kébir* (Editions Rouff, 1967), 46.
2. Photographs and documents relating to the Mers-el-Kébir affair, 1940–1941, NMM, Narrative of Events at Oran on 3 July 1940, Holland Family papers, HND/3/4.
3. Oran material from non-naval sources—Notes on Langer and Gleason's "The Challenge to Isolation," CAC, Undated Dudley Pound Papers, Extracts related to British attacks on French Fleet at Oran & Dakar, GBR/0014/DUPO 5/3.
4. Adm Dudley North to Adm Dudley Pound, CAC, Papers related to British attacks on French Fleet at Oran & Dakar, June 1940, DUPO 5/3.
5. Report on meeting at Oran, June 1940, CAC, Correspondence: Somerville, 1940–1947, NRTH 2/8.
6. War Cabinet Meeting, June 24, 1940, CAB, WM(40) 141, 65/7.
7. David Brown, *The Road to Oran* (Frank Cass, 2004), 104.
8. Henry H. Adams, *Years of Deadly Peril* (David McKay Company, 1974), 181.
9. War Cabinet Meeting, June 24, 1940, CAB, WM(40) 141, 65/7.
10. Brown, *Road to Oran*, 106.
11. Eleanor M. Gates, *End of the Affair* (University of California Press, 1981), 284.
12. Arthur J. Marder, *From the Dardanelles to Oran* (Oxford University Press, 1974), 203.

CHAPTER 10. IT IS EVENTS THAT MOVE THE WORLD

1. Albert Kammerer, *La Passion de la Flotte Française* (Librairie Arthéme Fayard, 1951), 133.
2. Rear Admiral Paul Auphan and Jacques Mordal, *The French Navy in World War II* (Naval Institute Press, 1959), 120.
3. War Cabinet Meeting, June 28, 1940, CAB, WM 187 (40), 65/13.
4. John Colville, *The Fringes of Power* (The Lyons Press, 1985), 174.
5. Colville, *Fringes of Power*, 175.
6. Colin Smith, *England's Last War Against France* (Phoenix, 2010), 60.
7. Admiral Sir W. M. James, *The Portsmouth Letters* (Macmillan & Co., 1946), 125.
8. Andrew Norman, *HMS Hood, Pride of the Royal Navy* (Stackpole Books, 2001), 3.

9. Final Report—Report of Proceedings—28 June–4 July 1940, CAC, Reports on Operation Catapult, Section 6, SMVL 7/19.
10. James Fownes Somerville Service Records, ADM, TNA, Royal Navy Service Records, 196/47/87.
11. Donald Macintyre, *Fighting Admiral—The Life and Battles of Admiral of the Fleet Sir James Somerville* (Evans Brothers, 1961), 12.
12. Recollections of Somerville by Commander William Boucher Edwards, CAC, Reports on Operation Catapult, SMVL 7/19.
13. Correspondence between Commander John Somerville and Martin Stephen about Stephen's book "The Fighting Admirals," CAC, SMVL 14/3.
14. Captain Herbert Layman to Marder, January 11, 1975, UCI, Arthur J. Marder papers, MS-F002, BA05-A-1. Box 8
15. Macintyre, *Fighting Admiral*, 247.
16. Macintyre, *Fighting Admiral*, 85.
17. Correspondence with Admiralty about Somerville's Request to be Restored to Active List, CAC, SMVL 6/4.
18. Derek House, *Radar at Sea: The Royal Navy in World War 2* (Naval Institute Press, 1993), 62.
19. Michael Simpson, ed., *The Somerville Papers* (Naval Records Society, 1995), 12 February 1940, letter from Somerville to Cunninghan, 28.
20. Letters from Listeners, CAC, Correspondence About Broadcasts, SMVL 12/5.
21. Macintyre, *Fighting Admiral*, 51.
22. Macintyre, *Fighting Admiral*, 51.
23. Simpson, *Somerville Papers*, May 30, 1940, letter from Somerville to his wife, Mary, 33.
24. Simpson, *Somerville Papers*, June 18, 1940, Report on Operation DYNAMO by Vice Admiral Betram Ramsay, 33.

CHAPTER 11. TRANSFORM A DEFEATED ALLY INTO AN ACTIVE ENEMY

1. William L. Shirer, *The Collapse of the Third Republic* (Simon and Schuster, 1969), 889.
2. Admiral George Collett to Marder, August 16, 1972, UCI, Arthur J. Marder papers, MS-F002, BA05-A-2. Box 7.
3. Henri Ballande, *De l'Amiraute a Bikini, Souvenirs des jours sans joie* (Presses de la Cite, 1957), 73.
4. Cedric Swinton Holland Service Records, ADM, TNA, Royal Navy Service Records, 196/52/257.
5. "The Attitude of the French Navy," NMM, Photographs and documents relating to the Mers-el-Kébir affair, 1940–1941, Narrative of Events at Oran on July 3, 1940, Holland Family papers, HND/3/4.
6. Arthur J. Marder, *From the Dardanelles to Oran: Studies of the Royal Navy in War and Peace, 1915–1940* (Oxford University Press, 1976), 210.
7. David Brown, *The Road to Oran* (Frank Cass, 2004), 168.
8. Final Report—Report of Proceedings—28 June–4 July 1940, CAC, Reports on Operation Catapult, Section 6, SMVL 7/19.
9. Warren Tute, *Deadly Stroke* (Coward, McCann & Geoghegan, 1973), 28.
10. Final Report—Report of Proceedings—28 June–4 July 1940, CAC, Reports on Operation Catapult, Section 6, SMVL 7/19.
11. Cypher Messages from Admiralty, CAC, Reports on Operation Catapult, SMVL 7/19.

12. Final Report—Report of Proceedings—28 June–4 July 1940, CAC, Reports on Operation Catapult, Section 6, SMVL 7/19.
13. Stephen Howarth, ed., *Men of War* (St. Martin's Press, 1992), 458.

CHAPTER 12. THE CHIEF CONQUERED PROVINCE OF GERMANY

1. Will Brownell and Richard N. Billings, *So Close to Greatness: The Biography of William C. Bullitt* (Macmillan, 1987), 207. After falling out with FDR, Bullitt returned to France on his own initiative in the summer of 1944 and served a largely ceremonial officer's role in Charles de Gaulle's Free French Forces through the end of the war.
2. Robert Murphy, *Diplomat Among Warriors* (Doubleday, 1964), 44.
3. William L. Shirer, *The Collapse of the Third Republic* (Simon and Schuster, 1969), 905.
4. Orville Bullitt, *For the President, Personal and Secret—Correspondence Between Franklin D. Roosevelt and William C. Bullitt* (Houghton Mifflin, 1972), 484.
5. Bullitt, *For the President*, 486.
6. Shirer, *Collapse of the Third Republic*, 906.
7. Andrew Roberts, *Walking with Destiny* (Viking, 2018), 552.
8. Major L. J. Ellis, *The War in France and Flanders: 1939–1940* (Her Majesty's Stationery Office, 1953), 327.
9. Winston Churchill, *The Second World War: Their Finest Hour* (Houghton Mifflin, 1949), 88.
10. Hugh Dalton, *Memoirs—1931–1945: The Fateful Years* (Frederick Muller, 1957), 335.
11. Churchill, *Their Finest Hour*, 100.

CHAPTER 13. ALMOST INEPT IN ITS UNWISDOM

1. Michael Simpson, ed., *The Cunningham Papers*, vol. 1: *The Mediterranean Fleet: 1939–1942* (The Naval Records Society, 1999), 3.
2. Admiral Andrew Cunningham, *A Sailor's Odyssey: The Autobiography of Admiral of the Fleet Viscount Cunningham of Hyndhope* (Seaforth Publishing, 1951), 9.
3. Admiral Sir W. M. James, *The Portsmouth Letters* (Macmillan & Co., 1946), 63.
4. Simpson, *Cunningham Papers*, 7.
5. "At Sea: Battle of the Mediterranean," *Time Magazine*, February 17, 1941, 34.
6. Robert Jameson, "Remembering Admiral Cunningham—The Great Insubordinate: Stick to your principles and disobey orders in style," Medium.com, April 14, 2019, https://rjameson.medium.com/remembering-admiral-cunningham-the-great-insubordinate-ca72640dfb1.
7. John Colville, *The Churchillians* (Weidenfeld and Nicolson, 1981), 141.
8. Dwight D. Eisenhower, *Crusade in Europe* (Doubleday & Company, 1948), 89.
9. Field Marshal Lord Alanbrooke, *War Diaries: 1939–1945* (University of California Press, 2001), xliii.
10. Cunningham, *Sailor's Odyssey*, 206.
11. Cunningham, *Sailor's Odyssey*, 203.
12. Simpson, *Cunningham Papers*, 45.
13. Vice Admiral René-Émile Godfroy, *L'Aventure de La Force X à Alexandrie (1940–1943)* (Librairie Plon, 1953), 5.
14. Cunningham, *Sailor's Odyssey*, 225.
15. Arthur J. Marder, *From the Dardanelles to Oran: Studies of the Royal Navy in War and Peace, 1915–1940* (Oxford University Press, 1974), 212.

16. Marder, *From the Dardanelles to Oran*, 263.
17. Cunningham, *Sailor's Odyssey*, 234.
18. Marder, *From the Dardanelles to Oran*, 212.
19. Simpson, *Cunningham Papers*, June 25, 1940, from Cunningham to Admiralty, 86.
20. Amirauté signal 5156, June 25, 1940, Service Historique de la Marine (SHM).
21. Minutes of Meeting Held in First Sea Lord's Room at the Admiralty, June 27, 1940, PRO, First Sea Lord's Personal War Records, ADM 205/4.
22. Odend'hal's Report, July 4, 1940, SHM.
23. First Sea Lord's Signal, 0006, June 28, 1940.
24. Simpson, *Cunningham Papers*, June 28, 1940, from Pound to Cunningham, 87.
25. Simpson, *Cunningham Papers*, June 28, 1940, from Cunningham to Admiralty, 87.
26. Simpson, *Cunningham Papers*, June 29, 1940, from Cunningham to Admiralty, 87.
27. Simpson, *Cunningham Papers*, June 29, 1940, from Cunningham to Pound, 82.
28. Henri Ballande, *De l'Amiraute a Bikini, Souvenirs des jours sans joie* (Presses de la Cite, 1957), 98.
29. Simpson, *Cunningham Papers*, 91.
30. Simpson, *Cunningham Papers*, June 30, 1940, from Cunningham to Admiralty, 89.
31. Simpson, *Cunningham Papers*, June 29, 1940, from Admiralty to Cunningham, 89.

CHAPTER 14. ONE OF THE MOST DISAGREEABLE AND DIFFICULT TASKS

1. Winston Churchill, *The Second World War: Closing the Ring* (Houghton Mifflin Company, 1951), 662.
2. COS (40) 510, "Implications of Action Contemplated in Respect of Certain French Ships. Aide Mémoire," June 30, 1940, CAB 80/14. Air Chief Marshal Sir Cyril Newall and General Sir John Dill were Pound's fellow chiefs of staff.
3. War Cabinet Meeting, July 1, 1940, WM(40) 1164, CAB 65/7.
4. John Colville, *The Churchillians* (Weidenfeld and Nicolson, 1981), 139.
5. Michael Simpson, ed., *Somerville Papers*, December 31, 1940, letter from Somerville to Mary Somerville, 233.
6. Admiral Sir Guy Grantham to Marder, May 4, 1973, UCI, Arthur J. Marder papers, MS-F002, BA05-A-2. Box 7. After the war, Churchill confidant Robert Boothby criticized a historian for writing that "Churchill never interfered with his admirals. The exact opposite is true. He never stopped."
7. Patrick Beesly, *Very Special Intelligence* (Doubleday and Company, 1978), 103.
8. Cypher Messages from Admiralty, CAC, Reports on Operation Catapult, SMVL 7/19.
9. Lord Ismay, *The Memoirs of General The Lord Ismay* (Heinemman, 1960), 149.
10. Operation Orders, CAC, Reports on Operation Catapult, Section 1, SMVL 7/19.
11. Operation Orders, CAC, Reports on Operation Catapult, Section 1, SMVL 7/19.
12. Operation Orders, CAC, Reports on Operation Catapult, Section 1, SMVL 7/19.
13. Operation Orders, CAC, Reports on Operation Catapult, Section 1, SMVL 7/19.
14. Major General Sir Edward Spears, *Two Men Who Saved France* (Stein and Day, 1966), 161.
15. Admiral Andrew Cunningham, *A Sailor's Odyssey: The Autobiography of Admiral of the Fleet Viscount Cunningham of Hyndhope* (Seaforth Publishing, 1951), 246.
16. Warren Tute, *Deadly Stroke* (Coward, McCann & Geoghegan, 1973), 66.
17. Field Marshal The Viscount Montgomery, *The Memoirs of Field-Marshal The Viscount Montgomery of Alamein* (The World Publishing Company, 1958), 63.

18. Cypher Messages from Admiralty, CAC, Reports on Operation Catapult, SMVL 7/19. In this time before italics and bold type in wireless communications, the use of "(R)" in this and the following message was employed to ensure that the recipient would understand that a word or phrase was intentionally repeated for emphasis. "(R)" was used to note that the word "not" was repeated to emphasize its importance and was not (R) not a typo.
19. Cypher Messages from Admiralty, CAC, Reports on Operation Catapult, SMVL 7/19.
20. Jürgen Rohwer, *Chronology of the War at Sea: 1939–1945* (Naval Institute Press, 1972), 22.
21. John Colville, *The Fringes of Power* (The Lyons Press, 1985), 183.
22. Anne Chisholm and Michael Davie, *Lord Beaverbrook, A Life* (Alfred A. Knopf, 1993), 349.
23. Edward R. Murrow, *This is London* (Simon & Schuster, 1941), 102.
24. Colville, *Fringes of Power*, 131.
25. A. J. P. Taylor, *Beaverbrook* (Simon & Schuster, 1972), 438.
26. Winston Churchill, *The Second World War: Their Finest Hour* (Houghton Mifflin Company, 1949), 235. This message appears only in Churchill's history of the war.

CHAPTER 15. MORE TOUCHY THAN EVER

1. John Jordan and Robert Dumas, *French Battleships: 1922–1956* (Seaforth Publishing, 2009), 75.
2. Colin Smith, *England's Last War Against France* (Phoenix, 2010), 58.
3. Narratives from Ships—Vice Admiral, Aircraft Carriers, CAC, Reports on Operation Catapult, Section 3, SMVL 7/19.
4. Narratives from Ships—Foxhound—G. H. Peters, Commander, CAC, Reports on Operation Catapult, Section 3, SMVL 7/19.
5. Report of Captain C. S. Holland, CAC, Reports on Operation Catapult, Section 4, SMVL 7/19.
6. Philippe Masson, *La Marine Française et la Guerre* 39/45 (Le Grand Livre du Mois, 1991), 144.
7. Warren Tute, *Deadly Stroke* (Coward, McCann & Geoghegan, 1973), 81.
8. "Mers El-Kebir, La Tragedie," *Paris Match*, July 12, 1990, 82.
9. Tute, *Deadly Stroke*, 83.
10. Philippe Lasterle, "La Tragique Parenthèse de Mers El-Kébir," *Relations Internationales* 117 (2004): 71–86. http://www.jstor.org/stable/45344950.
11. Report of Captain C. S. Holland, CAC, Reports on Operation Catapult, Section 4, SMVL 7/19.
12. Compte rendu des missions exécutées par le lieutenant de vaisseau Dufay, le 3 juillet 1940, SHM TTO 1.
13. Tute, *Deadly Stroke*, 90.
14. 3081 (1) Battle Summaries: Battle Summary—No. 1, Operations Against The French Fleet at Mers-el-Kebir (Oran), 3rd-6th July, Appendix B: Copy of Terms as sent to Admiral Gensoul, 3rd July 1940, C. B. 1940, Training and Staff Duties Division—Historical Section—Naval Staff, Admiralty, S.W. 1942, 22.
15. Operation Orders, CAC, Reports on Operation Catapult, Section 2, SMVL 7/19.

CHAPTER 16. DO NOT, REPEAT *NOT*, FAIL

1. Admiral Andrew Cunningham, *A Sailor's Odyssey: The Autobiography of Admiral of the Fleet Viscount Cunningham of Hyndhope* (Seaforth Publishing, 1951), 247.

2. Michael Simpson, ed., *The Cunningham Papers*, vol. I: *The Mediterranean Fleet, 1939–1942* (Naval Records Society, 1999), 91.
3. Cunningham, *Sailor's Odyssey*, 249.
4. Cunningham, *Sailor's Odyssey*, 250.
5. Simpson, *Cunningham Papers*, From the Admiralty to Cunningham, 3 July 1940, 93.
6. Cunningham, *Sailor's Odyssey*, 250.
7. Simpson, *Cunningham Papers*, From Cunningham to the Admiralty, 4 July 1940, 94.
8. Simpson, *Cunningham Papers*, From Godfroy to Cunningham, 3 July 1940, 93.
9. Vice Admiral René-Émile Godfroy, *L'Aventure de La Force X à Alexandrie (1940–1943)* (Librairie Plon, 1953), 62.
10. Cunningham, *Sailor's Odyssey*, 251.
11. Cunningham, *Sailor's Odyssey*, 251.
12. Cunningham, *Sailor's Odyssey*, 251.

CHAPTER 17. DISCUSS THE MATTER AS OLD FRIENDS

1. C.B. 3081 (1) Battle Summaries: Battle Summary—No. 1, Operations Against The French Fleet at Mers-el-Kebir (Oran), 3rd–6th July 1940, Appendix C: Admiral Gensoul's first written reply (copied by the Flag Lieutenant) received at 1000/3 by Captain Holland—(Enc. 4, M.016021/40); NMM, Training and Staff Duties Division—Historical Section—Naval Staff, Admiralty, S.W. 1942, 22.
2. Letter from Holland to Vice Admiral Aircraft Carriers, NMM, Photographs and documents relating to the Mers-el-Kébir affair, 1940–1941, Narrative of Events at Oran on 3 July 1940, NMM, Holland Family papers, HND/3/4.
3. Warren Tute, *Deadly Stroke* (Coward, McCann & Geoghegan, 1973), 96.
4. Compte rendu des missions exécutées par le lieutenant de vaisseau Dufay, le 3 juillet 1940, SHM TTO 1.
5. Tute, *Deadly Stroke*, 101.
6. Report of Captain C. S. Holland—Transcript for Interview with Admiral Gensoul, CAC, Reports on Operation Catapult, Section 4, SMVL 7/19.
7. Tute, *Deadly Stroke*, 106.
8. Compte rendu des missions exécutées par le lieutenant de vaisseau Dufay, le 3 juillet 1940, SHM TTO 1.
9. Second Written Reply Received from Adm. Gensoul, Report of Captain C. S. Holland, CAC, Reports on Operation Catapult, Section 4, SMVL 7/19.
10. Compte rendu des missions exécutées par le lieutenant de vaisseau Dufay, le 3 juillet 1940, SHM TTO 1.
11. Admiral J. H. Godfrey unpublished manuscript, "Chapter V. Oran, 3 July 1940: Mistaken Judgment, Tragic Misunderstanding, or Cruel Necessity," UCI, Arthur J. Marder papers, MS-F002, BA05-A-2. Box 8.
12. Colin Smith, *England's Last War Against France* (Phoenix, 2010), 39: "During his time in Paris he had acquired a French mistress." "Mers-el-Kebir was a bizarre and melancholy action," *Smithsonian*, Alistair Horne, July 1985, 130: "Holland . . . though, devoted to his wife, had recently been involved with an attractive Frenchwoman." Holland's archive includes a letter to his wife Barbara from Alistair Horne, apologizing for the delayed return of Holland's papers, which he had borrowed to write his article. Barbara Holland added a handwritten acknowledgment of the article in Smithsonian at the bottom of the letter.

13. Cunningham letter to Godfrey, 17 May, 1959, CAC, CUNN 5/4.
14. Michael Simpson, ed., *The Somerville Papers: Selections from the Private and Official Correspondence of Admiral of the Fleet Sir James Somerville* (Navy Records Society, 1999), 41.

CHAPTER 18. ASKED TO SHOOT HIS BEST FRIEND

1. Pierre Varillon, *Mers-el-Kébir* (Amiot-Dumont, 1949), 122.
2. Rear Admiral Paul Auphan and Jacques Mordal, *The French Navy in World War II* (Naval Institute Press, 1959), 130.
3. Rudy Cantel, *L'Attentat de Mers-El-Kébir* (La Technique du Livre, 1941), 187.
4. Alan Coles and Ted Briggs, *Flagship Hood: The Fate of Britain's Mightiest Warship* (Robert Hale, 1985), 162.
5. Narratives from Ships—Resolution, CAC, Reports on Operation Catapult, Section 3, SMVL 7/19.
6. Report of Captain C. S. Holland, CAC, Reports on Operation Catapult, Section 4, SMVL 7/19.
7. Admiral Andrew Cunningham, *A Sailor's Odyssey: The Autobiography of Admiral of the Fleet Viscount Cunningham of Hyndhope* (Seaforth Publishing, 1951), 250.
8. Conclusions, July 3, 1940, CAB, Minute 2, Confidential Annex, President Roosevelts Attitude, War Cabinet Meeting, WM 192 (40), 65/14/3.
9. Report of Captain C. S. Holland, Signal No. 6, CAC, Reports on Operation Catapult, Section 4, SMVL 7/19.
10. Report of Captain C. S. Holland, Signal No. 8, CAC, Reports on Operation Catapult, Section 4, SMVL 7/19.
11. Report of Captain C. S. Holland, Signal No. 9, CAC, Reports on Operation Catapult, Section 4, SMVL 7/19.
12. Report of Captain C. S. Holland, Signal No. 10, CAC, Reports on Operation Catapult, Section 4, SMVL 7/19.
13. Report of Captain C. S. Holland, Signal No. 11, CAC, Reports on Operation Catapult, Section 4, SMVL 7/19.
14. Final Report—Report of Proceedings—28 June–4 July 1940, CAC, Reports on Operation Catapult, SMVL 7/19.
15. Report of Captain C. S. Holland, CAC, Reports on Operation Catapult, Section 4, SMVL 7/19.
16. Cypher Messages from Admiralty, CAC, Reports on Operation Catapult, SMVL 7/19.
17. Final Report—Report of Proceedings—28 June–4 July 1940, CAC, Reports on Operation Catapult, SMVL 7/19.
18. Étienne Sicard, "The Battle of Mers-el-Kebir," *Life Magazine*, November 4, 1940, 14.
19. Ivan Maisky, *Memoirs of a Soviet Ambassador, The War: 1939–43* (Charles Scribner's Sons, 1967), 100.
20. John Colville, *The Fringes of Power* (The Lyons Press, 1985), 183.
21. Major General Sir Edward Spears, *Two Men Who Saved France* (Stein and Day, 1966), 163.
22. René Pierre Eugène Caroff, *Le Théâtre Méditerranée*, Tome 2: *du 25 juin 1940 au 8 novembre 1942* (Marine nationale E.-M. général, Service historique, 1960), 150.
23. David Brown, *The Road to Oran* (Frank Cass, 2004), 196.
24. Varillon, *Mers-el-Kébir*, 124.
25. Report of Captain C. S. Holland, Signal No. 12, CAC, Reports on Operation Catapult, Section 4, SMVL 7/19.

26. Varillon, *Mers-el-Kébir*, 122.
27. Report of Captain C. S. Holland, Signal No. 13, CAC, Reports on Operation Catapult, Section 4, SMVL 7/19.
28. Report of Captain C. S. Holland, Signal No. 14, CAC, Reports on Operation Catapult, Section 4, SMVL 7/19.
29. Final Report—Report of Proceedings—28 June–4 July 1940, CAC, Reports on Operation Catapult, SMVL 7/19.
30. Force 'H' signal, 1459, 3 July 1940 (War Diary, Vol. XVIII), 45.
31. Report of Captain C. S. Holland, CAC, Reports on Operation Catapult, Section 4, SMVL 7/19.
32. Report of Captain C. S. Holland, CAC, Reports on Operation Catapult, Section 4, SMVL 7/19.
33. Final Report—Report of Proceedings—28 June–4 July 1940, CAC, Reports on Operation Catapult, SMVL 7/19.
34. Final Report—Report of Proceedings—28 June–4 July 1940, CAC, Reports on Operation Catapult, SMVL 7/19.
35. Report of Captain C. S. Holland, CAC, Reports on Operation Catapult, Section 4, SMVL 7/19.
36. Report of Captain C. S. Holland, CAC, Reports on Operation Catapult, Section 4, SMVL 7/19.

CHAPTER 19. THE RED RIBBON OF THE FRENCH LEGION OF HONOR

1. Report of Captain C. S. Holland, CAC, Reports on Operation Catapult, Section 4, SMVL 7/19.
2. William L. Shirer, *The Collapse of the Third Republic* (Simon and Schuster, 1969), 916.
3. Report of Captain C. S. Holland, Signal No. 15, CAC, Reports on Operation Catapult, Section 4, SMVL 7/19.
4. Alan Coles and Ted Briggs, *Flagship Hood: The Fate of Britain's Mightiest Warship* (Robert Hale, 1985), 166.
5. Report of Captain C. S. Holland, Signal No. 16, CAC, Reports on Operation Catapult, Section 4, SMVL 7/19.
6. C.B. 3081 (1) Battle Summaries: Battle Summary—No. 1, Operations Against The French Fleet at Mers-el-Kebir (Oran), 3rd-6th July 1940, Appendix E: Final Statement from Admiral Gensoul, written on board the "Dunkerque," 1720/3/7/40, Training and Staff Duties Division—Historical Section—Naval Staff, Admiralty, S.W. 1942, 22.
7. Marder, *From the Dardanelles to Oran*, 249.
8. Report of Captain C. S. Holland, CAC, Reports on Operation Catapult, Section 4, SMVL 7/19.

CHAPTER 20. THE EVIL MINUTE

1. Alan Coles and Ted Briggs, *Flagship Hood: The Fate of Britain's Mightiest Warship* (Robert Hale, 1985), 167.
2. Narratives from Ships—Resolution, CAC, Reports on Operation Catapult, Section 3, SMVL 7/19.
3. Letters and diary entries relating to the Oran Episode, July 1940, CAC, Letters to His Wife, Written from Force H, SMVL 3/22.
4. Coles and Briggs, *Flagship Hood*, 168.
5. Étienne Sicard, "The Battle of Mers-el-Kebir," *Life Magazine*, November 4, 1940, 14.

6. Philippe Masson, *La Marine Française et la Guerre 39/45* (Le Grand Livre du Mois, 1991), 140.
7. Final Report—Report of Proceedings—28 June–4 July 1940, CAC, Reports on Operation Catapult, SMVL 7/19.
8. Rudy Cantel, *L'Attentat de Mers-El-Kébir* (La Technique du Livre, 1941), 42.
9. Pierre Varillon, *Mers-el-Kébir* (Amiot-Dumont, 1949), 139.
10. Sicard, "Battle of Mers-el-Kebir," 14.
11. Varillon, *Mers-el-Kébir*, 149.
12. Colin Smith, *England's Last War Against France* (Phoenix, 2010), 79.
13. Yves Rochas, *Pour En Savoir Plus Sur Mers El-Kébir* (Editions Lettres Du Monde, 1993), 259.
14. Jean Boutron, *An Honourable Sailor and Spy* (Plon, 1980), 104.
15. Smith, *England's Last War Against France*, 79.
16. Premier rapport de l'amiral Gensoul, July 4, 1940, SHM TTO 1.
17. John Jordan and Robert Dumas, *French Battleships: 1922–1956* (Seaforth Publishing, 2009), 77.
18. Jordan and Dumas, *French Battleships*, 80.
19. Varillon, *Mers-el-Kébir*, 150.
20. Jordan and Dumas, *French Battleships*, 80.
21. Smith, *England's Last War Against France*, 77.
22. Narratives from Ships—Hood, CAC, Reports on Operation Catapult, Section 3, SMVL 7/19.
23. Warren Tute, *Deadly Stroke* (Coward, McCann & Geoghegan, 1973),157.
24. Boutron, *Honourable Sailor and Spy*, 103.
25. Varillon, *Mers-el-Kébir*, 139. Varillon called the priest R. P. de "Geuser." Jean Boutron, in *An Honorable Sailor and Spy*, who had a close relationship with the priest while serving on the *Provence*, called him Father de "Gueuser," and mentioned that he was a Jesuit.
26. Coles and Briggs, *Flagship Hood*, 167 (*Dunkerque* and *Strasbourg*). Also: Narratives from Ships—Wrestler, CAC, Reports on Operation Catapult, Section 3, SMVL 7/19. (*Provence* and *Bretagne*).
27. Narratives from Ships—Enterprise, CAC, Reports on Operation Catapult, Section 3, SMVL 7/19.
28. Narratives from Ships—Wrestler, CAC, Reports on Operation Catapult, Section 3, SMVL 7/19.
29. Coles and Briggs, *Flagship Hood*, 169.
30. Final Report—Report of Proceedings—28 June–4 July 1940, CAC, Reports on Operation Catapult, SMVL 7/19.
31. C. S. Forester, *The Ship* (Michael Joseph LTD, 1949), 63.
32. Varillon, *Mers-el-Kébir*, 151.
33. Final Report—Report of Proceedings—28 June–4 July 1940, CAC, Reports on Operation Catapult, SMVL 7/19.

CHAPTER 21. THE WORST POSSIBLE OUTCOME

1. David Brown, *The Road to Oran* (Frank Cass, 2004), 200.
2. Henry H. Adams, *Years of Deadly Peril, The Coming of the War, 1939–1941* (David McKay Company, 1969), 211.
3. John Jordan and Robert Dumas, *French Battleships: 1922–1956* (Seaforth Publishing, 2009), 82.

4. Final Report—Report of Proceedings—28 June–4 July 1940, CAC, Reports on Operation Catapult, SMVL 7/19.
5. Premier rapport de l'amiral Gensoul, July 4, 1940, SHM TTO 1.
6. John Jordan and Jean Moulin, *French Destroyers: 1922–1956* (Naval Institute Press, 2015), 232.
7. Arthur J. Marder, *From the Dardanelles to Oran: Studies of the Royal Navy in War and Peace, 1915–1940* (Oxford University Press, 1974), 255.
8. Final Report—Report of Proceedings—28 June–4 July 1940, CAC, Reports on Operation Catapult, SMVL 7/19.
9. Jordan and Dumas, *French Battleships*, 83.
10. Rear Admiral Paul Auphan and Jacques Mordal, *The French Navy in World War II* (Naval Institute Press, 1959), 134.
11. Jordan and Dumas, *French Battleships*, 84.
12. Rapport du capitain de vaisseau Collinet, commandant le Strasbourg, SHM TTY 773.
13. Final Report—Report of Proceedings—28 June–4 July 1940, CAC, Reports on Operation Catapult, SMVL 7/19.
14. Final Report—Report of Proceedings—28 June–4 July 1940, CAC, Reports on Operation Catapult, SMVL 7/19.
15. Jordan and Dumas, *French Battleships*, 84.
16. John Colville, *The Fringes of Power* (The Lyons Press, 1985), 183.
17. Narratives from Ships—Resolution, CAC, Reports on Operation Catapult, Section 3, SMVL 7/19.
18. Final Report—Report of Proceedings—28 June–4 July 1940, CAC, Reports on Operation Catapult, SMVL 7/19.
19. Narratives from Ships—Hood, CAC, Reports on Operation Catapult, Section 3, SMVL 7/19.
20. Diary entry, July 4, 1940, CAC, Letters to His Wife, Written from Force H, SMVL 3/22.

CHAPTER 22. THIS IS NO TIME FOR DOUBT OR WEAKNESS

1. HC Deb. (4 July 1940) (362) cols 1043–1050.
2. "Churchill Grieved, Explains Fleet Had to Fight Erstwhile Ally to Thwart the Nazis," *New York Times*, July 5, 1940, 1.
3. John Colville, *The Fringes of Power* (The Lyons Press, 1985), 184.
4. Raymond Lee, *The London Journal of General Raymond E. Lee* (Little, Brown and Company, 1941), 12.
5. Colville, *Fringes of Power*, 185.
6. Andrew Roberts, *The Holy Fox* (Head of Zeus, 2014), 239.
7. HL Deb. (4 July 1940) (116) col 782.

CHAPTER 23. IT IS CRAZY TO FIGHT AMONG OURSELVES

1. Vice Admiral René-Émile Godfroy, *L'Aventure de La Force X à Alexandrie (1940–1943)* (Librairie Plon, 1953), 63.
2. Admiral Andrew Cunningham, *A Sailor's Odyssey: The Autobiography of Admiral of the Fleet Viscount Cunningham of Hyndhope* (Seaforth Publishing, 1951), 252.
3. Godfroy, *L'Aventure de La Force X à Alexandrie*, 63.
4. Cunninghan, *Sailor's Odyssey*, 252.

5. Godfroy, *L'Aventure de La Force X à Alexandrie*, 63.
6. Cunningham, *Sailor's Odyssey*, 252.
7. "At Sea: Friends Against Friends," *Time Magazine*, July 15, 1940, 28.
8. Michael Simpson, ed., *The Cunningham Papers*, vol. I: *The Mediterranean Fleet, 1939–1972* (Naval Records Society, 1999), From Cunningham to the Admiralty, July 4, 1940, 95.
9. Godfroy, *L'Aventure de La Force X à Alexandrie*, 67.
10. Godfroy, *L'Aventure de La Force X à Alexandrie*, 67.
11. Cunningham, *Sailor's Odyssey*, 253.
12. Godfroy, *L'Aventure de La Force X à Alexandrie*, 68.
13. Godfroy, *L'Aventure de La Force X à Alexandrie*, 68.
14. Cunningham, *Sailor's Odyssey*, 253.
15. Cunningham, *Sailor's Odyssey*, 254.
16. Hervé Coutau-Bégarie and Claude Huan, *Lettres et notes de l'amiral Darlan* (Economica, 1992), 168.
17. Cunningham, *Sailor's Odyssey*, 254.
18. Cunningham, *Sailor's Odyssey*, 254.
19. Cunningham, *Sailor's Odyssey*, 257.
20. Simpson, *Cunningham Papers*, 97.
21. Cunningham, *Sailor's Odyssey*, 657.
22. Cunningham, *Sailor's Odyssey*, 570.
23. Cunningham, *Sailor's Odyssey*, 663.

CHAPTER 24. THAT FILTHY JOB IS OVER AT LAST

1. Denis Baldensberger, *Mers-el-Kébir* (Editions Rouff, 1967), 119.
2. Letters and diary entries relating to the Oran Episode, July 1940, CAC, Letters to His Wife, Written from Force H, SMVL 3/22.
3. John Jordan and Robert Dumas, *French Battleships: 1922–1956* (Seaforth Publishing, 2009), 85.
4. Jordan and Dumas, *French Battleships*, 84.
5. Jordan and Dumas, *French Battleships*, 86.
6. Jordan and Dumas, *French Battleships*, 88.
7. Letter from Somerville to Vice Admiral Sir Geoffrey Blake, CAC, Misc Reports and Papers about Force H, SMVL 7/28.
8. Letter from James Somerville to his wife, CAC, Letters and diary entries relating to the Oran Episode, July 1940, SMVL 3/22.
9. Jordan and Dumas, *French Battleships*, 89.
10. Anthony Heckstall-Smith, *The Fleet That Faced Both Ways* (Anthony Blond, 1963), 121.
11. Personal message from author Vincent P. O'Hara.
12. C.B. 3081 (1) Battle Summaries: Battle Summary—No. 3, The Attack on the "Richelieu" At Dakkar, 8 July 1940, p. 62. Training and Staff Duties Division—Historical Section—Naval Staff, Admiralty, S.W. 1942, 22.
13. Colin Smith, *England's Last War Against France* (Phoenix, 2010), 96.
14. Jordan and Dumas, *French Battleships*, 126.
15. Jordan and Dumas, *French Battleships*, 127.
16. Heckstall-Smith, *Fleet That Faced Both Ways*, 114.
17. Heckstall-Smith, *Fleet That Faced Both Ways*, 115.
18. Smith, *England's Last War Against France*, 96.
19. Heckstall-Smith, *Fleet That Faced Both Ways*, 118.

20. Jordan and Dumas, *French Battleships*, 127.
21. Jordan and Dumas, *French Battleships*, 127.
22. Smith, *England's Last War Against France*, 98.
23. The full text—as well as an audio recording—of Churchill's "War of the Unknown Warriors" radio address, from which this extracted, appears on the website of America's National Churchill Museum: https://www.nationalchurchillmuseum.org/war-of-the-unknown-warriors-speech.html.

CHAPTER 25. YOU'RE NOT ALLOWED TO HAVE A HEART IN WARTIME

1. Richard Collier, *1940: The Avalanche* (The Dial Press, 1979), 156.
2. Paul Baudouin, *The Private Diaries of Paul Baudouin* (Eyre & Spottiswoode, 1948), 161.
3. Denis Baldensberger, *Mers-el-Kébir* (Editions Rouff, 1967), 148.
4. William Langer, *Our Vichy Gamble* (Alfred A. Knopf, 1947), 117.
5. "No Reproach," *Daily Herald*, July 5, 1940, 2.
6. "The French Fleet: The Soul of Tragedy," *The Observer*, July 7, 1940, 6.
7. "The French Fleet," *The Times*, July 5, 1940, 4.
8. "Tragic Necessity," *The Times*, July 6, 1940, 5.
9. "French Fleet: Several Ships Sunk Resisting English; New Fighting Hinted," *Boston Globe*, July 4, 1940, 1.
10. Philippe Masson, *La Marine Française et la Guerre 39/45* (Le Grand Livre du Mois, 1991), 178.
11. Robert Murphy, *Diplomat Among Warriors* (Doubleday & Company, 1964), 55.
12. Letter from James Somerville to his wife, CAC, Letters and diary entries relating to the Oran Episode, July 4, 1940, SMVL 3/22.
13. Note of Congratulation from Admiralty, CAC, Naval Messages to & from Force H, SMVL 7/27.
14. Note to Somerville from officers of the Dunkerque, CAC, Miscellaneous reports and papers about Force H, 1940–1941 SMVL 7/28.
15. Letter from James Somerville to his wife, CAC, Letters and diary entries relating to the Oran Episode, July 12, 1940, SMVL 3/22.
16. Letters and diary entries relating to the Oran Episode, July 1940, CAC, Letters to His Wife, Written from Force H, SMVL 3/22.
17. Letter from James Somerville to his wife, CAC, Letters and diary entries relating to the Oran Episode, July 6, 1940, SMVL 3/22.
18. Letter from Admiral Dudley North to the Secretary of the Admiralty, CAC, Section 6. Final Report—Vice Admiral, Commanding North Atlantic—Dudley North, SMVL 7/19. The definitive blemish on North's career was a later episode that involved the unchallenged passage of three French ships past Gibraltar in September 1940. North had credible reasons for not pursuing the ships. In addition, Somerville, who was stationed at Gibraltar with Force H, attempted to assume responsibility. North was relieved from his role as Flag Officer Commanding Gibraltar and Mediterranean Approaches.
19. A. V. Alexander's minute to Dudley Pound, July 15, 1940, ADM 1/19178.
20. Minute to First Lord of Admiralty, July 20 1940, ADM 1/10188 PRO.
21. The Circumstances Attending My Removal from My Command at Gibraltar by their Lordships, CAC, Dudley Pound: Oran, Dakar & Dismissal, DUPO 5/4.
22. Warren Tute, *Deadly Stroke* (Coward, McCann & Geoghegan, 1973), 150.
23. Henry H. Adams, *Years of Deadly Peril* (David McKay Company, 1974), 203.
24. Adams, *Years of Deadly Peril*, 203.

25. Baldensberger, *Mers-el-Kébir*, 179.
26. Herve Coutau-Bégarie and Cluade Huan, *Mers El-Kébir (1940), La rupture franco-britannique* (Economica, 1994), 152
27. Albert Kammerer, *La Passion de la Flotte Française* (Librairie Arthéme Fayard, 1951), 176.
28. Admiral Gensoul to Marder, September 9, 1972, UCI, Arthur J. Marder papers, MS-F002, BA05-A-2. Box 8.
29. Coutau-Bégarie and Huan, *Mers El-Kébir (1940)*, 4.
30. Philippe Lasterle, "Marcel Genoul (1880–1973), un amiral dans la tourmente," *Revue Historique Des Armees* 219 (2000): 91.
31. George Collett to Marder, August 24, 1972, UCI, Arthur J. Marder papers, MS-F002, BA05-A-2. Box 8.
32. Major General Sir Edward Spears, *Two Men Who Saved France* (Stein and Day, 1966), 164.
33. François Kersaudy, *Churchill and De Gaulle* (Atheneum, 1982), 85.
34. Robert E. Sherwood, *Roosevelt and Hopkins: An Intimate History* (Harper & Brothers, 1948), 149.
35. François Charles-Roux, *Cinq Mois Tragiques Aux Affaires Etrangéres (21 Mai—1 Novembre 1940)* (Librairie Plon, 1949), 130.
36. "Pittman Approves British Seizures," *New York Times*, July 5, 1940, 4.
37. Winston Churchill, *The Second World War: Their Finest Hour* (Houghton Mifflin Company, 1949), 238.
38. Count Galeazzo Ciano and Hugh Gibson, ed., *The Ciano Diaries, 1939–1943* (Howard Fertig, 1973), 273.
39. Anthony Heckstall-Smith, *The Fleet That Faced Both Ways* (Anthony Blond, 1963), 101.
40. Photographs and documents relating to the Mers-el-Kébir affair, 1940–1941, Narrative of Events at Oran on 3 July 1940, NMM, Holland Family papers, HND/3/4.
41. Report of Captain C. S. Holland, CAC, Reports on Operation Catapult, Section 4, SMVL 7/19.
42. Final Report—Report of Proceedings—28 June–4 July 1940, CAC, Reports on Operation Catapult, Section 6, SMVL 7/19.
43. Letter from Holland to Vice Admiral Aircraft Carriers, Photographs and documents relating to the Mers-el-Kébir affair, 1940–1941, Narrative of Events at Oran on 3 July 1940, NMM, Holland Family papers, HND/3/4.
44. Notes on Captain (later Vice Admiral) Cedric Holland, Naval Attache, Paris 1939 by Vice Admiral B. B. Schofield, UCI, Arthur J. Marder papers, MS-F002, BA05-A-2. Box 7.
45. Vice Admiral Brian Schofield to Marder, May 12, 1973, UCI, Arthur J. Marder papers, MS-F002, BA05-A-2. Box 7.
46. Jacques Benoist-Méchin, *Sixty Days That Shook the West—The Fall of France: 1940* (G. P. Putnam's Sons, 1963), 511.
47. The precise number of French victims at Mers-el-Kébir is uncertain. Published figures range from 1,250 to 1,312, with 1,297 being a widely used figure. The Association of Former Sailors of Mers-el-Kébir and Families of the Victims conducted an exhaustive study of documents and archives, and, as of the summer of 2025, have certified a total of 1,257 fatalities. https://www.perfectlytruestory.com/newsletter/his-grandfather-was-killed-by-the-british-at-mers-el-kbir-interview-with-pascal-landure-chosse.
48. "Churchill Statue Daubed in Paris," *The Guardian*, November 2, 1999, https://www.theguardian.com/world/1999/nov/03/1.

CHAPTER 26. YE ARE FORGERS OF LIES

1. William L. Shirer, *The Collapse of the Third Republic* (Simon and Schuster, 1969), 622.
2. Admiral Karl Doenitz, *Memoirs: Ten Years and Twenty Days* (The World Publishing Company, 1958), 42.
3. Vincent P. O'Hara, W. David Dickson, and Richard Worth, *On Seas Contested: The Seven Great Navies in the Second World War* (Naval Institute Press, 2010), 16, 55, and 96.
4. Keith Bird, *Erich Raeder: Admiral of the Third Reich* (Naval Institute Press, 2013), 127.
5. Stephen Howarth, *Men of War* (New York: St. Martin's Press, 1993), 45.
6. David J. Bercuson and Holger H. Herwig, *The Destruction of the Bismarck* (The Overlook Press, 2001), 24.
7. Winston Churchill, *The Second World War: The Gathering Storm* (Houghton Mifflin Company, 1948), 656.
8. *Fuehrer Conferences on Naval Affairs* (Naval Institute Press, 1990), 91.
9. "No 479, Unsigned Memorandum: Record of That Part of the Conversation Between The Führer and the Duce in Munich on June 18, 1940, which was Conducted in the Presence of the Reich Foreign Minister, Count Ciano, Colonel General Keitel, and General Roatta," *Documents on German Foreign Policy, Series D (1937–1945)*, vol. 9: *The War Years: March 18–June 22, 1940* (United States Government Printing Office, 1956), 609.
10. Count Galeazzo Ciano and Hugh Gibson, eds., *The Ciano Diaries, 1939–1943* (Howard Fertig, 1973), 266.
11. Robert Paxton, *Vichy France, Old Guard and New Order: 1940–1944* (Alfred A. Knopf, 1972), 118.
12. Robert Aron and Georgette Elgey, *The Vichy Regime, 1940–1944* (Putnam, 1958), 312.
13. *Fuehrer Conferences on Naval Affairs*, 250.
14. *Fuehrer Conferences on Naval Affairs*, 253.
15. Alain Darlan survived and was flown on a U.S. Air Force plane to the treatment center founded by Franklin D. Roosevelt in Warm Springs, Georgia.
16. Admiral Andrew Cunningham, *A Sailor's Odyssey: The Autobiography of Admiral of the Fleet Viscount Cunningham of Hyndhope* (Seaforth Publishing, 1951), 502.
17. Hervé Coutau-Begarie and Claude Huan, *Darlan* (Fayard, 1989), 625.
18. Cordell Hull, *Memoirs of Cordell Hull*, vol. 2 (Macmillan & co., 1948), 1200.
19. Merle Miller, *Ike the Soldier: As They Knew Him* (G. P. Putnam's, 1987), 426.
20. Charles Eade, *Secret Session Speeches by the Right Hon. Winston S. Churchill* (Cassell and Company, 1946), 100.
21. General Mark W. Clark, *Calculated Risk* (HarperCollins Publishers, 1950), 126.
22. "Algiers Describes Slaying of Darlan," *New York Times*, December 26, 1942, 3.
23. Charles W. Koburger Jr., *The Cyrano Fleet: France and Its Navy, 1940–1942* (Praeger, 1989), 105.
24. Dwight D. Eisenhower, *Crusade in Europe: A Personal Account of World War II* (Doubleday & Company, 1948), 116.
25. Colin Smith, *England's Last War Against France* (Phoenix, 2010), 422.
26. "195,000 Tons Sunk," *New York Times*, December 9, 1942, 1.
27. "Admiral at Toulon Reported Captive," *New York Times*, November 29, 1942, 10.
28. Winston Churchill, *The Second World War: Their Finest Hour* (Houghton Mifflin Company, 1949), 239.
29. John Colville, *The Fringes of Power* (The Lyons Press, 1985), 392.
30. HC Deb. (27 May 1941) (371) col 1718.

31. Vice Admiral Sir W. Kaye Edden to Marder, February 24, 1977, UCI, Arthur J. Marder papers, MS-F002, BA05-A-1. Box 1.
32. Simpson, *Somerville Papers*, September 27, 1944, letter from Somerville to North, 442.
33. John Jordan and Robert Dumas, *French Battleships: 1922–1956* (Seaforth Publishing, 2009),182, 188, 192.
34. Simpson, *Somerville Papers*, April 3, 1944, desk diary entry, 537.
35. Simpson, *Somerville Papers*, April 29, 1944, letter from Churchill to Alexander, 603.
36. Simpson, *Somerville Papers*, May 21, 1944, letter from Churchill to Alexander, 604.
37. Simpson, *Somerville Papers*, May 27, 1944, letter from Churchill to Alexander, 605.
38. Joan Bright Astley, *The Inner Circle: A View of War at the Top* (Little, Brown and Company, 1971), 138.
39. Donald Macintyre, *Fighting Admiral—The Life and Battles of Admiral of the Fleet Sir James Somerville* (Evans Brothers Limited, 1961), 259.
40. South West Heritage Trust: Somerset Archive Catalogue—Papers of the Somerville Family of Dinder, 1457–1949, September 29, 2023, https://somerset-cat.swheritage.org.uk/records/DD/SVL.

CODA

1. Winston Churchill, *The Second World War: The Gathering Storm* (Houghton Mifflin Company, 1948), iv. Churchill added, "There never was a war more easy to stop than that which has just wrecked what was left of the world from the previous struggle."
2. Winston Churchill, *The Second World War: Their Finest Hour* (Houghton Mifflin Company, 1949), 227.
3. Comments from Extracts from Churchill's Volume II, The Second World War, CAC, Admiral Godfrey, Naval Memoirs, Vol 7, Part 1, 1903–1946, GDFY 1/10.
4. Orville Bullitt, ed., *For the President, Personal and Secret—Correspondence Between Franklin D. Roosevelt and William C. Bullitt* (Houghton Mifflin Company, 1972), 488. This appeared in a July 5, 1940, letter from Ambassador Bullitt to Secretary of State Cordell Hull.
5. John Colville, *The Fringes of Power* (The Lyons Press, 1985), 335.
6. Warren Tute, *The Deadly Stroke* (Coward, McCann & Geoghegan, 1973), 17.
7. Colville, *Fringes of Power,* 175.

BIBLIOGRAPHY

ARCHIVAL MATERIAL

Churchill Archive Centre, Churchill College, University of Cambridge—CAC
Cambridge, U.K.
Admiral Sir Dudley Pound Papers
Admiral Sir James Somerville Papers
John Colville Papers
Major-General Sir Edward Spears Papers
Winston Churchill Papers
Special Collections and Archives, The UC Irvine Libraries—UCI
Irvine, CA
Arthur J. Marder Papers
National Maritime Museum—NMM
Greenwich
Cedric Holland Papers
Imperial War Museum—IWM
Commander P. F. Whinney Papers
Lt. Cdr. G. A. G. Brooke Papers
Franklin D. Roosevelt Presidential Library—FDRL
Hyde Park, NY
Eleanor Roosevelt Papers
Franklin D. Roosevelt Papers
Press Secretary Papers
Howard Gotlieb Archival Research Center, Boston University—HG
Boston, MA
Richard M. Watt Papers
Hansard, UK, Parliament (House of Commons / House of Lords)—HC / HL
Mr. Winston Churchill: Speeches in 1939 and 1940
Lord Halifax: Speeches in 1940
The National Archives—TNA
Public Records Office / The National Archive—PRO

MAGAZINES, JOURNALS, NEWSPAPERS, AND ONLINE

Cau, Jean. "Mers el-Kébir, La Tragedie." *Paris Match*, July 12, 1990. 82–94.

Dilks, Laila. "The Twilight War and the Fall of France: Chamberlain and Churchill in 1940." *Transactions of the Royal Historical Society*, 1978. Vol. 28, 61–86.

———. "Mers-el-Kébir Was a Bizarre and Melancholy Action." *Smithsonian Magazine*, July 1985, 122–38.

Horne, Alistair. "Mers-el-Kébir, 1940." *The Daily Mail*, November 25, 1999.

Jameson, Robert. "Remembering Admiral Cunningham—The Great Insubordinate." Medium.com, April 14, 2019. https://rjameson.medium.com/remembering-admiral-cunningham-the-great-insubordinate-ca72640dfb1.

Lasterle, Philippe. "Could Admiral Gensoul Have Averted the Tragedy of Mers el-Kébir?" *The Journal of Military History* 67, no. 3 (July 2003): 835–44.

———. "Marcel Gensoul (1880–1973), un amiral dans la tourmente." *Revue historique des armées* 219 (2000): 71–91.

Life Magazine

The New Yorker

The New York Times

The Saturday Evening Post

Time Magazine

BOOKS

Adam, Colin Forbes. *Life of Lord Lloyd*. London: MacMillan, 1948.

Adams, Henry H. *Witness to Power: The Life of Fleet Admiral William D. Leahy*. Annapolis: Naval Institute Press, 1985.

———. *Years of Deadly Peril, The Coming of the War, 1939–1941*. New York: David McKay Company, 1969.

Addison, Paul. *Churchill on the Home Front, 1900–1955*. London: Pimlico, 1993.

Agar, Herbert. *The Darkest Year: Britain Alone, June 1940-June 1941*. London: The Bodley Head, 1972.

Alanbrooke, Field Marshal Lord. *War Diaries: 1939–1945*. Berkeley: University of California Press, 1957.

Amery, Leo. *My Political Life: The Unforgiving Years, 1929–1940*. London: Hutchinson, 1955.

Armstrong, Hamilton Fish. *Chronology of Failure: The Last Days of the French Republic*. New York: Macmillan & Co., 1941.

Aron, Robert, and Georgette Elgey. The *Vichy Regime, 1940–1944*. London: Putnam, 1958.

Arthur, Max. *Lost Voices of the Royal Navy*. London: Hodder and Stoughton, 1966.

Ashley, Maurice. *Churchill as Historian*. New York: Charles Scribner's Sons, 1968.

Aspinall-Oglander, Cecil. *Roger Keyes: Being the Biography of Admiral of the Fleet Lord Keyes*. London: The Hogarth Press, 1951.

Astley, Joan Bright. *The Inner Circle: A View of the War at the Top*. Boston: Little Brown, 1971.

Atkinson, Rick. *An Army at Dawn, The War in North Africa—1942–1943*. New York: Henry Holt and Company, 2002.

———. *The Day of Battle: The War in Sicily and Italy, 1943–1944*. New York: Henry Holt and Company, 2005.

Auphan, Rear Admiral Paul, and Jacques Mordal. *The French Navy in World War II*. Annapolis: Naval Institute Press, 1959.

Baldensperger, Denis. *Mers-el-Kébir*. Paris: Editions Rouff, 1967.

Ballande, Henri. *De L'Amiraute A Bikini: Souvenirs des jours sans joie*. Paris: Presses de la Cité, 1957.

Barber, Noel. *The Week France Fell*. New York: Stein and Day, 1976.

Bardens, Dennis. *Churchill in Parliament*. London: Robert Hale, 1967.

Barnes, John, and David Nicholson, eds. *The Empire at Bay—The Leo Amery Diaries: 1929–1945*. London: Hutchinson & Co., 1988.

Barres, Philippe. *Charles De Gaulle*. London: Hutchinson & Co., 1941.

Baudouin, Paul. *The Private Diaries of Paul Baudouin*. London: Eyre & Spottiswoode, 1948.
Beaufre, André. *1940: The Fall of France*. London: Cassell & Co., 1965.
Beesly, Patrick. *Very Special Intelligence: The Story of the Admiralty's Operational Intelligence Centre, 1939–1945*. Garden City: Doubleday & Company, 1978.
Bekker, Cajus. *Hitler's Naval War*. Garden City: Doubleday & Company, 1974.
Bell, P. M. H. *A Certain Eventuality: Britain and the Fall of France*. Westmead: Saxon House, 1974.
Benoist-Méchin, Jacques. *Sixty Days that Shook the West—The Fall of France: 1940*. New York: G.P. Putnam's Sons, 1963.
Bercuson, David, and Holger Herwig. *The Destruction of the Bismarck*. Woodstock: The Overlook Press, 2001.
Berlin, Isaiah. *Mr. Churchill in 1940*. Boston: Houghton Mifflin, 1964.
Berthon, Simon. *Allies at War*. New York: Carroll & Graff Publishers, 2001.
Bird, Keith. *Erich Raeder: Admiral of the Third Reich*. Annapolis: Naval Institute Press, 2013.
Birkenhead, Earl of. *Halifax*. Boston: Houghton Mifflin Company, 1966.
———. *The Professor and the Prime Minister: The Official Life of Professor F.A. Lindemann*. Cambridge: The Riverside Press, 1962.
Black, Conrad. *Franklin Delano Roosevelt*. New York: Public Affairs, 2003.
Bloch, Michael. *Ribbentrop, A Biography*. New York: Crown Publishers, 1992.
Bois, Elie. *Truth on the Tragedy of France*. London: Hodder and Stoughton, 1941.
Bond, Brian. *Britain, France, and Belgium: 1939–1940*. London: Brassey's, 1975.
Bonham-Carter, Violet. *Winston Churchill: An Intimate Portrait*. New York: Harcourt, Brace & World, 1965.
Boothe, Clare. *Europe in the Spring*. New York: Alfred A. Knopf, 1941.
Boothby, Robert. *I Fight to Live*. London: Victor Gollancz, 1947.
———. *Recollections of a Rebel*. London: Hutchinson, 1975.
Boutron, Jean. *An Honourable Sailor and Spy*. Paris: Plon, 1980.
Bouverie, Tim. *Appeasement*. New York: Tim Duggan Books, 2019.
Bradford, Sarah. *George VI*. London: Penguin Books, 1989.
Brodhurst, Robin. *Churchill's Anchor: The Biography of Admiral of the Fleet Sir Dudley Pound*. London: Pen and Sword Military, 2001.
Brown, David. *The Road to Oran: Anglo-French Naval Relations, September 1939–July 1940*. London: Frank Cass, 2004.
———. *The Royal Navy and the Mediterranean*. Vol. III: *November 1940–December 1941*. London: Taylor & Francis, 2013.
Brownell, Will. *So Close to Greatness: The Biography of William C. Bullitt*. New York: Macmillan & Co., 1987.
Bryant, Arthur. *The Turn of the Tide. Based on the Diaries of Field-Marshal Lord Alanbrooke*. Garden City: Doubleday & Company, 1957.
Bullitt, Orville, ed. *For the President, Personal and Secret—Correspondence Between Franklin D. Roosevelt and William C. Bullitt*. Boston: Houghton Mifflin Company, 1972.
Butler, Evan. *Keep the Memory Green: The Story of Dunkirk*. London: Hutchinson & Co., 1942.
Butler, J. R. M. *Lord Lothian*. New York: St. Martin's Press, 1960.
Calder, Angus. *The People's War: Britain 1939–45*. New York: Pantheon Books, 1969.
Cantel, Rudy. *L'Aattentat de Mers-el-Kébir*. Paris: La Technique du Livre, 1941.
Caroff, René Pierre Eugène. *Les Forces Maritimes de l'Ouest*. Vincennes: Service historique de la Marine, 1954.

———. *Le Théâtre Atlantique*. Tome 2: *aprés le 25 juin 1940*. Paris: Marine nationale E. M. général, Service historique, 1959.

———. *Le Théâtre Méditerranée*. Tome 2: *du 25 juin 1940 au 8 novembre 1942*. Paris: Marine nationale E. M. général, Service historique, 1960.

Chapman, Guy. *Why France Fell: The Defeat of the French Army in 1940*. New York: Holt, Reinhart and Winston, 1968.

Charmley, John. *Duff Cooper—The Authorized Biography*. London: Weidenfeld and Nicolson, 1986.

Charles-Roux, François. *Cinq Mois Tragiques Aux Affaires Etrangéres (21 Mai—1er Novembre 1940)*. Paris: Librairie Plon, 1949.

Chatfield, Admiral of the Fleet Sir Ernle. *It Might Happen Again: The Navy and Defence*. London: William Heineman LTD, 1947.

Chisholm, Anne, and Michael Davie. *Lord Beaverbrook: A Life*. New York: Alfred A. Knopf, 1993.

Churchill, Winston. *Great Contemporaries*. London: Thornton Butterworth Ltd, 1937.

———. *Never Give In—The Best of Winston Churchill's Speeches*. New York: Hyperion, 2003.

———. *The Second World War: Closing the Ring*. Boston: Houghton Mifflin Company, 1951.

———. *The Second World War: The Gathering Storm*. Boston: Houghton Mifflin Company, 1948.

———. *The Second World War: Their Finest Hour*. Boston: Houghton Mifflin Company, 1949.

Ciano, Count Galeazzo, and Hugh Gibson, eds. *The Ciano Diaries, 1939–1943*. New York: Howard Fertig, 1973.

Clark, Mark. *Calculated Risk*. New York: HarperCollins Publishers, 1950.

Clayton, Tim, and Phil Craig. *Finest Hour: The Battle of Britain*. New York: Simon & Schuster, 1999.

Cockett, Richard. *My Dear Max: The Letters of Brendan Bracken to Lord Beaverbrook, 1925–1958*. London: The Historian's Press, 1990.

Coles, Alan, and Ted Briggs. *Flagship Hood: The Fate of Britain's Mightiest Warship*. London: Robert Hale, 1985.

Collier, Richard. *1940: The Avalanche*. New York: The Dial Press, 1979.

Colville, John. *The Churchillians*. London: Weidenfeld and Nicolson, 1981.

———. *Footprints in Time*. London: Collins, 1976.

———. *The Fringes of Power*. Guilford, CT: The Lyons Press, 1985.

———. *Winston Churchill and His Inner Circle*. New York: Wyndham Books, 1981.

Cooper, Duff. *Old Men Forget: The Autobiography of Duff Cooper*. London: Rupert Hart-Davis, 1953.

Coote, Colin. *Editorial: The Memoirs of Colin R. Coote*. London: Eyre & Spottiswoode, 1965.

Coutau-Bégarie, Hervé, and Claude Huan. *Lettres et notes de l'Amiral Darlan*. Paris: Economica, 1953.

———. *Darlan*. Paris: Fayard, 1989.

———. *Mers El-Kébir (1940), La rupture franco-britannique*. Paris: Economica, 1994.

Crozier, W. P. *Off the Record: Political Interviews—1933–1943*. London: Hutchinson of London, 1973.

Cudahy, John. *The Armies March: A Personal Report*. New York: Charles Scribner's Sons, 1941.

Cumming, Anthony, ed. *In Action with Destroyers: 1939–1945*. South Yorkshire: Pen & Sword, 2017.

Cunningham, Admiral Andrew Browne. *A Sailor's Odyssey: The Autobiography of Admiral of the Fleet, Viscount Cunningham or Hyndhope*. London: Hutchinson & Co., Ltd, 1951.

Daladier, Edouard. *Edouard Daladier: Prison Journal, 1940–1945*. Boulder: Westview Press, 1995.
Dalton, Hugh. *Memoirs—1931–1945: The Fateful Years*. London: Frederick Muller Ltd., 1957.
Darlan, Alain. *L'Amiral Darlan Parle*. Paris: Amiot-Dumont, 1952.
D'Este, Carlo. *Warlord: A Life of Winston Churchill at War*. New York: HarperCollins Publishers, 2008.
de Chambrun, René. *I Saw France Fall*. New York: William Morrow & Company, 1940.
de Gaulle, Charles. *The Complete War Memoirs of Charles de Gaulle*. New York: Simon & Schuster, 1955.
de Gramont, Sanche. *The French: Portrait of a People*. New York: G. P. Putnam's Sons, 1969.
de Montmorency, Alec. *The Enigma of Admiral Darlan*. New York: E. P. Dutton, 1943.
de Roussy de Sales, Raoul. *The Making of Yesterday: The Diaries of Raoul de Roussy de Sales*. New York: Reynal & Hitchcock, 1947.
de Saint-Exupery, Antoine. *Flight to Arras*. Melbourne: William Heinemann LTD, 1942.
Dear, I. C. B., ed. *The Oxford Companion to World War II*. Oxford: Oxford University Press, 1995.
Dietrich, Otto. *Hitler*. Chicago: Henry Regnery Company, 1955.
Dilks, David, ed. *The Diaries of Sir Alexander Cadogan: 1938–1945*. New York: G. P. Putnam's Sons, 1972.
Divine, A. D. *Navies in Exile*. New York: E. P. Dutton & Company, 1944.
Divine, David. *The Nine Days of Dunkirk*. London: Faber and Faber. 1959.
Docteur, Vice Admiral Jules-Théophile. *La Grande Énigme de la Guerre : Darlan—Amiral de la Flotte*. Paris: Editions de la Couronne, 1949.
———. *La Vérité sur les Amiraux*. Paris: Editions de la Couronne, 1949.
Doenitz, Admiral Karl. *Memoirs: Ten Years and Twenty Days*. Cleveland: The Word Publishing Co., 1959.
Draper, Theodore. *The Six Weeks' War: May 10–June 26, 1940*. New York: Book Find Club, 1944.
Eade, Charles. *Churchill—By His Contemporaries*. London: The Reprint Society, 1953.
———. *Secret Sessions of the Right Hon. Winston S. Churchill*. London: Cassel & Co, 1946.
Eden, Anthony. *The Memoirs of Sir Anthony Eden*. Vol. 1: *Facing the Dictators*. London: Cassell & Co, 1962.
———. *The Memoirs of Sir Anthony Eden*. Vol. 2: *The Reckoning*. London: Cassell & Co, 1965.
Egremont, Max. *Under Two Flags: The Life of General Sir Edward Spears*. London: Weidenfeld & Nicolson, 1997.
Eisenhower, Dwight D. *Crusade in Europe*. Garden City: Doubleday & Company, 1948.
Ellis, Major L. J. *The War in France and Flanders: 1939–1940*. London: Her Majesty's Stationery Office, 1953.
Evans, Richard J. *The Third Reich in Power, 1933–1939*. New York: The Penguin Press, 2005.
Farrere, Claude. *François Darlan, Amiral de France et sa flotte*. Paris: Flammarion, 1940.
Feiling, Sir Keith. *The Life of Neville Chamberlain*. London: Macmillan & Co., 1946.
Fisher, David E. *A Summer Bright and Terrible: Winston Churchill, Lord Dowding, Radar and the Impossible Triumph of the Battle of Britain*. Washington: Shoemaker and Hoard, 2005.
Forester, C. S. *The Ship*. London: Michael Joseph, 1943.
François-Poncet, André. *The Fateful Years: Memoirs of a French Ambassador in Berlin, 1931–1938*. New York: Harcourt, Brace and Co., 1949.
Friedman, Norman. *The British Battleship: 1906–1946*. South York: Seaforth Publishing, 2015.

Frischauer, William, and Robert Jackson. *The Altmark Affair.* New York: Macmillan & Co., 1955.

Fuehrer Conferences on Naval Affairs: 1939–1945. Annapolis: Naval Institute Press, 1990.

Gates, Eleanor. *End of the Affair: The Collapse of the Anglo-French Alliance, 1939–40*. Berkeley: University of California Press, 1940.

Gilbert, G. M. *Nuremberg Diary*. Cambridge: Da Capo Press, 1995.

Gilbert, Martin. *The Churchill War Papers.* Vol. 1: *At the Admiralty, September 1939–May 1940.* New York: W. W. Norton & Company, 1993.

———. *The Churchill War Papers.* Vol. 2: *Never Surrender, May 1940–December 1940.* New York: W. W. Norton & Company, 1995.

———. *Finest Hour: Winston Churchill, 1939–1941.* London: Heinemann, 1983.

———. *Road to Victory. Winston S. Churchill 1941–1945.* Toronto: Stoddart, 1986.

———. *Winston Churchill, The Wilderness Years.* Boston: Houghton Mifflin Company, 1982.

Godfroy, René-Émile. *L'Aventure de la Force X.* Paris: Librairie Plon, 1953.

Grenfell, Russell. *The Bismarck Episode.* New York: MacMillan & Co., 1949.

Gretton, Peter. *Former Naval Person: Winston Churchill & The Royal Navy.* New York: Coward McCann Inc., 1968.

Guderian, Heinz. *Panzer Leader.* Cambridge: DaCapo Press, 1996.

Halifax, Lord. *Fullness of Days.* New York: Dodd, Mead & Company, 1957.

Harrison, Tom, and Charles Madge. *Britain: by Mass Observation.* London: The Cresset Library, 1986.

Harvey, John. *The Diplomatic Diaries of Oliver Harvey: 1937–1940.* London: Collins, 1970.

Heckstall-Smith, Anthony. *The Fleet That Faced Both Ways.* London: Anthony Blond, 1963.

Henderson, Sir Nevile. *Failure of a Mission: by the British Ambassador to Berlin 1937–1939.* New York: G. P. Putnam's Sons, 1940

———. *Water Under the Bridges.* London: Hodder & Stoughton, 1945.

Herman, John. *The Paris Embassy of Sir Eric Phipps: Anglo-French Relations and the Foreign Office.* Brighton: Sussex Academic Press, 1998.

Hering, Général Pierre. *La Vie Exemplaire de Philippe Pétain.* Paris: Paris-Livres, 1956.

Hickman, Tom. *Churchill's Bodyguard.* London: Headline Book Publishing, 2005.

Hinsley, F. H. *Command of the Sea: British Naval History 1918–45.* London: Christophers, 1950.

Hitler, Adolf. *Hitler's Second Book—The Unpublished Sequel to* Mein Kampf. New York: Enigma Books, 2003.

Hobbs, David. *Taranto.* South Yorkshire: Seaforth Publishing, 2020.

Holland, James. *The Battle of Britain: Five Months that Changed History. May–October 1940.* New York: St. Martin's Press, 2010.

Horne, Alistair. *Seven Ages of Paris.* New York: Alfred A. Knopf, 2003.

———. *To Lose a Battle: France 1940.* Boston: Little Brown and Company, 1969.

Howarth, Stephen. *Men of War.* New York: St. Martin's Press, 1993.

Howse, Derek. *Radar at Sea: The Royal Navy in World War 2.* Annapolis: Naval Institute Press, 1993.

Hull, Cordell. *The Memoirs of Cordell Hull. 2 vols.* New York: Macmillan & Co., 1948.

Hytier, Adrienne Doris. *Two Years of French Foreign Policy: Vichy, 1940–1942.* Paris: Librairie Armand Colin, 1958.

Ickes, Harold. *The Secret Diary of Harold Ickes. Vol. 3: The Lowering Clouds, 1939–1941.* New York: Simon & Schuster, 1953.

Ismay, Lord. *The Memoirs of General The Lord Ismay*. London: Heinemann, 1960.

Jackson, Julian. *The Fall of France: May–June 1940*. Oxford: Arthur Barker Limited, 1975.

James, Robert Rhodes. *Chips: The Diaries of Sir Henry Channon*. London: Weidenfeld and Nicolson, 1967.

James, W. M. Sir Admiral. *The Portsmouth Letters*. London: Macmillan & Co., 1946.

Jenkins, Roy. *Churchill: A Biography*. New York: Farrar, Straus and Giroux, 2001.

Jones, Matthew. *Britain, the United States and the Mediterranean War, 1942–44*. London: Macmillan Press, 1996.

Jordan, John, and Robert Dumas. *French Battleships, 1922–1956*. Yorkshire: Seaforth Publishing, 2009.

Jordan, John, and Jean Moulin. *French Destroyers—Torpilleurs d'Escadre & Contre-Torpilleurs, 1922–1956*. Annapolis: Naval Institute Press, 2015.

Kammerer, Albert. *La Passion de la Flotte Français*. Paris: Librairie Artheme Fayard, 1951.

———. *La Vérité Sur l'Armistice*. Paris: Editions Médicis, 1944.

Karslake, Basil. *1940: The Last Act: The Story of the British Forces in France After Dunkirk*. Hamden: Archon Books, 1979.

Kaufman, J. E., and H. W. *The Maginot Line: None Shall Pass*. Westport: Praeger, 1997.

Kemp, Anthony. *The Maginot Line: Myth and Reality*. Briarcliff Manor: Stern and Day, 1982.

Kemp, Lieutenant Commander P. K. *Key to Victory: The Triumph of British Sea Power in World War II*. Boston: Little, Brown & Company, 1957.

Kersaudy, François. *Churchill and De Gaulle*. New York: Atheneum, 1982.

Kimball, Warren. *Churchill and Roosevelt: The Complete Correspondence*. Princeton: Princeton University Press, 1984.

Koburger, Charles, Jr. *The Cyrano Fleet: France and Its Navy, 1940–1942*. Westport: Praeger, 1989.

Korda, Michael. *With Wings Like Eagles: The History of the Battle of Britain*. New York: Harper Perennial, 2009.

Lacouture, Jean. *De Gaulle, The Rebel, 1890–1944*. New York: W. W. Norton & Company, 1990.

Lamb, Richard. *Churchill as War Leader*. New York: Carroll & Graf Publishers, 1991.

Langer, William. *Our Vichy Gamble*. New York: Alfred A. Knopf, 1947.

Lash, Joseph P. *Roosevelt and Churchill: 1939–1941. The Partnership that Saved the West*. New York: W. W. Norton, 1976.

Lavery, Brian. *In Which They Served: The Royal Navy Officer Experience in the Second World War*. London: Conway, 2008.

Lazareff, Pierre. *Deadline: The Behind-the-Scenes Story of the Last Decade in France*. New York: Random House, 1942.

Leasor, James. *The Clock with Four Hands*. New York: Reynal and Company, 1958.

———. *War at the Top—Based on the Experiences of General Sir Leslie Hollis*. London: House of Stratus, 1959.

Lee, Raymond. *The London Journal of General Raymond E. Lee, 1940–1941*. Boston: Little, Brown and Company, 1941.

Liebling, A. J. *Liebling's War: World War II Dispatches of A. J. Liebling*. New York: The Library of America, 2011.

Longmate, Norman. *The Home Front: An Anthology of Personal Experience, 1938–1945*. London: Chatto & Windus, 1981.

Lottman, Herbert. *The Fall of Paris: June 1940*. New York: HarperCollins Publishers, 1992.

Lukacs, John. *The Duel*. New Haven: Yale University Press, 1990.

———. *Five Days in London. May 1940*. New Haven: Yale University Press, 1999.
Macintyre, Donald. *Fighting Admiral—The Life and Battles of Admiral of the Fleet Sir James Somerville*. London: Evans Brothers Limited, 1961.
Macmillan, Harold. *The Blast of War: 1939–1945*. New York: Harper & Row Publishers, 1967.
Maisky, Ivan. *Memoirs of a Soviet Ambassador, The War: 1939–43*. New York: Charles Scribner's Sons, 1967.
Manchester, William. *The Last Lion: Winston Spencer Churchill, Alone, 1932–1940*. Boston: Little, Brown and Company, 1988.
Manchester, William, and Paul Reid. *The Last Lion: Winston Spencer Churchill, Defender of the Realm, 1940–1965*. Boston: Little, Brown and Company, 2012.
Marder, Arthur. *From the Dardanelles to Oran: Studies of the Royal Navy in War and Peace, 1915–1940*. London: Oxford University Press, 1974.
———. *Operation Menace: The Dakar Expedition and the Dudley North Affair*. London: Oxford University Press, 1976.
Masson, Philippe, *La Marine Française et la Guerre 39/45*. Paris: Le Grand Livre du Mois, 1991.
Maurois, Andre. *Tragedy in France*. New York: Harper & Brothers, 1940.
———. *Why France Fell*. London: John Lane, 1940.
McKee, Alexander. *Black Saturday: The Tragedy of the Royal Oak*. London: Souvenir Press, 1959.
Meacham, Jon. *Franklin and Winston: An Intimate Portrait of an Epic Friendship*. New York: Random House, 2004.
Melton, George. *Darlan: Ambassador and Statesman of France*. Westport: Praeger, 1998.
———. *From Versailles to Mers el-Kébir: The Promise of Anglo-French Naval Cooperation, 1919–1940*. Annapolis: Naval Institute Press, 2015.
Miller, Merle. *Ike the Soldier: As They Knew Him*. New York: G. P. Putnam's Sons, 1987.
Moch, Jules. *Rencontres Avec . . . Darlan et Eisenhower*. Paris: Plon, 1968.
Montgomery, Field Marshal Lord. *The Memoirs of Field-Marshal The Viscount Montgomery of Alamein, K. G.* Cleveland: The World Publishing Company, 1958.
Moran, Lord. *Churchill at War 1940–45*. New York: Carroll & Graf Publishers, 2002.
Mosley, Leonard. *On Borrowed Time: How World War II Began*. New York: Random House, 1969.
Murfett, Malcolm. *The First Sea Lords: From Fisher to Mountbatten*. Westport: Prager, 1995.
Murphy, Robert. *Diplomat Among Warriors*. New York: Doubleday & Company, 1964.
Murrow, Edward R. *This is London*. New York: Simon & Schuster, 1941.
Nicolson, Sir Harold. *The Diaries and Letters of Harold Nicolson: The War Years, 1939–1945*. New York : Atheneum, 1967.
Nogueres, Henri. *La Suicide de la Flotte Francaise a Toulon*. Paris: Robert Laffont, 1961.
Norman, Andrew. *HMS Hood, Pride of the Royal Navy*. Mechanicsburg: Stackpole Books, 2001.
O'Conor, Rory. *Running a Big Ship*. Oxford: Casemate Publishers, 2017.
O'Hara, Vincent P., W. David Dickson, and Richard Worth. *On Seas Contested: The Seven Great Navies in the Second World War*. Annapolis: Naval Institute Press, 2010.
Olson, Lynne. *Last Hope Island*. New York: Random House, 2017.
———. *Troublesome Young Men*. New York. Farrar, Strauss and Giroux, 2007.
Ousby, Ian. *Occupation: The Ordeal of France—1940–1944*. New York: St. Martin's Press, 1997.
Packwood, Allen. *How Churchill Waged War*. Yorkshire: Frontline Books, 2019.

Panter-Downes, Mollie. *London War Notes, 1939–1945*. New York: Farrar, Straus and Giroux, 1971.
Parkinson, Roger. *Blood, Toil, Tears and Sweat: The War History from Dunkirk to Alamein, based on the War Cabinet Papers, 1940 to 1941*. New York: David McKay Company, 1973.
Patat, Jean-Pierre, and Michael Lutfalla. *A Monetary History of France in the Twentieth Century*. New York: St. Martin's Press, 1990.
Pawle, Gerald. *The Secret War: 1939–45*. New York: William Sloan Associates, Inc., 1957.
———. *The War and Colonel Warden: Based on the Recollections of Commander C. R. Thompson, Personal Assistant to the Prime Minister, 1940–1945*. New York: Alfred A. Knopf, 1963.
Paxton, Robert O. *Parades and Politics at Vichy, The French Officer Corps Under Marshal Petain*. Princeton: Princeton University Press, 1966.
Pertinax. *The Gravediggers of France*. Garden City: Doubleday, Doran & Company, 1944.
Playfair, Major General I. S. O. *The Mediterranean and Middle East*. Vol. I: *The Early Successes Against Italy (to May 1941)*. London: Her Majesty's Stationery Office, 1954.
Poolman, Kenneth. *Ark Royal*. London: William Kimber: 1956.
———. *The British Sailor, Experiences of War*. London: Arms and Armour Press, 1989.
———. The Kelly. New York: W. W. Norton & Company, Inc., 1954.
Porch, Douglas. *The Path to Victory*. New York: Farrar, Straus and Giroux, 2004.
Prysor, Glyn. *Citizen Sailors: The Royal Navy in the Second World War*. London: Penguin Books, 2012.
Reynaud, Paul. *In the Thick of the Fight: 1930–1945*. New York: Simon & Schuster, 1956.
Reynolds, Paul. *In Command of History*. London: Penguin, 2004.
Ribbentrop, Joachim. *The Ribbentrop Memoirs*. London: Weidenfeld & Nicolson, 1954.
Richards, Denis. *Royal Air Force 1939–1945*. Vol. 1: *The Fight at Odds*. London: Her Majesty's Stationery Office, 1953.
Roberts, Andrew. *Churchill, Walking with Destiny*. New York: Viking, 2018.
———. *Emminent Churchillians*. New York: Simon & Schuster, 1995.
———. *The Holy Fox*. London: Weidenfeld and Nicolson, 1991.
———. *Masters and Commanders*. New York: HarperCollins, 2009.
———. *The Storm of War: A New History of the Second World War*. New York: HarperCollins, 2011.
Rochas, Yves. *Pour En Savoir Plus Sur Mers El-Kébir*. Paris: Editions Lettres Du Monde, 1993.
Rohwer, Jürgen. *Chronology of the War at Sea: 1939–1945*. Annapolis: Naval Institute Press, 1972.
Rosbottom, Ronald C. *When Paris Went Dark: The City of Light Under German Occupation, 1940–1944*. New York: Little, Brown and Company, 2014.
Rosenman, Samuel, ed. *The Public Papers and Addresses of Franklin D. Roosevelt—1940 Volume*. New York: MacMillan & Co., 1941.
Roskill, Stephen. *Churchill and the Admirals*. New York: William Morrow and Company, 1960.
———. *HMS Warspite: The Story of a Famous Battleship*. Annapolis: Naval Institute Press, 1957.
———. *The War at Sea: 1939–1945*. Vol. 1: *The Defensive*. London: Her Majesty's Stationery Office, 1954.
———. *White Ensign: The British Navy at War, 1939–1945*. Annapolis: Naval Institute Press, 1960.

Ruge, Vice Admiral Friedrich. *Der Seekrieg: The German Navy's Story, 1939–1945*. Annapolis: Naval Institute Press, 1957.

Schmidt, Dr. Paul. *Hitler's Interpreter.* London: William Heinemann Ltd., 1951.

Schofield, Vice Admiral B. B. *With the Royal Navy in War and Peace: O'er the Dark Blue Sea*. Yorkshire: Pen & Sword, 2018.

Sebag-Montefiore, Hugh. *Dunkirk: Fight to the Last Man*. Cambridge: Harvard University Books, 2006.

Self, Robert. *The Neville Chamberlain Diary Letters*. Vol. 4: *The Downing Street Years, 1934–1940*. London: Ashgate, 2005.

Sevareid, Eric. *Not So Wild a Dream*. New York: Alfred A. Knopf, 1947.

Sheean, Vincent. *Between the Thunder and the Sun*. London: Random House, 1943.

Sherwood, Robert. *Roosevelt and Hopkins: An Intimate History*. New York: Harper and Brothers, 1948.

Shirer, William H. *Berlin Diary*. New York: Knopf, 1941.

———. *The Collapse of the Third Republic*. New York: Simon & Schuster, 1969.

———. *The Nightmare Years: 1930–1940*. Boston: Little, Brown and Company, 1984.

———. *The Rise and Fall of the Third Reich*. New York: Simon & Schuster, 1960.

———. *The Sinking of the Bismarck*. New York: Random House, 1962.

———. *"This is Berlin." Radio Broadcasts form Nazi Germany*. Woodstock, NY: The Overlook Press, 1999.

Simpson, Michael, ed. *The Cunningham Papers: Selections from the Private and Official Correspondence of Admiral of the Fleet Viscount Cunningham of Hyndhope*. Vol. I: *The Mediterranean Fleet, 1939–1942*. Aldershot: Navy Records Society, 1999.

———, ed. *The Somerville Papers: Selections from the Private and Official Correspondence of Admiral of the Fleet Sir James Somerville*. Aldershot: Navy Records Society, 1995.

Slessor, Sir John. *The Central Blue: Recollections and Reflections by Marshal of the Royal Air Force Sir John Slessor*. London: Cassell and Company, 1956.

Slimming, Jan. *Codebreaker Girls: A Secret Life at Bletchley Park*. Yorkshire: Pen and Sword, 2021.

Smith, Colin. *England's Last War Against France*. London: Orion Books, 2009.

Smith, Dennis Mack. *Mussolini*. New York: Knopf, 1982.

Smith, Peter. *The Great Ships, British Battleships in WWII*. Mechanicsburg: Stackpole Books, 1977.

Soames, Mary. *Clementine Churchill: The Biography of a Marriage*. Boston: Houghton, Mifflin Company, 1979.

Somerville, Christopher. *Our War: How the British Commonwealth Fought the Second World War*. London: Weidenfeld & Nicolson, 1998.

Spears, Major General Sir Edward. *Assignment to Catastrophe*. Vol. I: *Prelude to Dunkirk, June 1939–May 1940*. New York: A. A. Wyn, Inc., 1954.

———. *Assignment to Catastrophe*. Vol. II: *The Fall of France, June 1940*. New York: A. A. Wyn, Inc. 1955.

———. *Two Men Who Saved France: Pétain and de Gaulle*. New York: Stein and Day, 1966.

Taylor, A. J. P. *Beaverbrook*. New York: Simon & Schuster, 1972.

———. *English History, 1914–1945*. New York: Oxford University Press, 1965.

Taylor, Robert Lewis. *Winston Churchill: An Informal Study of Greatness*. Garden City: Doubleday & Company, 1952.

Taylor, Telford. *Munich: The Price of Peace*. New York: Vantage Books, 1979.

———. *Sword and Swastika*. New York: Simon & Schuster, 1952.

Thompson, Inspector Walter Henry. *Assignment: Churchill.* New York: Farrar, Straus and Young, 1955.

Thompson, Laurence. *1940.* New York: William Morrow & Company, 1966.

Thursfield, Rear Admiral H. G., ed. *Brassey's Naval Annual—1948.* London: William Clowes & Sons, 1948.

Toland, John. *Adolf Hitler.* New York: Ballantine Books, 1976.

Tombs, Robert, and Isabelle. *That Sweet Enemy: The French and the British from the Sun King to the Present.* London: William Heinemann, 2006.

Tompkins, Peter. *The Murder of Admiral Darlan.* New York: Simon and Schuster, 1965.

Trevor-Roper, H. R. *Blitzkrieg to Defeat—Hitler's War Directives: 1939–1945.* New York: Holt, Rinehart and Winston, 1964.

Tucker-Jones, Anthony. *Churchill, Master and Commander: Winston Churchill at War 1895–1945.* London: Osprey Publishing, 2023.

Tute, Warren. *The Deadly Stroke.* New York: Coward, McCann & Geoghegan, 1973.

———. *The Reluctant Enemies.* London: Collins, 1989.

U.S. Government Printing Office. *Documents on German Foreign Policy, Series D (1937–1945).* Vol. 9: *The War Years: March 18–June 22, 1940.* Washington: United States Government Printing Office, 1956.

Vader, John. *The Fleet Without a Friend.* London: New English Library, 1971.

Van Der Vat, Dan. *The Grand Scuttle.* Staplehurst: Spellmount Limited, 1994.

Vansittart, Robert. *Lessons of My Life.* New York: A. A. Knopf, 1943.

Varillon, Pierre. *Mers-el-Kébir, Avec de nombreux documents.* Paris: Amiot-Dumont, 1949.

Verrier, Anthony. *Assassination in Algiers: Churchill, Roosevelt, de Gaulle, and the Murder of Admiral Darlan.* New York: W. W. Norton & Company, 1990.

Vian, Sir Philip. *Action This Day: A War Memoir.* London: Frederick Muller Limited, 1960.

Von Below, Nicolaus. *At Hitler's Side: The Memoirs of Hitler's Luftwaffe Adjutant, 1937–45.* London: Greenhill Books, 1980.

Warlimont, Walter. *Inside Hitler's Headquarter, 1939–1945.* Novato: Presidio, 1964.

Warner, Geoffrey. *Pierre Laval and the Eclipse of France, 1931–1945.* New York: Macmillan & Co., 1968.

Waterfield, Gordon. *Professional Diplomat: Sir Percy Loraine of Kirkharle Bt.* London: John Murray, 1973.

Watt, Richard M. *Dare Call It Treason.* New York: Simon & Schuster, 1963.

———. *The King's Depart: The Tragedy of Germany: Versailles and the German Revolution.* New York: Simon & Schuster, 1968.

Weber, Thomas. *Hitler's First War.* Oxford: Oxford University Press, 1994.

Weinberg, Gerhard. *A World at Arms: A Global History of World War II.* Cambridge: Cambridge University Press, 1994.

Weitz, John. *Hitler's Diplomat: The Life and Times of Joachim von Ribbentrop.* New York: Ticknor & Fields, 1992.

Welles, Sumner. *The Time for Decision.* New York: Harper & Brothers, 1944.

Werth, Alexander. *France: 1940–1955.* New York: Henry Holt and Company, 1956.

———. *The Last Days of Paris, A Journalist's Diary.* London: Hamish Hamilton, 1940.

———. *The Twilight of France, 1933–1940. A Journalist's Chronicle.* New York: Harper Brothers, 1942.

Weygand, General Maxime. *Recalled to Service: The Memoirs of General Maxime Weygand.* Garden City: Doubleday, 1952.

Weygand, J. W. *The Role of General Weygand: Conversations with His Son*. London: Eyre & Spottiswoode, 1948.

Wheeler-Bennett, Sir John W. *King George VI, His Life and Reign*. New York: St. Martin's Press, 1958.

Williams, Charles. *The Last Great Frenchman, A Life of General de Gaulle*. New York: John Wiley & Sons, 1993.

———. *Pétain: How the Hero of France Became a Convicted Traitor and Changed the Course of History*. New York: Palgrave Macmillan, 2005.

Wilt, Alan F. *War from the Top: German and British Military Decision Making During World War II*. Bloomington: Indiana University Press, 1990.

Winton, John, ed. *The War at Sea: 1939–1945*. London: Hutchinson & Co., 1967.

Woodward, David. *Ramsay at War: The Fighting Life of Admiral Sir Bertram Ramsay*. London: Willian Kimber, 1957.

Woodward, Sir Llewellyn. *History of the Second World War: British Foreign Policy in the Second World War*. Vol. 1. London: Her Majesty's Stationery Office, 1970.

Wright, Robert. *The Man Who Won the Battle of Britain*. New York: Scribner's, 1970.

Ziegler, Philip. *London at War, 1939–1945*. London: Pimlico, 2002.

———. *Mountbatten*. New York: Alfred A. Knopf, 1985.

INDEX

ABOUT THE AUTHOR

Bill Whiteside, a member of the International Churchill Society, is a writer and researcher focused on Winston Churchill and the Royal Navy. After a thirty-year career in sales and marketing, he shifted his interest to history, with a particular focus on a little-known naval clash during Churchill's second month as Britain's prime minister. This infatuation led to his book and numerous articles on the subject. Whiteside holds a BS in management from the University of Notre Dame and lives in Lancaster, Pennsylvania.

The Naval Institute Press is the book-publishing arm of the U.S. Naval Institute, a private, nonprofit, membership society for sea service professionals and others who share an interest in naval and maritime affairs. Established in 1873 at the U.S. Naval Academy in Annapolis, Maryland, where its offices remain today, the Naval Institute has members worldwide.

Members of the Naval Institute support the education programs of the society and receive the influential monthly magazine *Proceedings* or the colorful bimonthly magazine *Naval History* and discounts on fine nautical prints and on ship and aircraft photos. They also have access to the transcripts of the Institute's Oral History Program and get discounted admission to any of the Institute-sponsored seminars offered around the country.

The Naval Institute's book-publishing program, begun in 1898 with basic guides to naval practices, has broadened its scope to include books of more general interest. Now the Naval Institute Press publishes about seventy titles each year, ranging from how-to books on boating and navigation to battle histories, biographies, ship and aircraft guides, and novels. Institute members receive significant discounts on the Press' more than eight hundred books in print.

Full-time students are eligible for special half-price membership rates. Life memberships are also available.

For more information about Naval Institute Press books that are currently available, visit www.usni.org/press/books. To learn about joining the U.S. Naval Institute, please write to:

Member Services
U.S. Naval Institute
291 Wood Road
Annapolis, MD 21402-5034
Telephone: (800) 233-8764
Fax: (410) 571-1703
Web address: www.usni.org